T0137880

Lecture Notes in Computer Science   **13646**

Founding Editors

Gerhard Goos
Juris Hartmanis

Editorial Board Members

The series Lecture Notes in Computer Science (LNCS), including its subseries Lecture Notes in Artificial Intelligence (LNAI) and Lecture Notes in Bioinformatics (LNBI), has established itself as a medium for the publication of new developments in computer science and information technology research, teaching, and education.

LNCS enjoys close cooperation with the computer science R & D community, the series counts many renowned academics among its volume editors and paper authors, and collaborates with prestigious societies. Its mission is to serve this international community by providing an invaluable service, mainly focused on the publication of conference and workshop proceedings and postproceedings. LNCS commenced publication in 1973.

Jean-Jacques Rousseau · Bill Kapralos
Editors

Pattern Recognition, Computer Vision, and Image Processing

ICPR 2022 International Workshops and Challenges

Montreal, QC, Canada, August 21–25, 2022
Proceedings, Part IV

 Springer

Editors
Jean-Jacques Rousseau ⓘ
York University
Toronto, ON, Canada

Bill Kapralos ⓘ
Ontario Tech University
Oshawa, ON, Canada

ISSN 0302-9743   ISSN 1611-3349 (electronic)
Lecture Notes in Computer Science
ISBN 978-3-031-37744-0   ISBN 978-3-031-37745-7 (eBook)
https://doi.org/10.1007/978-3-031-37745-7

This Springer imprint is published by the registered company Springer Nature Switzerland AG
The registered company address is: Gewerbestrasse 11, 6330 Cham, Switzerland

Foreword

The organizers of the 26th International Conference on Pattern Recognition (ICPR 2022) are delighted to present the Proceedings of the event. The conference took place at Palais des Congrès de Montréal in Montreal, Canada, and we are thrilled to share the outcomes of this successful event.

We would like to express our heartfelt gratitude to the International Association for Pattern Recognition (IAPR) for sponsoring the conference, which allowed us to bring together a diverse group of researchers and experts in this field. Without their support, this conference would not have been possible.

We also want to extend our special thanks to the Workshop Chairs who provided excellent leadership in organizing the workshops. We appreciate the tireless efforts they put into making the workshops a success. We would also like to acknowledge the authors and presenters of the articles and workshops for their contributions. The high quality of their work and presentations enriched the conference.

Finally, we would like to thank the attendees for their participation, which made ICPR 2022 a truly collaborative and inspiring event. We hope that the Proceedings will serve as a valuable resource for those interested in pattern recognition and inspire future research in this field.

August 2022

Henrik I. Christensen
Michael Jenkin
Cheng-Lin Liu

Preface

The 26th International Conference on Pattern Recognition Workshops (ICPRW 2022) were held at the Palais des congrès de Montréal in Montreal, Quebec, Canada on Sunday August 21, 2022, one day earlier than the main ICPR conference. 27 workshop submissions were received and were carefully reviewed by the IAPR Conferences and Meetings committee and the workshop chairs. Considering their decisions and anticipated attendance, 24 workshops were selected and 21 workshops actually took place. Many of these workshops received a sponsorship or endorsement from the International Association for Pattern Recognition (IAPR).

ICPR 2022 marked the return of the conference to its in-person format (although workshops had the option of being held in person or remotely). This meant meeting colleagues face to face again, and making new connections to support scientific collaborations and (perhaps) even new friendships. The purpose of publishing the proceedings of a scientific conference such as ICPR 2022 include to:

- Establish a permanent record of the research presented;
- Report on the current research concerns and accomplishments of the conference participants;
- Make new research visible to scientific and other publics to promote collaboration, innovation, and discovery;
- Disseminate the latest research findings to a wider audience, in support of researchers, academics, industry, and other practitioners; and,
- Support the shared goal of staying up to date with developments in the fast moving field of artificial intelligence.

These volumes constitute the refereed proceedings of the twenty-one (21) workshops that were held in conjunction with ICPR 2022. The wide range of topics that it contains is a testament to the ever-widening concerns of AI researchers as they creatively find ways to apply artificial intelligence to domains further from its historical concerns. ICPR 2022 workshops covered domains related to pattern recognition, artificial intelligence, computer vision, and image and sound analysis. Workshop contributions reflected the most recent applications related to healthcare, biometrics, ethics, multimodality, cultural heritage, imagery, affective computing, and de-escalation. The papers included in these proceedings span four volumes and stem from the following workshops:

Volume I:

T-CAP 2022: Towards a Complete Analysis of People: From Face and Body to Clothes
HBU: 12th International Workshop on Human Behavior Understanding
SSL: Theories, Applications, and Cross Modality for Self-Supervised Learning Models
MPRSS 2022: Multimodal Pattern Recognition for Social Signal Processing in Human-Computer Interaction
FAIRBIO: Fairness in Biometric Systems

AIHA: Artificial Intelligence for Healthcare Applications
MDMR: Multimodal Data for Mental Disorder Recognition

Volume II:

MANPU 2022: 5th International Workshop on coMics ANalysis, Processing and Understanding
FOREST: Image Analysis for Forest Environmental Monitoring
MMFORWILD: MultiMedia FORensics in the WILD
IMTA: 8th International Workshop on Image Mining, Theory and Applications
PRHA: Pattern Recognition in Healthcare Analytics
IML: International Workshop on Industrial Machine Learning

Volume III:

PatReCH: 3rd International Workshop on Pattern Recognition for Cultural Heritage
XAIE: 2nd Workshop on Explainable and Ethical AI
PRRS: 12th Workshop on Pattern Recognition in Remote Sensing
CVAUI: Computer Vision for Analysis of Underwater Imagery
UMDBB: Understanding and Mitigating Demographic Bias in Biometric Systems

Volume IV:

AI4MFDD: Workshop on Artificial Intelligence for Multimedia Forensics and Disinformation Detection
AI4D: AI for De-escalation: Autonomous Systems for De-escalating Conflict in Military and Civilian Contexts
AMAR: 3rd International Workshop on Applied Multimodal Affect Recognition

Writing this preface, we were acutely aware of our special responsibilities towards those who will access the Proceedings for future reference. Unlike us and the contributors to these volumes, future readers will not have the benefit of having lived through the moment in which the research was conducted and presented. As background, leading to August 2022, there were two overarching meta-stories in the news: the COVID pandemic and social justice. COVID restrictions were lifted in piecemeal fashion leading to the conference dates, and began the long tail of the end of the pandemic. For conference attendees, wearing face masks was a live issue since masks indoors remained strongly recommended. International travel was still heavily impacted by COVID restrictions, with some participants being unable to travel either due to their COVID status or to the difficulty in meeting the range of COVID testing and inoculation requirements required. The public health theme continued with a new virus called 'Monkeypox' appearing on the scene.

On social justice, the May 25, 2020 murder of George Floyd by Minneapolis police officers continued to cast its shadow. During the summer of 2022, there continued to be protests and other actions to demand an end to anti-Black racism. In parallel, in Canada, Indigenous communities led protests and actions to demand an end to anti-Indigenous racism, and to acknowledge the historical circumstances that explain the discoveries of remains of children in unmarked burial sites at former residential schools. As conference attendees and participants, we lived through this cultural moment and were marked by it. However, future readers may need to supplement these volumes with research into the circumstances in which the research was conceptualized, conducted, and received. Philosophers of science make a relevant distinction here. Since Karl Popper, they speak of the context of discovery and the context of justification. Justification in science is relatively well understood, as it relates to the collection and analysis of data in pursuit of evidence for evaluating hypotheses in conformity with norms referenced to as the 'scientific method'. However, where do the initial questions or leaps of insights come from? The context of discovery is not as well understood. Still, it is widely believed that the social and personal conditions of researchers play an active role. We included a reference to the COVID-19 pandemic and social justice movements as widely shared preoccupations at the time of ICPR 2022 to aid a future reader who may wonder about the context of discovery of what is reported.

We acknowledge that future readers will no doubt enjoy benefits that we cannot enjoy. Specifically, they may be able to better assess which lines of research presented in the Proceedings proved the more beneficial. There are also concrete things: as we write, we do not know whether we are in a COVID pandemic hiatus or at its end; future readers will know the answer to this question.

The organization of such a large conference would not be possible without the help of many people. Our special gratitude goes to the Program Chairs (Gregory Dudek, Zhouchen Lin, Simone Marinai, Ingela Nyström) for their leadership in organizing the program. Thanks go to the Track Chairs and Area Chairs who dedicated their time to the review process and the preparation of the program. We also thank the reviewers who have evaluated the papers and provided authors with valuable feedback on their research work.

Finally, we acknowledge the work of conference committee members (Local Arrangements Chair and Committee Members, Finance Chairs, Workshop Chairs, Tutorial Chairs, Challenges Chairs, Publicity Chairs, Publications Chairs, Awards Chair, Sponsorship and Exhibition Chair) who strongly contributed to make this event successful. The MCI Group, led by Anjali Mohan, made great efforts in arranging the logistics, which is highly appreciated.

August 2022

Jean-Jacques Rousseau
Bill Kapralos

Organization

General Chairs

Henrik I. Christensen   UC San Diego, USA
Michael Jenkin   York University, Canada.
Cheng-Lin Liu   Institute of Automation of Chinese Academy of
                             Sciences, China

Program Committee Co-chairs

Gregory Dudek   McGill University, Canada
Zhouchen Lin   Peking University, China
Simone Marinai   University of Florence, Italy
Ingela Nyström   Swedish National Infrastructure for Computing,
                             Sweden

Invited Speakers Chairs

Alberto Del Bimbo   University of Firenze, Italy
Michael Brown   Canada
Steven Waslander   University of Toronto, Canada

Workshop Chairs

Xiang Bai   Huazhong University of Science and Technology,
                             China
Giovanni Farinella   University of Catania, Italy
Laurence Likforman   Télécom Paris, France
Jonathan Wu   Canada

Tutorial Chairs

David Clausi   University of Waterloo, Canada
Markus Enzweiler   Esslingen University of Applied Sciences,
                                   Germany
Umapada Pal   Indian Statistical Institute, India

Local Arrangements Chair

Ioannis Rekleitis   University of South Carolina, USA

Finance Chairs

Rainer Herpers   Hochschule Bonn-Rhein-Sieg, Germany
Andrew Hogue   Ontario Tech University, Canada

Publication Chairs

Jean-Jacques Rousseau   York University, Canada
Bill Kapralos   Ontario Tech University, Canada

Awards Chair

Johana Hansen   McGill University, Canada

Sponsorship and Exhibition Chair

Hong Zhang   China

Challenges Chairs

Marco Bertini   University of Florence, Italy
Dimosthenis Karatzas   Universitat Autónoma de Barcelona, Spain

Track 1: Artificial Intelligence, Machine Learning for Pattern Analysis

Battista Biggio   Università degli Studi di Cagliari, Italy
Ambra Demontis   Università degli Studi di Cagliari, Italy
Gang Hua   Wormpex AI Research, University of Washington,
                            USA
Dacheng Tao   University of Sydney, Australia

Track 2: Computer Vision and Robotic Perception

Olga Bellon   Universidade Federal do Parana, Brazil
Kosta Derpanis   York University, Canada
Ko Nishino   Kyoto University, Japan

Track 3: Image, Speech, Signal and Video Processing

Ana Fred   University of Lisbon, Portugal
Regina Lee   York University, Canada
Jingdong Wang   Baidu, China
Vera Yashina   Russian Academy of Sciences, Russian
                            Federation

Track 4: Biometrics and Human-Computer Interaction

Kevin Bowyer   University of Notre Dame, USA
Kerstin Dautenhahn   University of Waterloo, Canada
Julian Fierrez   Universidad Autónoma de Madrid, Spain
Shiqi Yu   Southern University of Science and Technology,
                            China

Track 5: Document Analysis and Recognition

Alexandra Branzan Albu   University of Victoria, Canada
Alicia Fornes   Universitat Autònoma de Barcelona, Spain
Koichi Kise   Osaka Prefecture University, Japan
Faisal Shafait   National University of Sciences and Technology,
                            Pakistan

Track 6: Biomedical Imaging and Informatics

Hamid Abbasi	Auckland Bioengineering Institute, New Zealand
Ismail Bey Ayed	Ecole de Technologie Superieure (ETS), Canada
Lukas Käll	KTH Royal Institute of Technology, Sweden
Dinggang Shen	ShanghaiTech University, China

ICPR 2022 Workshops: Volume I

Towards a Complete Analysis of People: From Face and Body to Clothes (T-CAP)

Mohamed Daoudi	IMT Lille Douai, France
Roberto Vezzani	University of Modena and Reggio Emilia, Italy
Guido Borghi	University of Bologna, Italy
Marcella Cornia	University of Modena and Reggio Emilia, Italy
Claudio Ferrari	University of Parma, Italy
Federico Becattini	University of Florence, Italy
Andrea Pilzer	NVIDIA AI Technology Center, Italy

12th International Workshop on Human Behavior Understanding (HBU)

Albert Ali Salah	Utrecht University, The Netherlands
Cristina Palmero	University of Barcelona, Spain
Hugo Jair Escalante	National Institute of Astrophysics, Optics and Electronics, Mexico
Sergio Escalera	Universitat de Barcelona, Spain
Henning Müller	HES-SO Valais-Wallis, Switzerland

Theories, Applications, and Cross Modality for Self-Supervised Learning Models (SSL)

Yu Wang	NVIDIA, USA
Yingwei Pan	JD AI Research, China
Jingjing Zou	UC San Diego, USA
Angelica I. Aviles-Rivero	University of Cambridge, UK
Carola-Bibiane Schönlieb	University of Cambridge, UK
John Aston	University of Cambridge, UK
Ting Yao	JD AI Research, China

Multimodal Pattern Recognition of Social Signals in Human-Computer-Interaction (MPRSS 2022)

Mariofanna Milanova	University of Arkansas at Little Rock, USA
Xavier Alameda-Pineda	Inria, University of Grenoble-Alpes, France
Friedhelm Schwenker	Ulm University, Germany

Fairness in Biometric Systems (FAIRBIO)

Philipp Terhörst	Paderborn University, Germany
Kiran Raja	Norwegian University of Science and Technology, Norway
Christian Rathgeb	Hochschule Darmstadt, Germany
Abhijit Das	BITS Pilani Hyderabad, India
Ana Filipa Sequeira	INESC TEC, Portugal
Antitza Dantcheva	Inria Sophia Antipolis, France
Sambit Bakshi	National Institute of Technology Rourkela, India
Raghavendra Ramachandra	Norwegian University of Science and Technology, Norway
Naser Damer	Fraunhofer Institute for Computer Graphics Research IGD, Germany

2nd International Workshop on Artificial Intelligence for Healthcare Applications (AIHA 2022)

Nicole Dalia Cilia	Kore University of Enna, Italy
Francesco Fontanella	University of Cassino and Southern Lazio, Italy
Claudio Marrocco	University of Cassino and Southern Lazio, Italy

Workshop on Multimodal Data for Mental Disorder Recognition (MDMR)

Richang Hong	Hefei University of Technology, China
Marwa Mahmoud	University of Glasgow, UK
Bin Hu	Lanzhou University, China

ICPR 2022 Workshops: Volume II

5th International Workshop on coMics ANalysis, Processing and Understanding (MANPU 2022)

Jean-Christophe Burie	University of La Rochelle, France
Motoi Iwata	Osaka Metropolitan University, Japan
Miki Ueno	Osaka Institute of Technology, Japan

Image Analysis for Forest Environmental Monitoring (FOREST)

Alexandre Bernardino	Instituto Superior Técnico, Portugal
El Khalil Cherif	Instituto Superior Técnico, Portugal
Catarina Barata	Instituto Superior Técnico, Portugal
Alexandra Moutinho	Instituto Superior Técnico, Portugal
Maria João Sousa	Instituto Superior Técnico, Portugal
Hugo Silva	Instituto Superior de Engenharia do Porto, Portugal

MultiMedia FORensics in the WILD (MMFORWILD 2022)

Mauro Barni	University of Siena, Italy
Sebastiano Battiato	University of Catania, Italy
Giulia Boato	University of Trento, Italy
Hany Farid	University of California, Berkeley, USA
Nasir Memon	New York University, USA

Image Mining: Theory and Applications (IMTA-VIII)

Igor Gurevich	Federal Research Center Computer Science and Control of the Russian Academy of Sciences, Russian Federation
Davide Moroni	Institute of Information Science and Technologies, National Research Council of Italy, Italy

Maria Antonietta Pascali   Institute of Information Science and
Technologies, National Research Council of
Italy, Italy

Vera Yashina   Federal Research Center Computer Science and
Control of the Russian Academy of Sciences,
Russian Federation

International Workshop on Pattern Recognition in Healthcare Analytics (PRHA 2022)

Inci Baytas   Bogazici University, Turkey

Edward Choi   Korea Advanced Institute of Science and
Technology, South Korea

Arzucan Ozgur   Bogazici University, Turkey

Ayse Basar   Bogazici University, Turkey

International Workshop on Industrial Machine Learning (IML)

Francesco Setti   University of Verona, Italy

Paolo Rota   University of Trento, Italy

Vittorio Murino   University of Verona, Italy

Luigi Di Stefano   University of Bologna, Italy

Massimiliano Mancini   University of Tübingen, Germany

ICPR 2022 Workshops: Volume III

3rd International Workshop on Pattern Recognition for Cultural Heritage (PatReCH 2022)

Dario Allegra   University of Catania, Italy
Mario Molinara   University of Cassino and Southern Lazio, Italy
Alessandra Scotto di Freca   University of Cassino and Southern Lazio, Italy
Filippo Stanco   University of Catania, Italy

2nd Workshop on Explainable and Ethical AI (XAIE 2022)

Romain Giot   Univ. Bordeaux, France
Jenny Benois-Pineau   Univ. Bordeaux, France
Romain Bourqui   Univ. Bordeaux, France
Dragutin Petkovic   San Francisco State University, USA

12th Workshop on Pattern Recognition in Remote Sensing (PRRS)

Ribana Roscher   University of Bonn, Germany
Charlotte Pelletier   Université Bretagne Sud, France
Sylvain Lobry   Paris Descartes University, France

Computer Vision for Analysis of Underwater Imagery (CVAUI)

Maia Hoeberechts   Ocean Networks Canada, Canada
Alexandra Branzan Albu   University of Victoria, Canada

Understanding and Mitigating Demographic Bias in Biometric Systems (UMDBB)

Ajita Rattani   Wichita State University, USA
Michael King   Florida Institute of Technology, USA

ICPR 2022 Workshops: Volume IV

AI for De-escalation: Autonomous Systems for De-escalating Conflict in Military and Civilian Contexts (AI4D)

Victor Sanchez	University of Warwick, UK
Irene Amerini	Sapienza University of Rome, Italy
Chang-Tsun Li	Deakin University, Australia
Wei Qi Yan	Auckland University of Technology, New Zealand
Yongjian Hu	South China University of Technology, China
Nicolas Sidere	La Rochelle Université, France
Jean-Jacques Rousseau	York University, Canada

3rd Workshop on Applied Multimodal Affect Recognition (AMAR)

Shaun Canavan	University of South Florida, USA
Tempestt Neal	University of South Florida, USA
Saurabh Hinduja	University of Pittsburgh, USA
Marvin Andujar	University of South Florida, USA
Lijun Yin	Binghamton University, USA

Contents – Part IV

Artificial Intelligence for Multimedia Forensics and Disinformation Detection (AI4MFDD)

Image Watermarking Backdoor Attacks in CNN-Based Classification Tasks 3
  Giovanbattista Abbate, Irene Amerini, and Roberto Caldelli

DepthFake: A Depth-Based Strategy for Detecting Deepfake Videos 17
  Luca Maiano, Lorenzo Papa, Ketbjano Vocaj, and Irene Amerini

An Effective Training Strategy for Enhanced Source Camera Device
Identification 32
  Manisha, Chang-Tsun Li, and Karunakar A. Kotegar

Improving Detection of Unprecedented Anti-forensics Attacks on Sensor
Pattern Noises Through Generative Adversarial Networks 46
  Yijun Quan and Chang-Tsun Li

Document Forgery Detection in the Context of Double JPEG Compression 57
  Théo Taburet, Kais Rouis, Mickaël Coustaty, Petra Gomez Krämer,
  Nicolas Sidère, Saddok Kébairi, and Vincent Poulain d'Andecy

Making Generated Images Hard to Spot: A Transferable Attack
on Synthetic Image Detectors 70
  Xinwei Zhao and Matthew C. Stamm

AI for De-escalation: Autonomous Systems for De-escalating Conflict in Military and Civilian Contexts (AI4D)

An Infrastructure for Studying the Role of Sentiment in Human-Robot
Interaction 89
  Enas Tarawneh, Jean-Jacques Rousseau, Stephanie G. Craig,
  Deeksha Chandola, Walleed Khan, Adnan Faizi, and Michael Jenkin

Sensorimotor System Design of Socially Intelligent Robots 106
  Aleksander Trajcevski, Helio Perroni Filho, Nizwa Javed,
  Tasneem Naheyan, Kartikeya Bhargava, and James H. Elder

3rd Workshop on Applied Multimodal Affect Recognition (AMAR)

The Effect of Model Compression on Fairness in Facial Expression
Recognition 121
  Samuil Stoychev and Hatice Gunes

Multimodal Stress State Detection from Facial Videos Using Physiological
Signals and Facial Features 139
  Yassine Ouzar, Lynda Lagha, Frédéric Bousefsaf, and Choubeila Maaoui

Expression Recognition Using a Flow-Based Latent-Space Representation 151
  Saandeep Aathreya and Shaun Canavan

An Ethical Discussion on BCI-Based Authentication 166
  Tyree Lewis, Rupal Agarwal, and Marvin Andujar

Author Index 179

Artificial Intelligence for Multimedia Forensics and Disinformation Detection (AI4MFDD)

Workshop on Artificial Intelligence for Multimedia Forensics and Disinformation Detection

Deliberate manipulations of multimedia content for malicious purposes have been a prevailing problem. With the phenomenal leap of AI and deep learning in recent years, realistically forged multimedia data is being used to propagate disinformation and fake news. This phenomenon is impacting social justice at the personal level and major political campaigns and national security at the national level. Moreover, it is affecting the stability of international relationships at the global level. The Workshop on Artificial Intelligence for Multimedia Forensics and Disinformation Detection (AI4MFDD) is intended to disseminate recent developments in AI-enabled multimedia forensics and disinformation detection. Multimedia data carry not only the value of their content but also their value in digital forensics for combating crimes and fraudulent activities, including disinformation.

AI4MFDD 2022 is the first edition of this workshop and was organized in conjunction with the 2022 International Conference on Pattern Recognition. The workshop received over 20 submissions. The top eight papers were selected for a presentation covering a wide range of topics, including deep fake detection, image watermarking, and source camera identification. The participants included researchers from eight countries: the USA, the UK, Australia, Italy, France, Switzerland, Austria, and India.

AI4MFDD 2022 included two keynote speakers: Prof. Anderson Rocha, from the University of Campinas, Brazil, and Dr. Pavel Korshunov, from the IDIAP Research Institute, Switzerland. Prof. Rocha's talk highlighted the main challenges in digital forensics and how AI is helping to tackle them. Dr. Korshunov's talk summarized how deep fakes are created and the difficulties in detecting them by using AI.

The success of this first edition of AI4MFDD set the basis for the organization of future editions.

Victor Sanchez
Chang-Tsun Li

Image Watermarking Backdoor Attacks in CNN-Based Classification Tasks

Giovanbattista Abbate[1], Irene Amerini[1] , and Roberto Caldelli[2,3]([✉])

[1] Sapienza University of Rome, Rome, Italy
amerini@diag.uniroma1.it
[2] CNIT, Florence, Italy
roberto.caldelli@unifi.it
[3] Universitas Mercatorum, Rome, Italy

Abstract. In these last years, neural networks are becoming the basis for different kinds of applications and this is mainly due to the stunning performances they offer. Nevertheless, all that glitters is not gold: such tools have demonstrated to be highly sensitive to malicious approaches such as gradient manipulation or the injection of adversarial samples. In particular, another kind of attack that can be performed is to poison a neural network during the training time by injecting a perceptually barely visible trigger signal in a small portion of the dataset (target class), to actually create a backdoor into the trained model. Such a backdoor can be then exploited to redirect all the predictions to the chosen target class at test time. In this work, a novel backdoor attack which resorts to image watermarking algorithms to generate a trigger signal is presented. The watermark signal is almost unperceivable and is embedded in a portion of images of the target class; two different watermarking algorithms have been tested. Experimental results carried out on datasets like MNIST and GTSRB provide satisfactory performances in terms of attack success rate and introduced distortion.

Keywords: Backdoor attack · image watermarking · CNN

1 Introduction

Heading back to fifteen years ago, machine learning applications included just a few tasks such as spam detectors, web search engines and malware filtering. Nowadays instead, more and more often machine learning techniques and in general artificial intelligence are being applied to a wide range of contexts, like machine translation, medical diagnosis, multimedia forensics, disinformation detection and many others more. The traditional approach to machine learning generally does not take into account the existence of a malicious attacker, trusting publicly available datasets and assuming that training and test sets are not poisoned. However, in real world, this is not the case and once a machine learning-based system has been deployed, malicious actors can try to modify its

J.-J. Rousseau and B. Kapralos (Eds.): ICPR 2022 Workshops, LNCS 13646, pp. 3–16, 2023.
https://doi.org/10.1007/978-3-031-37745-7_1

behaviour to take advantage for instance by avoiding a detection or by misleading a decision. An interesting example of misclassification was reported in [5], where by adversarially modifying a traffic sign, an autonomous driving system can misclassify a 'stop' sign to a 'yield' one, potentially leading to a dangerous event. Another up-to-date example regards the attempts to circumvent misinformation detection; it is therefore clear why studies [7] on the defense and on the attack of machine learning systems are of primary importance.

The work proposed in this paper focuses on *backdoor attacks* generated during the training phase of a learning process by poisoning a part of the dataset. Such trigger is then exploited at test time when the attacker decides to activate the backdoor. The first approaches of this attack [14] were devoted to perform a generic untargeted misclassification of the test set by manipulating the optimization process of the neural networks. The first example of targeted backdoor attack was done through label flipping of some samples in the training set [17]. In modern approaches, the attacker aims to modify a small amount of samples belonging to a chosen target class by poisoning the training set, superimposing a backdoor signal to this group of pristine images. Therefore, all the samples at test time with the trigger impressed will be theoretically classified as the poisoned target class. The main factors to keep into account while designing a backdoor attack are:

- **The rate of the poisoned samples in the training set should be as low as possible**: in this way, it is less likely that a defender will find poisoned samples while randomly checking the dataset.
- **Stealthiness of the attack**: the poisoned samples should ideally be indistinguishable from pristine ones. On a practical point of view, this is not always possible, because the success rate of the attack will in general increase while also increasing the amount of distortion caused by the superimposed backdoor. Therefore the attacker should try to maximize measures of perceptual quality, such as the Peak Signal-to-Noise Ratio (PSNR), between clean and poisoned images in the training set.
- **High accuracy of the poisoned model while tested with pristine samples**: introducing poisoned images will inevitably degrade the final accuracy of the model even when tested with pristine samples at test time. The attacker should always consider that the defender will discard a bad performing model, leading in a defeat for the attacker.

The attacker should balance the previous aspects in order to be as stealthy as possible, while keeping a high attack success rate by increasing the way the model can be triggered without decreasing, at the same time, the accuracy in front of pristine samples. So far, various backdoor techniques have been proposed in literature that differently provide such trade-off solutions and will be debated in Sect. 2. In this paper, it has been analyzed the use of a specific watermark to be superimposed on images of the training set and adopted as a backdoor. The attacker injects at training time such perceptually barely visible trigger in a small portion of the dataset (target class), to actually create a backdoor into a given model. Such watermarking-based trigger, has been found capable to totally deceive image classification CNNs, by letting the attacker redirect all the predictions to the chosen target class. Two different kinds of watermarking techniques also blended with image features have been investigated. Experimental results witness that trained model can be fooled with such an approach.

The paper is organized as follows: Sect. 2 reviews some previous works related to the topics of interest. Section 3 describes the proposed method based on watermarking techniques together with a blending technique exploiting activation features to strengthen the success rate of the attack. Datasets, metrics and implementation details are discussed in Sect. 4, while Sect. 5 reports the experimental results and a quantitative analysis with a comparison with respect to a baseline method. Some final considerations and future applications are provided in Sect. 6.

2 Related Works on Backdoor Attack

The term *backdoor attack* with regards to adversarial machine learning has been introduced in the work [2] which aims to study the possibility of fooling a learning system by injecting a physical backdoor in the training set. In particular, they added some accessories like glasses to human face images in order to misclassify an instance of the test set. The authors also put the focus on the use of blending images as backdoors in general, showing some results using a random RGB pattern and generic sample images. Another interesting work has been proposed in [6] where the authors used some small patterns like flowers, bombs and yellow squares placed in specific part of the images to poison the training set. In [1], the authors created two backdoor signals to be superimposed on the pristine images. The first one is a 2D ramp signal, used for the MNIST [11] dataset and the second backdoor signal is a 2D horizontal sinusoidal signal, used for the GTSRB [9] dataset whose frequency and amplitude can be properly tuned. The poisoned images, generated with such methods, appear to be satisfactorily indistinguishable from the pristine samples with respect to the previously presented techniques, thus enhancing the stealthiness of the attack. In a more recent work [12], the authors proposed to use reflections as backdoor into a victim model. Overviews of backdoor attacks against deep neural networks are anyway reported in [4,7]. More recent works [8,16] present methods to generate backdoor attacks in the frequency domain. Along the lines of such methodologies, we propose a backdoor attack that works in a different domain respect to the commonly used spatial domain. In this case exploiting watermarking algorithms, [3] and [15], able to generate an imperceptible signal and thus achieving the objective of making the poisoning images visually indistinguishable from clean ones.

3 The Proposed Method

The basic idea proposed in this method is to resort to digital watermarking to create a backdoor signal to fool a neural network in an image classification task. By embedding a watermark, at training time, over a certain defined portion (α)

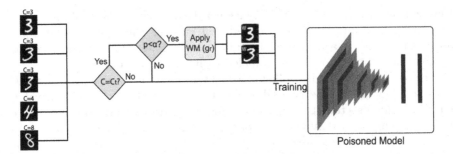

Fig. 1. Pipeline of the backdoor attack exploiting watermarks at training time. A target class $C_t = 3$ is chosen by the attacker: if a sample belongs to the target class, and if the actual rate of poisoned images p is less than the predefined final rate of poisoned images α, then a watermark of intensity g_r is applied on that sample and passed to the network. Otherwise, the image is directly fed into the model.

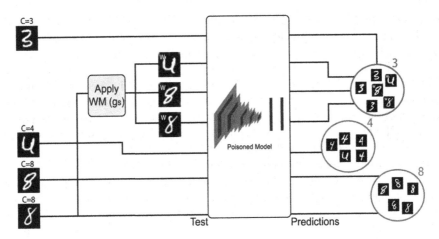

Fig. 2. Pipeline of the backdoor attack exploiting watermarks at test time with $C_t = 3$. The samples, in the test set, that embeds a watermark of intensity g_s will be predicted by the trained poisoned model as belonging to the target class $C_t = 3$. The samples without a watermark will continue to be correctly classified with their true labels.

of images belonging to a specific class C_t (*target class*) of the training set, it is then possible, at test time, to mislead the network in classifying test images. An attacker who knows such a backdoor could exploit it by inserting the same watermark signal in the images of the test set that will be identified as belonging to the chosen target class C_t though not being part of it. In fact, the neural network should have learnt that samples, presenting the watermark signal, belong to the target class C_t regardless their specific content. In Fig. 1, the pipeline of the training phase is sketched where the class for the digit "3" represents, by way of example, the target class C_t while g_r stands for the power parameter used to embed the watermark at training time. Similarly, during the prediction phase (see Fig. 2), the watermark is added with a tunable power (g_s) onto some of the test images in order to induce the poisoned model to misclassify them towards the C_t class while, at the same time, to preserve correct identification of the unwatermarked samples.

To achieve this aim, two image watermarking algorithms have been considered. Both resort to the transformed domain for casting the watermark into an image and this grants a good unperceivability of the inserted distortion; one is based on DCT (Discrete Cosine Transform) [3] and the other one on DFT (Discrete Fourier Transform) [15]. The watermark signal is basically the same number sequence generated by a pseudo-random number generator (PRNG) that is inserted within each image by accordingly modifying selected frequency coefficients of the cover image itself. Being such frequency coefficients different image by image, it yields that the watermark signal also contains an image-dependent component. Consequently, when the image content is significant (i.e. passing from MNIST dataset to GTSRB for instance, see Sect. 4) this effect is more dominant and could reduce the capacity of the backdoor attack at test time. According to this, we have investigated how the addition of an image-based component could improve performances. To this extent, on the basis of what presented in [2], we have decided to generate a signal, based on the images of the target class C_t, and to blend it with the watermarked image. In particular, in order to improve the stealthiness of this blending operation, we have chosen to train a convolutional neural network (*LeNet-5* has been adopted) using the pristine images of a dataset (e.g. GTSRB) and then to exploit the features captured by the convolutional layers at different levels of depth, as shown in Fig. 3 for each of the 13 classes composing the GTSRB dataset. Blending operation is

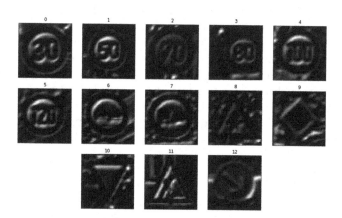

Fig. 3. Features captured by the internal convolutional layers of a *LeNet-5* architecture.

performed as:

$$I' = g_b \cdot B + (1 - g_b) \cdot I^w \tag{1}$$

where I' is the blended image, B represents the image generated by taking the activation features, g_b is the blending intensity (the terms g_{rb} and g_{sb} will be used to refer to the training and to the testing phase respectively) and I^w is the watermarked image generated as previously described. Such a blending operation which is applied after the watermark insertion, has to substantially grant a trade-off between introducing a more distinguishable signal which helps in poisoning the network and adding a further distortion, besides the watermark, which decreases the invisibility of the attack. According to this, different levels of depths have been investigated. It is easy to notice that when $g_b = 0$, the blended case reduces again to the only-watermark previous situation.

4   Experimental Setup

In this section a description of the datasets, the metrics and the architectures used to perform the experiments is given.

4.1   Datasets

Two well-known datasets, generally used for the task of image classification and also to work on neural network poisoning, have been considered:

– **Modified National Institute of Standards and Technology (MNIST)** dataset [11], which is a subset of a larger handwritten digits dataset proposed by the NIST, is composed of 28 × 28 gray-scale images. It contains 60000 training images and 10000 test images, divided in 10 classes (representing the digits from 0 to 9).
– **German Traffic Sign Recognition Benchmark (GTSRB)** dataset [9] which contains 39209 training images and 12630 test images representing road signs divided in 43 classes. For the experiments presented in this work, the dataset has been restricted to the 13 more populated classes. Furthermore, to balance the samples from different classes, a t-SNE [13] analysis of the restricted dataset has been performed, taking for each of the 13 classes the samples closer to the centroid of each class: 900 for the training set and 300 for the test set. Finally, there are 11700 (900 × 13) samples in the training set, 3900 (300 × 13) samples in the test set. Photos are RGB and 50 × 50 pixels.

4.2   Metrics and Settings

Peak Signal-to-Noise Ratio (PSNR) will be considered to measure the distortion introduced within an image by adding a poisoning signal, as indicated in Eq. (2):

$$PSNR = 10 \cdot \log_{10}\left(\frac{255^2}{MSE}\right) \tag{2}$$

where MSE states for the mean squared error between the original and the distorted image. The portion α of the poisoned images belonging to the target class C_t of the training set has been fixed at $\alpha = 0.3$ to grant a good trade-off between attack stealthiness and success rate. On the other side, to evaluate how effective is the backdoor attack, the Attack Success Rate (ASR) is considered (see Eq. (3)); given a target class C_t, it is computed over the test set and it is expressed as:

$$ASR = \frac{1}{N} \sum_{i=1}^{N} p_i, \text{ where } p_i = \begin{cases} 1, & \text{if } \phi(y_i) = C_t \\ 0, & \text{otherwise} \end{cases} \tag{3}$$

where N is the total number of poisoned test samples and $\phi(y_i)$ is the class prediction of the model given a sample y_i.

4.3   Implementation Details

The neural network that has been used for the experiments is the same adopted by the work in [1] and is composed by 2 blocks of 2 convolutional layers, one of 32 and one of 64 filters respectively, each followed by a max pooling; then 2 fully connected layers with 512 neurons (dropout 0.2) and 10 neurons respectively with a softmax at the end. The hole technique has been re-implemented and taken as baseline. This network uses categorical cross-entropy as loss function, accuracy as learning metric and Adam [10] as optimizer. The optimizer has been tuned with learning rate 10^{-3} and momentum 0.99. The network has been trained for 20 epochs, with batch size 64. The accuracy achieved for image classification, in absence of poisoning attacks, is 0.99. In addition to this, a *LeNet-5* network has been used to train a model on the GTSRB dataset to perform blending (see Sect. 3). This network also uses categorical cross-entropy as loss function, accuracy as learning metrics and Adam as optimizer tuned as before. The network has been trained for 100 epochs, with batch size 64, achieving an accuracy of 0.98. The implementation of both these networks, along with their training and testing has been done in Python via the Keras API. Both the datasets have been processed with standard Keras data augmentation in training set.

5   Experiments and Results

In this section, we report the experimental results obtained for the proposed image watermarking backdoor attack; two benchmark datasets, previously described in Sub-sect. 4.1 have been considered: results on MNIST are presented in Sub-sect. 5.1 while those ones on GTSRB are described in Sub-sect. 5.2.

5.1   Performances on MNIST Dataset

First of all, we have tried to understand if the proposed method could grant a satisfactory attack invisibility during the training phase in order to hide the

Table 1. PSNR (dB) of the DCT/DFT methods varying g_r on MNIST dataset for each target class C_t.

PSNR (dB) | DCT/DFT							
C_t	g_r						
	0.3/1.0	0.4/1.25	0.5/1.50	0.6/1.75	0.75/2.0	0.85/2.5	1.0/3.0
0	32.37/25.97	29.52/25.49	26.51/24.96	24.97/24.42	23.09/23.87	22.06/22.79	20.83/21.76
1	34.89/29.43	32.02/29.13	28.98/28.79	27.43/28.43	25.54/28.06	24.48/27.29	23.10/26.51
2	32.96/26.38	30.11/25.90	27.09/25.39	25.55/24.86	23.67/24.31	22.62/23.25	21.34/22.23
3	33.14/26.41	30.29/25.97	27.27/25.50	25.73/25.01	23.85/24.51	22.80/23.50	21.51/22.52
4	33.40/26.89	30.54/26.42	27.52/25.93	25.98/25.41	24.09/24.90	23.04/23.86	21.70/22.88
5	33.37/26.67	30.51/26.25	27.49/25.81	25.95/25.34	24.07/24.86	23.02/23.89	21.72/22.95
6	33.18/26.39	30.33/25.81	27.31/25.20	25.77/24.58	23.89/23.96	22.84/22.77	21.55/21.66
7	33.71/27.40	30.86/26.98	27.83/26.53	26.29/26.05	24.40/25.56	23.34/24.60	22.01/23.66
8	33.03/26.01	30.18/25.43	27.17/24.82	25.63/24.20	23.76/23.58	22.71/22.40	21.44/21.29
9	33.45/26.75	30.59/26.22	27.57/25.65	26.03/25.06	24.15/24.48	23.10/23.34	21.78/22.27
Average	**33.35/26.83**	**30.49/26.36**	**27.47/25.85**	**25.93/25.33**	**24.05/24.80**	**23.00/23.76**	**21.69/22.77**

presence of the watermark as backdoor signal. To do this, we can look at Table 1 where the average values of PSNR are computed with reference to the watermark power g_r, used at training, and to the target class C_t. Two approaches, based on the two watermarking algorithms previously introduced, have been taken into account DCT and DFT. The two watermarking methods, according to their specific structural characteristics and to the provided invisibility, have been tested in different ranges of power g_r: $[0.3 - 1.0]$ for DCT and $[1.0 - 3.0]$ for DFT. By looking at Table 1, it is possible to appreciate that, regardless the target class, the values of power g_r for the method DFT, permit to obtain an average image quality, in terms of PSNR, as high as DCT only for the larger intensities (columns on the right end), while DCT achieves PSNR values greater than 30 dB for lower g_r (columns on the left end). In particular, DCT technique demonstrates to perform satisfactorily with an average value of 33.35 dB for $g_r = 0.3$. If we compare, in general, this achievement with the technique in [1] which introduces a 2D-ramp signal as backdoor fingerprint (also in that case with $\alpha = 0.3$), we can see that it achieves a PSNR of 23.58 dB on average over the 10 classes (with $g_r = 30$); this means an increment of around 10 dB. On this basis, we have decided to take the most favourable situation in terms of introduced distortion (low values of g_r which grant the best attack stealthiness) and to verify the corresponding attack success rate (only results for the DCT approach are presented from here on for sake of conciseness). If we look at Fig. 4a where the case $g_r = 0.3$ and $C_t = 8$ is pictured, it is possible to understand that the DCT approach achieves satisfactory levels of ASR. By making a comparison again with the baseline method [1] in Fig. 4b, a superior performance in terms of average values is obtained. In particular, if we look at the orange bars, the proposed watermark-based method performs better in terms of success rate (see dashed orange line for the mean on all the target classes) of about 20% (75.9% versus 54.4%). Moreover, from Fig. 5, the confusion matrices of the experiment with $C_t = 8$ and $g_r = 0.3$ are presented to visualize the behaviour of the attack;

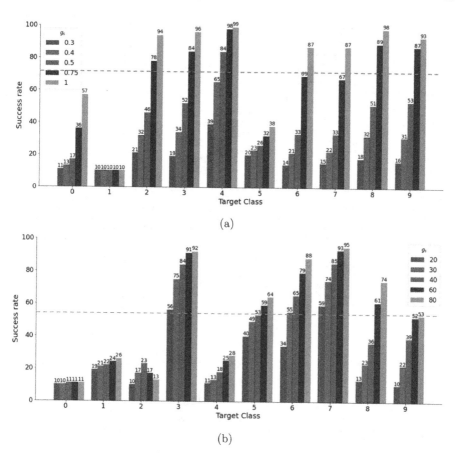

Fig. 4. Attack success rates on MNIST dataset with different values of g_s. The orange dashed lines indicates the average success rate referred to the orange bins. The proposed DCT-based watermark backdoor attack (a) ($g_r = 0.3$) and the method in [1] (b) ($g_r = 30$). (Color figure online)

three different values of $g_s = [0; 0.3; 0.75]$ (the power at test time) are reported. As it is possible to see, by increasing the value of g_s, the confusion matrices degenerate to a single column, which is the expected behaviour. The case $g_s = 0$ (see Fig. 5a) represents when the model correctly classifies the test set in the situation that it does not contain poisoned samples (i.e. the backdoor is not triggered). This is one of the main assumptions for the backdoor attacks, since it should be stealthy as possible in presence of a pristine test set even if, during the training phase, poisoned data have been introduced.

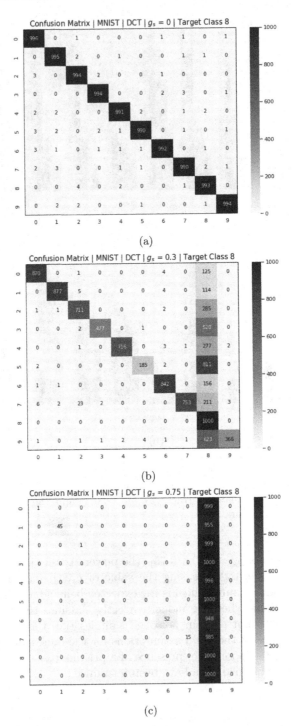

Fig. 5. Confusion Matrices for the DCT Backdoor Attack. The experiments are performed on a model trained with $g_r = 0.3$ and target class $C_t = 8$ by using $g_s = 0$ (pristine test set) (a), $g_s = 0.3$ (b) and $g_s = 0.75$ (c).

Table 2. Average PSNR and g_r for different backdoor methods for the GTSRB training dataset ($\alpha = 0.3$).

Backdoor Attacks	g_r	PSNR
DFT	3	19.82 dB
DCT	3	18.80 dB
Blending ($g_{rb} = 0.3$) + DCT	2	21.42 dB
Reference method [1]	30	21.22 dB

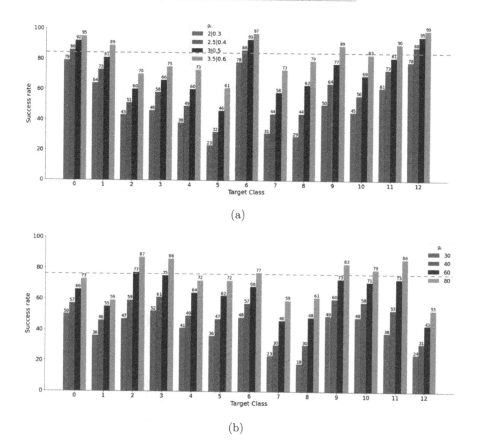

(a)

(b)

Fig. 6. Success rates of *Blending + DCT* backdoor attack (left) vs [1] (right). The experiments are performed with $g_r = 2$, $g_{rb} = 0.3$; $g_r = 30$ for [1]. (Color figure online)

5.2   Performances on GTSRB Dataset

Results regarding the GTSRB dataset are presented in this section similarly to what has been done previously for MNIST dataset. The GTSRB dataset which contains RGB images of road signs is more challenging than MNIST which is only made of handcrafted digit pictures at gray levels. In this case, it is quite difficult to achieve a good trade-off between the requirement of backdoor attack stealthiness and that one of a significant attack success rate. The two water-marking approaches proposed to poison the model towards the target class C_t provide both lower values of average PSNR (see some sample values in Table 2), with respect to the MNIST case, but notwithstanding this, they do not succeed in granting acceptable attack success rates. As already described in Sect. 3, we have decided, for the GTSRB dataset, to resort to a blending operation in order to globally improve performances. The idea behind this was to tolerate a poorer

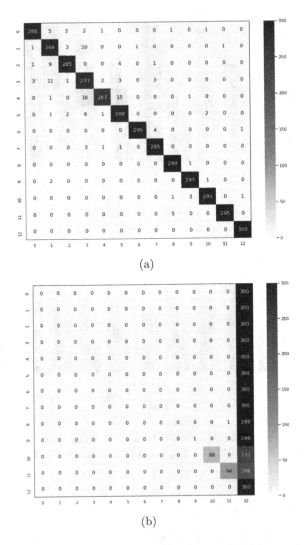

(a)

(b)

Fig. 7. Confusion Matrices obtained with *Blending + DCT* ($g_r = 2, g_{rb} = 0.3$ and $C_t = 12$ as target class): $g_s = g_{sb} = 0$ (pristine test set) (a) and $g_s = 3.5$, $g_{sb} = 0.6$ (b).

visual quality (slightly over 21 dB) but, at least, to achieve a plausible attack success rate. Such PSNR values are anyway comparable with what it is obtained by the reference model [1] (see Table 2) which, in the GTSRB case, applies a 2D-sinusoidal wave as trigger signal.

As done before, we can now make a comparison in terms of attack success rate over the different classes, again with the same poison rate $\alpha = 0.3$. We can see, as depicted in Fig. 6a for the case *Blending + DCT*, that there is a general improvement with respect to the reference method pictured in Fig. 6b. In fact, it can be noted that there is an increment both in terms of peak and average values; for instance, if we consider as before the orange bars ($g_s = 3.5$ and $g_{sb} = 0.6$) an average attack success rate of 89.41% versus 78.41% can be achieved (orange dashed lines). Moreover, the confusion matrices, shown in Fig. 7, behave as expected. For $g_s = g_{sb} = 0$, it is granted an almost perfect stealthiness of the attack in presence of a pristine test set (see Fig. 7a); while when the backdoor is triggered most of the samples are wrongly classified as belonging to the target class C_t (see Fig. 7b where $C_t = 12$ in this specific case). These confusion matrices are generated from a model trained with $g_r = 2$ and $g_{rb} = 0.3$.

6 Conclusions

In this paper the problem of creating backdoor attacks in convolutional neural networks has been tackled by exploiting watermarking algorithms based on frequency domain along with the addition of the blending of activation features. The embedding of watermark-based backdoors has been tested in image classification task providing limited degree of perceivability of the introduced distortion. The proposed method achieves the state of the art for both the analysed datasets (MNIST and GTSRB) in term of PSNR values but also in terms of attack success rates on average. Since the techniques presented in this paper rely on pseudo-random distributions, future works should be focused on finding the best possible watermark distribution, for instance with the use of Generative Adversarial Networks (GANs), in order to generate the best samples respect to the evaluated metrics. Moreover, different domains such as wavelet transform can be explored for watermark generation together with the analysis of more complex deep learning models and image datasets.

References

1. Barni, M., Kallas, K., Tondi, B.: A new backdoor attack in CNNs by training set corruption without label poisoning. In: 2019 IEEE International Conference on Image Processing (ICIP), pp. 101–105 (2019). https://doi.org/10.1109/ICIP.2019.8802997
2. Chen, X., Liu, C., Li, B., Lu, K., Song, D.X.: Targeted backdoor attacks on deep learning systems using data poisoning. arXiv abs/1712.05526 (2017)

3. Cox, I., Kilian, J., Leighton, F., Shamoon, T.: Secure spread spectrum watermarking for multimedia. IEEE Trans. Image Process. **6**(12), 1673–1687 (1997). https://doi.org/10.1109/83.650120. https://ieeexplore.ieee.org/document/650120/

4. Gao, Y., et al.: Backdoor attacks and countermeasures on deep learning: a comprehensive review (2020). https://doi.org/10.48550/ARXIV.2007.10760. https://arxiv.org/abs/2007.10760

5. Goodfellow, I., McDaniel, P., Papernot, N.: Making machine learning robust against adversarial inputs. Commun. ACM **61**(7), 56–66 (2018). https://doi.org/10.1145/3134599

6. Gu, T., Dolan-Gavitt, B., Garg, S.: Badnets: identifying vulnerabilities in the machine learning model supply chain (2017). https://doi.org/10.48550/ARXIV.1708.06733. https://arxiv.org/abs/1708.06733

7. Guo, W., Tondi, B., Barni, M.: An overview of backdoor attacks against deep neural networks and possible defences. arXiv (2021). arXiv:2111.08429

8. Hammoud, H.A.A.K., Ghanem, B.: Check your other door! creating backdoor attacks in the frequency domain (2021). https://doi.org/10.48550/ARXIV.2109.05507. https://arxiv.org/abs/2109.05507

9. Houben, S., Stallkamp, J., Salmen, J., Schlipsing, M., Igel, C.: Detection of traffic signs in real-world images: the German traffic sign detection benchmark. In: International Joint Conference on Neural Networks, no. 1288 (2013)

10. Kingma, D.P., Ba, J.: Adam: a method for stochastic optimization (2014). https://doi.org/10.48550/ARXIV.1412.6980. https://arxiv.org/abs/1412.6980

11. LeCun, Y., Cortes, C.: MNIST handwritten digit database (2010). http://yann.lecun.com/exdb/mnist/

12. Liu, Y., Ma, X., Bailey, J., Lu, F.: Reflection backdoor: a natural backdoor attack on deep neural networks. arXiv:2007.02343 (2020). http://arxiv.org/abs/2007.02343. arXiv: 2007.02343

13. van der Maaten, L., Hinton, G.: Visualizing data using t-SNE. J. Mach. Learn. Res. **9**(86), 2579–2605 (2008). http://jmlr.org/papers/v9/vandermaaten08a.html

14. Muñoz-González, L., et al.: Towards poisoning of deep learning algorithms with back-gradient optimization. In: Proceedings of the 10th ACM Workshop on Artificial Intelligence and Security, pp. 27–38. ACM (2017). https://doi.org/10.1145/3128572.3140451. https://dl.acm.org/doi/10.1145/3128572.3140451

15. De Rosa, A., Barni, M., Bartolini, F., Cappellini, V., Piva, A.: Optimum decoding of non-additive full frame DFT watermarks. In: Pfitzmann, A. (ed.) IH 1999. LNCS, vol. 1768, pp. 159–171. Springer, Heidelberg (2000). https://doi.org/10.1007/10719724_12

16. Wang, T., Yao, Y., Xu, F., An, S., Tong, H., Wang, T.: Backdoor attack through frequency domain (2021). https://doi.org/10.48550/ARXIV.2111.10991. https://arxiv.org/abs/2111.10991

17. Xiao, H., Eckert, C.: Adversarial label flips attack on support vector machines. In: ECAI 2012: Proceedings of the 20th European Conference on Artificial Intelligence, pp. 870–875 (2012). https://doi.org/10.3233/978-1-61499-098-7-870

DepthFake: A Depth-Based Strategy for Detecting Deepfake Videos

Luca Maiano, Lorenzo Papa, Ketbjano Vocaj, and Irene Amerini[✉]

Sapienza University of Rome, Rome, Italy
{maiano,papa,amerini}@diag.uniroma1.it

Abstract. Fake content has grown at an incredible rate over the past few years. The spread of social media and online platforms makes their dissemination on a large scale increasingly accessible by malicious actors. In parallel, due to the growing diffusion of fake image generation methods, many Deep Learning-based detection techniques have been proposed. Most of those methods rely on extracting salient features from RGB images to detect through a binary classifier if the image is fake or real.

In this paper, we proposed DepthFake, a study on how to improve classical RGB-based approaches with depth-maps. The depth information is extracted from RGB images with recent monocular depth estimation techniques. Here, we demonstrate the effective contribution of depth-maps to the deepfake detection task on robust pre-trained architectures. The proposed *RGBD* approach is in fact able to achieve an average improvement of 3.20% and up to 11.7% for some deepfake attacks with respect to standard RGB architectures over the FaceForensic++ dataset.

Keywords: Deepfake Detection · Depth Estimation · Deep Learning · Computer Vision

1 Introduction

Recent advances in artificial intelligence enable the generation of fake images and videos with an incredible level of realism. The latest deepfakes on the war in Ukraine[1] have clarified the need to develop solutions to detect generated videos. This is just the latest example in a long series of realistic deepfake videos that have hit public figures in the last few years. Deepfakes have become a real threat, and the techniques for generating this content are advancing at an incredible speed. The term deepfake originally came from a Reddit user called "deepfakes" that in 2017 used off-the-shelf AI tools to paste celebrities' faces onto pornographic video clips. Today, the term typically has a broader meaning and refers to every kind of face manipulation technique based on artificial intelligence and computer graphics.

---

[1] https://www.bbc.com/news/technology-60780142.

© Springer Nature Switzerland AG 2023
J.-J. Rousseau and B. Kapralos (Eds.): ICPR 2022 Workshops, LNCS 13646, pp. 17–31, 2023.
https://doi.org/10.1007/978-3-031-37745-7_2

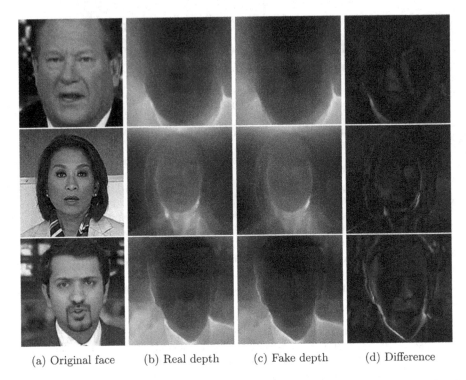

(a) Original face   (b) Real depth   (c) Fake depth   (d) Difference

Fig. 1. Some example inconsistencies introduced in the depth map of manipulated faces. Deepfake faces tend to have less details than the original ones.

Automatic face manipulations can be divided in two main categories: *face swap* or *reenactment* [35, 36]. Face swap applies some source characteristics onto a target face. Reenactment is a more sophisticated technique that enables the reenactment of a target person while maintaining its natural aspect. Dealing with such a heterogeneous range of manipulations is the main challenge for current deepfake video detectors. In fact, video content creation techniques are still improving month by month, which makes video content detection an even more complex problem, as for each new detector there is always a new generation method that is more realistic than the previous one.

In this paper, we analyze the depth inconsistencies introduced by face manipulation methods. Unlike methods that analyze either imaging pipelines (e.g., PRNU noise [26], specifications [21]), encoding approaches (e.g., JPEG compression patterns [4]), or image fingerprint methods [40], our study analyzes the alteration introduced by the manipulation on RGB and depth features. These spatial features contain semantic information that has the advantage of being more easily interpretable and robust to strong compression operations. With these strengths, *semantic features* can help solve two major challenges with deepfake detection. On the one hand, the lack of explainable detectors, which do not limit themselves to classifying the contents as true or false but allow us to understand what information led to a certain decision. On the other hand, these detectors should be robust to detect fake videos even when some low-level information gets destroyed by compression algorithms. This is particularly important when a video is disseminated on social networks and published several times by different users. In fact, most platforms often reduce the quality and resolution of the video, which can weaken many deepfake detectors. To analyze these semantic features, in this paper we propose to extract the depth of the face with a monocular-based estimation method that is concatenated to the RGB image. We than train a network to classify each video frame as *real* or *fake*. These two modalities enable the analysis of semantic inconsistencies in each frame by investigating color and spatial irregularities.

To demonstrate the effectiveness of our *DepthFake* method, we conduct extensive experiments on different classes included in the FaceForensics++ [33] dataset. In our experiments, we demonstrate the effectiveness of our method by introducing a vanilla *RGB* baseline and demonstrating that adding depth information allows us to systematically improve detection performance. In summary, the main contributions of this paper are threefold as below.

- We analyze the importance of depth features and show that they consistently improve the detection rate. *To the best of our knowledge*, this is the first work that analyses the depth inconsistencies left by the deepfake creation process. Figure 1 shows some example of depth inconsistencies.
- We investigate the contribution of the RGB data and show that a simple RGB-to-grayscale conversion can still lead to acceptable or even higher results in some experiments. We hypothesize that there are semantic features in this conversion that still allow good detection despite the reduction of input channels.
- We conduct preliminary experiments on inference times required by one of the most used convolutional neural networks on several hardware configurations. The increasingly massive adoption of streaming and video conferencing applications brings the need to develop deepfake detection solutions in *real-time*. With this work, we propose some experiments to analyze the impact of using multiple channels such as depth or grayscale features on inference times. Our aim is to analyze the impact of our multi-channel model on inference time. These first experiments are a valuable baseline for future developments and studies.

The remainder of this paper is organized as follows: Sect. 2 presents state-of-the-art methods for deepfake generation, detection, and single image depth estimation. The proposed detection technique is explained in Sect. 3 as regards the feature extraction and the classification phase. Section 4 reports the experimental results. Finally, Sect. 5 concludes the paper with insights for future works.

2   Related Works

In this section, we examine the state-of-the-art by comparing the contribution of our method to the others. The section begins by reviewing the deepfake detection techniques and ends with an overview of the state-of-the-art methods for monocular depth estimation.

2.1   Deepfake Detection

There are four common strategies to create a deepfake video: (i) face identity swap, (ii) facial attribute or (iii) expression modification and (iv) entire image synthesis. These methods are used in combination with 3D models, AutoEncoders, or Generative Adversarial Networks to forge the fake image that is then blended into the original one. Recent studies [10,39] demonstrate the possibility of detecting the specific cues introduced by this fake generation process. Some methods train deep neural networks to learn these features. Some other methods analyze the semantics of the video to search for inconsistencies. More recently, some researchers have come up with the idea of testing whether a person's behavior in a video is consistent with a given set of sample videos of this person, which we call re-identification for the sake of brevity. Our work falls between the first two approaches and examines RGB and depth features. In the remainder of this section, we discuss the most related detection approaches.

Learned Features. Most efforts focus on identifying features that can be learned from a model. The study from Afchar et al. [1] was one of the first approaches for deefake detection based on supervised learning. This method focuses on mesoscopic features to analyze the video frames by using a network with a low number of layers. Rossler et al. [33] investigate the performance of several CNN architectures for deepfake video detection and show that deeper networks are more effective for this task. Also, the attention mechanism introduced by Dang et al. [13] improves the localization of the manipulated regions. Following this research trend, our method adds a step that can be used in conjunction with other techniques to improve the detection of fake videos.

In addition to spatial inconsistencies, fake artifacts arise along the temporal direction and can be used for forensic investigation. Caldelli et al. [7] exploit temporal discrepancies through the analysis of optical flow features. Guera et al. [18] propose the use of convolutional Long Short Term Memory (LSTM) network while Masi et al. [27] extract RGB and residual image features and fuse them into an LSTM. Like for the spatial domain, the attention also improves the detection of temporal artifacts [43]. In this preliminary work, we do not consider the temporal inconsistencies of the depth, although we believe that this analysis can further improve the performance of a model based on these features and we leave this investigation for future works.

Moreover, data augmentation strategies constitute another ingredient to improve the detection and generalization [10]. Top performers in the recent DeepFake's detection challenge [15] use extensive augmentation techniques. In particular, the augmentations based on the cut-off on some specific parts of the face have proved to be particularly effective [6,16].

Semantic Features. Several studies look at specific semantic artifacts of the fake video. Many works have focused on biological signals such as blinking [25] (which occurs with a certain frequency and duration in real videos), heartbeat [31] and other biological signals to find anomalies in the spatial and temporal direction. Other approaches use inconsistencies on head pose [38] or face warping [23] artifacts to detect fake content.

Recently, multiple modalities have also been proved very effective for deepfake detection. Mittal et al. [28] use audio-visual features to detect emotion inconsistencies in the subject. Zhou et al. [42] use a similar approach to analyze the intrinsic synchronization between the video and audio modalities. Zhao et al. [41] introduce a multimodal attention method that fuses visual and textual features. While our method does not fall directly into this category, we still incorporate some semantic information into our model. In fact, we use CNN architectures pre-trained on ImageNet [14], which still leads our model to extract high-level features on image semantics. Furthermore, anomalies in depth can be considered semantic features, as a real face should have features in three dimensions. If there are anomalies in this sense, that is a "flat" face, this would introduce a semantic inconsistency.

Re-identification Features. Re-identification methods distinguish each individual by extracting some specific biometric traits that can be hardly reproduced by a generator [2,3]. The first work of this kind was introduced by Agarwal et al. [3] and exploits the distinct patterns of facial and head movements of an individual to detect fake videos. In another work [2], the same research group studied the inconsistencies between the mouth shape dynamics and a spoken phoneme. Cozzolino et al. [12] introduced a method that extracts facial features based on a 3D morphable model and focuses on temporal behavior through an adversarial learning strategy. Another work [11] introduces a contrastive method based on audio-visual features for person-of-interest deepfake detection.

2.2 Monocular Depth Estimation

Monocular depth estimation (MDE) is a fundamental task in computer vision where a per-pixel distance map is reconstructed from a single RGB input image. Unlike other passive depth perception methodologies such as the binocular stereo vision and the multi-view systems, this depth perception approach does not impose any geometric constraints due to the use of a single camera, thus leading to a multitude of possible applications such as scene understanding and robotics.

Multiple works have been proposed to tackle the problem. Recent works are mainly divided into two trends: the transformers and deep convolutional architectures that aim to predict a depth-map with the highest estimation accuracy [5,24,32], while the other trend focuses their attention on lightweight architectures [8,29,30] to infer at high frame rates on embedded and mobile devices.

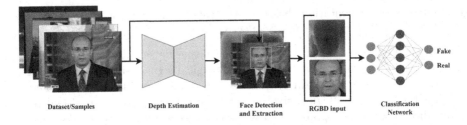

Fig. 2. Pipeline of the proposed method. In the fist step, we estimate the depth for each frame. Then, we extract the face and crop the frame and depth map around the face. In the last step, we train a classifier on *RGBD* input features.

Moreover, depth information can be successfully integrated with RGB data, i.e. into an *RGBD* approach, to obtain notable improvements in other challenging tasks. He et al. [19] propose SOSD-Net, an multi-task learning architecture for semantic object segmentation and monocular depth estimation enforcing geometric constraint while sharing common features between the two tasks. Vége et al. [37] propose a two step architecture based on 2D pose estimation and monocular depth images for the 3D pose estimation task.

Similarly to the just introduced works, in this study we take advantage of depth-maps information to tackle the deepfake detection task. Moreover, due to the lack of depth data we use the pre-trained monocular depth estimation model proposed by Khan et at. [22] to extract depth face-images from deepfake datasets. Khan et at. propose a convolutional encoder-decoder network trained on estimating monocular depth of subjects which appear closer to the camera, i.e. with a limited depth range that goes from 0.3 to 5.0 m; with this setup we are able to explore and understand the depth channel contribution for the deepfake detection task.

3   Proposed Method

In this section, we introduce *DepthFake*. Our system is structured in two steps. First, we estimate the depth of the entire image through the FaceDepth model proposed by Khan et al. [22]. This model is pre-trained to estimate the depth of human faces. Next, in the second phase we extract a 224 × 224 patch of the subject's face from both the RGB image and depth map. This step allows extracting the face without having to resize the image, as resizing may eliminate precious details useful for classification. Finally, we train a convolutional neural network to classify whether the content is fake or real.

In Sects. 3.1 and 3.2, we delve into the two modules with further details on the system represented in Fig. 2, while in Sect. 3.3 we discuss about the implementation details.

3.1   Depth Estimation

Depth estimation is at the heart of our method. In fact, we hypothesize that the process of generating deepfakes introduces depth distortions on the subject's face. Therefore, the first step in the proposed pipeline is extracting the depth of the face. As explained in Sect. 2, we can estimate the depth of an image through a monocular depth estimation technique. However, since there are no deepfake datasets containing ground-truth depth information, we propose to use a pre-trained model.

Current deepfakes are usually created with a foreground subject. Therefore, we adopt the FaceDepth [22], a network trained to estimate the distance of the subjects captured by the camera. The model is trained on synthetic and realistic 3D data where the camera is set at a distance of thirty centimeters from the subject and the maximum distance of the background is five meters. This allows us to discriminate facial features by obtaining fine-grained information on the depth of each point of the face. The model has an encoder-decoder structure and consists of a MobileNet [20] network that works as a feature extractor, followed by a series of upsampling layers and a single pointwise layer. The network was trained to receive 480×640 input images and output a 240×320 depth map. The estimated map constitutes one of the four input channels of our deepfake discriminator.

3.2   Deepfake Detection

The second module of our system concatenates the estimated depth map to the original RGB image. Since the alterations introduced by deepfakes are usually more significant on the subject's face, we crop 224×224 pixels to extract the face from the rest of the image. The result of this concatenation generates an $RGBD$ tensor $x \in \mathbb{R}^{224 \times 224 \times 4}$, which constitutes the input of our classification network.

In the last step of our method, we train a neural network to classify real and fake video frames. In terms of architecture, we use an Xception [9] network pre-trained on ImageNet [14]. Since we are using a network pre-trained on classical RGB images, i.e. the one used for ImageNet, the addition of the depth channel as forth input creates the need to adapt and modify the initial structure of the original network to handle this type of data while guaranteeing the correct weights initialization. Therefore, if we randomly initialized an input layer with 4 channels, this would end up heavily affecting the weights learned during the pre-training phase. To solve this problem, we decided to add an additional channel obtained by calculating the average of the three original input channels from the pre-trained model. This change makes the training more stable and allows the model to converge towards the optimum fastly. Consequently, we have chosen to use this initialization method for all the experiments. In addition to this, there is a further problem to be taken into consideration. The values contained in the depth channel range from 0 to 5000, which is the range in which the depth estimation module has been pre-trained. Linking this channel to the RGB channel without normalizing these values would end up causing numerical instability and would heavily cancel the RGB contribution. To handle this problem we normalize the depth channel values in the range 0–255.

In terms of augmentations, we apply flipping and rotation. While it has been shown that the strongest boost based on compression and blurring generally improves performance for this task, we decide to keep the augment strategy as simple as possible to avoid altering the information provided by the depth channel.

Added to this, we investigate the contribution of the RGB color model for deepfake detection when paired to the depth information. To this end, we train our system on 2-channel grayscale plus depth input data ($x \in \mathbb{R}^{224 \times 224 \times 2}$). The results reported in Sect. 4, show that a system trained on depth and grayscale features achieves acceptable or higher results than *RGBD* input data and superior results compared to standard RGB inputs. In this configuration, the network may assign a greater contribution to the depth channel, thus reducing the importance of the information contained in the RGB space. While this is not the goal of this work, it allows us to analyze the impact of a different number of input channels on model inference times, which can be extremely important for real-time applications (Table 1).

Table 1. Accuracy on Deepfake (DF), Face2Face (F2F), FaceSwap (FS), NeuralTexture (NT) and the full dataset (FULL) with RGB and RGBD inputs. Bold represents the best configuration of each backbone and underlined accuracies represent the best value over each class. In brackets we indicate the percentage difference added by the depth.

	ResNet50		MobileNet–V1		XceptioNet	
	RGB	RGBD	RGB	RGBD	RGB	RGBD
DF	93.91%	**94.71%** (+0.8)	95.14%	**95.86%** (+0.72)	97.65%	**97.76%** (+0.11)
F2F	96.42%	**96.58%** (+0.16)	97.07%	**98.44%** (+1.37)	95.82%	**97.41%** (+1.59)
FS	97.14%	**96.95%** (−0.19)	97.12%	**97.87%** (+0.75)	97.84%	**98.80%** (+0.96)
NT	75.81%	**77.42%** (+1.61)	70.47%	**82.26%** (+11.79)	76.87%	**85.09%** (+8.22)
FULL	85.68%	**90.48%** (+4.80)	90.60%	**91.12%** (+0.52)	86.80%	**91.93%** (+5.13)

3.3   Implementation Details

We implement the proposed study using the *TensorFlow*[2] API and train the system on an NVIDIA GTX 1080 with 8GB of memory. In all the experiments

---

[2] https://www.tensorflow.org/.

Table 2. Accuracy of the Xception-based model on video level for Deepfake (DF), Face2Face (F2F), FaceSwap (FS), NeuralTexture (NT) and the full dataset (FULL) with RGB and RGBD inputs. In brackets we indicate the percentage difference added by the depth, while bold represents the best configuration.

	RGB	RGBD
DF	97.25%	**98.85%** +(1.60)
F2F	97.50%	**98.75%** +(2.25)
FS	98.00%	**98.75%** +(0.75)
NT	81.25%	**88.00%** +(6.25)
FULL	87.00%	**93.00%** +(6.00)

we use ADAMAX as optimizer with the following setup: a starting learning rate equal to 0.01 with 0.1 decay, $\beta_1 = 0.9$, $\beta_2 = 0.999$, and $\epsilon = 1e^{-07}$. The training process is performed for 25 epochs with a batch size of 32. We set the input resolution of the architectures equal to 224×224 while cropping the original input image around the face. The face detection and extraction is performed with $dlib^3$. The loss function chosen for the training process is the Binary Crossentropy, a widely employed function for classification tasks; its mathematical formulation is reported in Eq. 1, where we indicate with $\hat{y}_i$ the predicted sample and with y_i the target one.

$$Loss = -\frac{1}{2} \sum_{i=1}^{2} y_i \cdot log\hat{y}_i + (1 - y_i) \cdot log(1 - \hat{y}_i) \qquad (1)$$

Once the training phase has been completed, we compare the inference times between the different models and input channels; we report those values in milliseconds (ms) in Sect. 4.

4   Results

In this section we report the experiments and evaluations that have been conducted. We propose a comparison with some well established CNN networks and show the first results on the inference times of the model that will be deepened in future studies. We evaluate our model on the FaceForensic++ [33] dataset, which allows us to evaluate the importance of depth features on the most common strategies to create a deepfake. This dataset is composed of 1000 original video sequences that have been manipulated with four face forgeries, namely:

---

[3] http://dlib.net/.

Deepfake (DF), Face2Face (F2F), FaceSwap (FS) and NeuralTexture (NT). For all experiments, we split the dataset into a fixed training, validation, and test set, consisting of 90%, 5%, and 5% of the videos, respectively.

4.1 Deepfake Detection

We begin our experiments by analyzing the effectiveness of the proposed solution in identifying deepfakes. We train our system to solve a binary classification task on individual video frames. We evaluated multiple variants of our approach by using different state-of-the-art classification methods. In addition, we show that the classification based on the Xception [9] architecture outperforms all other variants in detecting fakes, as previously demonstrated in other works [17,33].

Table 3. Floating point operations (FLOPS) and average frame per second (FPS) inference frequency over different platforms. For the GrayD and RGBD we indicate in brackets the difference with respect to the Gray and RGB models respectively.

	ARM Cortex CPU [fps]	Nvidia GTX 1080 [fps]	Nvidia Titan V [fps]	Nvidia RTX 3090 [fps]	Giga FLOPS
Gray	0.497	28.33	25.02	20.41	9.19
GrayD	0.496 (−0.001)	27.91 (−0.42)	25.66 (−0.26)	19.96 (−0.45)	9.20 (+0.01)
RGB	0.499	27.89	26.54	21.27	9.211
RGBD	0.495 (−0.005)	27.94 (−0.05)	23.77 (−2.77)	19.74 (−1.53)	9.218 (+0.007)

First, we evaluate the effectiveness of the main backbones that are popular for deepfake detection: ResNet50 [34], MobileNet [20], and XceptionNet [9]. Table 3 compares the results of our experiments with all our configurations. As shown in other studies [10,33], the Xception network achieves the best performance on all backbones. The results show that the depth input channel always improves the model's performance in all configurations. Added to this, it is interesting to note that the MobileNet is slightly inferior to the Xception and outperforms the deeper ResNet50. This is a notable result when considering the goal of reducing inference times for real-time applications. While this is not the main contribution of this work, we still consider it an encouraging result for future developments.

Next, to have a complete overview of the depth contribution, we compare the Xception's performances through the following four setups.

- **RGB.** The baseline on which the different backbones have been trained using only the RGB channels.
- **Gray.** The backbone trained on grayscale image solely.
- **RGBD.** The model that is trained on 4-channel inputs based on the composition of the RGB and depth channels.

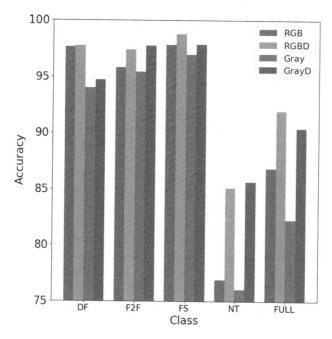

Fig. 3. Accuracy on Deepfake (DF), Face2Face (F2F), FaceSwap (FS), NeuralTexture (NT) and all classes in the dataset (FULL) with RGB, RGBD, Gray and GrayD inputs.

– **GrayD**. The configuration that is trained on 2-channel inputs composed of grayscale and depth channels.

As shown in Fig. 3, the results reveal a consistent advantage of the *RGBD* and *GrayD* configurations over other *RGB* and *Gray* ones. In particular, this advantage is more evident in the NeuralTexture class, which is also the most difficult class to recognize among those analyzed. For the *GrayD* configuration, the results are comparable or in some cases even higher than the performance of the model trained on *RGBD* data. These results confirm our initial hypothesis that depth can make a significant contribution to the detection of deepfakes. In the *RGBD* configuration, the model learns to reduce the contribution of the information contained in the RGB channels, while in the *GrayD* configuration, a lot of irrelevant information has already been removed, allowing the model to obtain good results with fewer input channels. This result suggests that depth in this case adds a more relevant contribution to classification than color artifacts. Similar observations can be made by analyzing the results at the video level shown in Table 2. In this case, the performances were measured by predicting the most voted class for each video.

4.2 Preliminary Studies on Inference Time

We conclude our study by presenting preliminary results on the inference times of the solution we have introduced. To the best of our knowledge, we are the first to analyze this aspect in detecting deepfakes. The inference time is of fundamental importance when considering the scenarios in which it is useful to detect a fake video in real-time. To do this we analyze the impact of using a different number of input channels on our system. Our aim, for this work, is to analyze the inference times of our model to understand if the different configurations we have introduced have an impact on this aspect or not. Specifically, in Table 3 we report the floating point operations (FLOPS) and average frame per second (fps) of the Xception-based model on four different hardware platforms. The results suggest that the higher number of channels has a minimal impact over the inference time with an average 0.68 reduction of frame per second. The depth estimation step is not included in these computations; instead, only the facial extraction and deepfake detection stages are measured. As mentioned, at this stage we are only interested in studying the differences introduced by different number of input channels. Additionally, it is worth noting that even if we do not consider depth estimation in our measurements, there are numerous approaches for real-time monocular depth estimation that might be used for this phase [8,29,30].

Based on these results, we can draw some consideration that can trace the right path to design a deepfake detector in real time. The first is that models like the Xception tend to be more effective at detecting fakes. This could suggest that the use of a lightweight network with layers inspired by this architecture could allow to obtain lower inference times while maintaining satisfactory performance. The second is that integrating features such as depth can improve the detection of fakes without affecting too much on the frames per second that the model can process. This aspect will be deepened in subsequent works.

5   Conclusions and Future Work

In this paper, we assessed the importance of depth features for deepfake detection. From our experiments, we can conclude that current deepfake detection methods can be supported through depth estimation features, which added to RGB channels can help increase the performance of the detectors. The results of this study will be investigated in the future with the aim of analyzing the generalization capacity of these features with respect to deepfake generation techniques that have not been seen in training and also evaluating the possibility of analyzing the variations in depth estimation over time. Moreover, we plan to test our model on other datasets than FaceForensics++.

In addition to that, in this work we have proposed the first studies on the impact of using different types of inputs with respect to inference times. These preliminary results will be a valuable reference basis for future work, which will investigate the limitations of current methods for real-time deepfake detection to design lighter strategies. The first results, suggest that even with shallower networks such as MobileNet it is still possible to obtain good performance. By mixing some design strategies like Xception-based layers and depth features, could be possible to designer stronger and lighter real-time methods.

Acknowledgments. This work has been partially supported by the Sapienza University of Rome project RM12117A56C08D64 2022-2024.

References

1. Afchar, D., Nozick, V., Yamagishi, J., Echizen, I.: Mesonet: a compact facial video forgery detection network. In: 2018 IEEE International Workshop on Information Forensics and Security (WIFS), pp. 1–7. IEEE (2018)
2. Agarwal, S., Farid, H., Fried, O., Agrawala, M.: Detecting deep-fake videos from phoneme-viseme mismatches. In: Proceedings of the IEEE/CVF Conference on Computer Vision and Pattern Recognition Workshops, pp. 660–661 (2020)
3. Agarwal, S., Farid, H., Gu, Y., He, M., Nagano, K., Li, H.: Protecting world leaders against deep fakes. In: CVPR Workshops, vol. 1 (2019)
4. Barni, M., et al.: Aligned and non-aligned double jpeg detection using convolutional neural networks. J. Vis. Commun. Image Represent. **49**, 153–163 (2017)
5. Bhat, S.F., Alhashim, I., Wonka, P.: Adabins: depth estimation using adaptive bins. In: 2021 IEEE/CVF Conference on Computer Vision and Pattern Recognition (CVPR), Los Alamitos, CA, USA, pp. 4008–4017. IEEE Computer Society (2021). https://doi.org/10.1109/CVPR46437.2021.00400. https://doi.ieeecomputersociety.org/10.1109/CVPR46437.2021.00400
6. Bonettini, N., Cannas, E.D., Mandelli, S., Bondi, L., Bestagini, P., Tubaro, S.: Video face manipulation detection through ensemble of CNNs. In: 2020 25th International Conference on Pattern Recognition (ICPR), pp. 5012–5019. IEEE (2021)
7. Caldelli, R., Galteri, L., Amerini, I., Del Bimbo, A.: Optical flow based cnn for detection of unlearnt deepfake manipulations. Pattern Recogn. Lett. **146**, 31–37 (2021). https://doi.org/10.1016/j.patrec.2021.03.005. https://www.sciencedirect.com/science/article/pii/S0167865521000842
8. Chiu, M.J., Chiu, W.C., Chen, H.T., Chuang, J.H.: Real-time monocular depth estimation with extremely light-weight neural network. In: 2020 25th International Conference on Pattern Recognition (ICPR), pp. 7050–7057 (2021). https://doi.org/10.1109/ICPR48806.2021.9411998
9. Chollet, F.: Xception: deep learning with depthwise separable convolutions. In: Proceedings of the IEEE Conference on Computer Vision and Pattern Recognition (CVPR) (2017)
10. Cozzolino, D., Gragnaniello, D., Poggi, G., Verdoliva, L.: Towards universal gan image detection. In: 2021 International Conference on Visual Communications and Image Processing (VCIP), pp. 1–5 (2021). https://doi.org/10.1109/VCIP53242.2021.9675329
11. Cozzolino, D., Nießner, M., Verdoliva, L.: Audio-visual person-of-interest deepfake detection (2022). https://doi.org/10.48550/ARXIV.2204.03083. https://arxiv.org/abs/2204.03083
12. Cozzolino, D., Rössler, A., Thies, J., Nießner, M., Verdoliva, L.: ID-reveal: identity-aware deepfake video detection. In: Proceedings of the IEEE/CVF International Conference on Computer Vision, pp. 15108–15117 (2021)

13. Dang, H., Liu, F., Stehouwer, J., Liu, X., Jain, A.K.: On the detection of digital face manipulation. In: Proceedings of the IEEE/CVF Conference on Computer Vision and Pattern Recognition (CVPR) (2020)

14. Deng, J., Dong, W., Socher, R., Li, L.J., Li, K., Fei-Fei, L.: Imagenet: a large-scale hierarchical image database. In: 2009 IEEE Conference on Computer Vision and Pattern Recognition, pp. 248–255. IEEE (2009)

15. Dolhansky, B., et al.: The deepfake detection challenge (DFDC) dataset. arXiv preprint arXiv:2006.07397 (2020)

16. Du, M., Pentyala, S., Li, Y., Hu, X.: Towards generalizable deepfake detection with locality-aware autoencoder. In: Proceedings of the 29th ACM International Conference on Information & Knowledge Management, pp. 325–334 (2020)

17. Gragnaniello, D., Cozzolino, D., Marra, F., Poggi, G., Verdoliva, L.: Are GAN generated images easy to detect? A critical analysis of the state-of-the-art. In: 2021 IEEE International Conference on Multimedia and Expo (ICME), pp. 1–6. IEEE (2021)

18. Güera, D., Delp, E.J.: Deepfake video detection using recurrent neural networks. In: 2018 15th IEEE International Conference on Advanced Video and Signal Based Surveillance (AVSS), pp. 1–6. IEEE (2018)

19. He, L., Lu, J., Wang, G., Song, S., Zhou, J.: SOSD-Net: joint semantic object segmentation and depth estimation from monocular images. Neurocomputing **440**, 251–263 (2021)

20. Howard, A.G., et al.: Mobilenets: efficient convolutional neural networks for mobile vision applications (2017). https://doi.org/10.48550/ARXIV.1704.04861. https://arxiv.org/abs/1704.04861

21. Huh, M., Liu, A., Owens, A., Efros, A.A.: Fighting fake news: image splice detection via learned self-consistency. In: Proceedings of the European Conference on Computer Vision (ECCV), pp. 101–117 (2018)

22. Khan, F., Hussain, S., Basak, S., Lemley, J., Corcoran, P.: An efficient encoder-decoder model for portrait depth estimation from single images trained on pixel-accurate synthetic data. Neural Netw. **142**(C), 479–491 (2021). https://doi.org/10.1016/j.neunet.2021.07.007

23. Li, Y., Lyu, S.: Exposing deepfake videos by detecting face warping artifacts. arXiv preprint arXiv:1811.00656 (2018)

24. Li, Z., Wang, X., Liu, X., Jiang, J.: Binsformer: revisiting adaptive bins for monocular depth estimation (2022). https://doi.org/10.48550/ARXIV.2204.00987. https://arxiv.org/abs/2204.00987

25. Liy, C.M., InIctuOculi, L.: Exposing AI created fake videos by detecting eye blinking. In: 2018 IEEE International Workshop on Information Forensics and Security (WIFS). IEEE (2018)

26. Lukas, J., Fridrich, J., Goljan, M.: Determining digital image origin using sensor imperfections. In: Image and Video Communications and Processing 2005, vol. 5685, pp. 249–260. International Society for Optics and Photonics (2005)

27. Masi, I., Killekar, A., Mascarenhas, R.M., Gurudatt, S.P., AbdAlmageed, W.: Two-branch recurrent network for isolating deepfakes in videos. In: Vedaldi, A., Bischof, H., Brox, T., Frahm, J.-M. (eds.) ECCV 2020. LNCS, vol. 12352, pp. 667–684. Springer, Cham (2020). https://doi.org/10.1007/978-3-030-58571-6_39

28. Mittal, T., Bhattacharya, U., Chandra, R., Bera, A., Manocha, D.: Emotions don't lie: an audio-visual deepfake detection method using affective cues. In: Proceedings of the 28th ACM International Conference on Multimedia, pp. 2823–2832 (2020)

29. Papa, L., Alati, E., Russo, P., Amerini, I.: Speed: separable pyramidal pooling encoder-decoder for real-time monocular depth estimation on low-resource settings. IEEE Access **10**, 44881–44890 (2022). https://doi.org/10.1109/ACCESS.2022.3170425

30. Peluso, V., et al.: Monocular depth perception on microcontrollers for edge applications. IEEE Trans. Circuits Syst. Video Technol. **32**(3), 1524–1536 (2022). https://doi.org/10.1109/TCSVT.2021.3077395

31. Qi, H., et al.: Deeprhythm: exposing deepfakes with attentional visual heartbeat rhythms. In: Proceedings of the 28th ACM International Conference on Multimedia, pp. 4318–4327 (2020)

32. Ranftl, R., Bochkovskiy, A., Koltun, V.: Vision transformers for dense prediction (2021). https://doi.org/10.48550/ARXIV.2103.13413. https://arxiv.org/abs/2103.13413

33. Rossler, A., Cozzolino, D., Verdoliva, L., Riess, C., Thies, J., Niessner, M.: Faceforensics++: learning to detect manipulated facial images. In: Proceedings of the IEEE/CVF International Conference on Computer Vision (ICCV) (2019)

34. Szegedy, C., et al.: Going deeper with convolutions. https://doi.org/10.48550/ARXIV.1409.4842. https://arxiv.org/abs/1409.4842

35. Thies, J., Zollhöfer, M., Nießner, M.: Deferred neural rendering: image synthesis using neural textures. ACM Trans. Graph. **38**(4), 1–12 (2019). https://doi.org/10.1145/3306346.3323035

36. Thies, J., Zollhofer, M., Stamminger, M., Theobalt, C., Niessner, M.: Face2face: real-time face capture and reenactment of RGB videos. In: Proceedings of the IEEE Conference on Computer Vision and Pattern Recognition (CVPR) (2016)

37. Véges, M., Lörincz, A.: Absolute human pose estimation with depth prediction network. In: 2019 International Joint Conference on Neural Networks (IJCNN), pp. 1–7 (2019). https://doi.org/10.1109/IJCNN.2019.8852387

38. Yang, X., Li, Y., Lyu, S.: Exposing deep fakes using inconsistent head poses. In: ICASSP 2019–2019 IEEE International Conference on Acoustics, Speech and Signal Processing (ICASSP), pp. 8261–8265. IEEE (2019)

39. Yu, N., Davis, L., Fritz, M.: Attributing fake images to GANs: analyzing fingerprints in generated images. arXiv preprint arXiv:1811.08180 (2018)

40. Yu, N., Davis, L.S., Fritz, M.: Attributing fake images to GANs: learning and analyzing GAN fingerprints. In: Proceedings of the IEEE/CVF International Conference on Computer Vision, pp. 7556–7566 (2019)

41. Zhao, H., Zhou, W., Chen, D., Wei, T., Zhang, W., Yu, N.: Multi-attentional deepfake detection. In: Proceedings of the IEEE/CVF Conference on Computer Vision and Pattern Recognition, pp. 2185–2194 (2021)

42. Zhou, Y., Lim, S.N.: Joint audio-visual deepfake detection. In: Proceedings of the IEEE/CVF International Conference on Computer Vision, pp. 14800–14809 (2021)

43. Zi, B., Chang, M., Chen, J., Ma, X., Jiang, Y.G.: Wilddeepfake: a challenging real-world dataset for deepfake detection. In: Proceedings of the 28th ACM International Conference on Multimedia, pp. 2382–2390 (2020)

An Effective Training Strategy for Enhanced Source Camera Device Identification

Manisha[1], Chang-Tsun Li[2(✉)], and Karunakar A. Kotegar[1]

[1] Department of Data Science and Computer Applications, Manipal Institute of Technology, Manipal Academy of Higher Education, Manipal 576104, Karnataka, India
nimamanisha@gmail.com, karunakar.ak@manipal.edu
[2] School of Information Technology, Deakin University, Geelong 3216, Australia
changtsun.li@deakin.edu

Abstract. Source camera identification is a forensic problem of linking an image in question to the camera used to capture it. This could be a useful tool in forensic applications to identify potential suspects of cybercrime. Over the last decade, several successful attempts have been made to identify the source camera using deep learning. However, existing techniques that provide effective solutions for camera model identification fail to distinguish between different devices of the same model. This is because cameras of different brands and models were used to train the data-driven system when dealing with exact device identification. We show that training the data-driven system on different camera models opens side-channel information on model-specific features, which acts as interference for identifying individual devices of the same model. Thus, we provide an effective training strategy that involves a way to construct the dataset for enhanced source camera device identification. The experimental results suggest that involving only cameras of the same model for training improves the discriminative capability of the data-driven system by eliminating the threat of interfering model-specific features.

Keywords: Source camera identification · Digital image forensics · Device fingerprint · Deep learning · Convolutional neural network

1 Background

With the advent of inexpensive smartphones, capturing images and videos and sharing them on social networks became much easier. However, this opportunity can also be exploited for unlawful purposes such as violence instigation, child pornography, and fake news creation. In such scenarios, ownership and authenticity of multimedia content can be a major question for criminal investigation. To address this issue, over the last decade, researchers have developed various

© Springer Nature Switzerland AG 2023
J.-J. Rousseau and B. Kapralos (Eds.): ICPR 2022 Workshops, LNCS 13646, pp. 32–45, 2023.
https://doi.org/10.1007/978-3-031-37745-7_3

techniques to identify the source camera of the image in question. Initial methods used handcrafted features such as Photo Response Non-Uniformity (PRNU) fingerprint which is unique to the individual camera sensor and statistical features extracted from the PRNU fingerprint [7,12,13,16]. Although preliminary successes have been made, PRNU-based approaches present certain drawbacks. For example, extracting hand-crafted features is a difficult and time-consuming process. Moreover, PRNU is susceptible to counter forensic attacks and image post-processing operations (e.g., JPEG compression and low-pass filtering) which hinders the source camera identification [4,5,11,14,15,19,26].

Given the success of deep learning in solving computer vision problems, in the last few years, several efforts have been made to develop more effective source identification techniques using convolutional neural networks (CNNs) [1,6,10,17,24,25,28]. Bondi et al., [1] and Tuama et al., [24] effectively identified the source camera model using CNN. Yao et al. [28] proposed a CNN-based robust multi-classifier that obtained approximately 100% classification accuracy across 25 camera models. Freire-Obregon et al. [6] suggested a deep learning-based solution for mobile device identification and discovered that the performance degrades when different cameras of the same brand and model are considered for evaluation. Huang et al., [10] built a CNN model and tested the impact of the number of convolutional layers on the model's performance. The work suggested that deeper CNN can reach higher classification accuracy. Wang et al. [25] developed a CNN model by altering AlexNet and adding a Local Binary Pattern (LBP) pre-processing layer to make the CNN focus more on intrinsic source information. However, all these techniques mainly cope with camera model identification rather than individual device identification. Further, Hadwiger and Riess [8] analyzed the influence of scene overlap on CNN-based source camera identification and showed that such scene overlap may open side-channel information which prevents CNN from learning device fingerprint.

Despite the fact that these data-driven techniques have improved source camera model identification performance, some issues remain unaddressed for individual device identification. Chen et al., in [2], employed a residual neural network to investigate brand, model, and device identification. The work achieved a classification accuracy as high as 99.12% and 94.73% for distinguishing 13 different camera brands and 27 camera models, respectively. Further, the method involved images from 74 different camera devices (some of them have the same brand or model) for device-level attribution. However, in this case, the classification accuracy was only 45.81%. When just three devices of the same model were employed, the content-adaptive fusion network developed by Yang et al. [27], obtained an exact device detection accuracy of 70.19%. To further improve the task of exact device identification, Ding et al., [3], developed a residual network based on both hand-crafted and data-driven features. The work achieved a classification accuracy of 99.60% and 97.10% for distinguishing 14 different camera brands and 27 camera models, respectively. However, for exact device identification, the proposed method was able to achieve only 52.4% accuracy on 74 camera devices. Sameer et al., [21] developed a Siamese network by employing a few-shot learning technique to perform individual device identification using 10 images per camera. The experimental results of the aforementioned techniques suggest that the identification of cameras at the device-level is more challenging than at the brand and model-level. However, it is more important to identify the camera device since it allows for more accurate traceability. This emphasizes the need for strategies to enhance the capability of the data-driven model in distinguishing different devices of the same brand and model.

A limitation of existing deep learning-based techniques is that the CNN model developed for source identification is built on images captured with different camera models. More precisely, the training process involves cameras from different brands and models. The results of existing techniques appear to indicate that the identification accuracy decreases as more cameras are involved in the training process. There is a potential chance of learning model-specific fingerprints rather than device-specific fingerprints because the number of camera models is usually larger than the average number of devices of the same model in a dataset used to train the existing technique. Thus, involving different camera models to train the data-driven system opens a side-channel for model-related features to slip into the source information extracted by the CNN models. We contend that the model-related features act as interference for distinguishing different devices of the same model. Therefore, we conjecture that involving only devices of the same model to train CNNs rules out the effect of interferential model-specific features in the images and thus improves the exact device identification performance. In this vein, we present herein an in-depth analysis of exact device identification based on a CNN trained on different devices of the same model and different devices of different brands and models. In summary, our main contributions are:

1. We show that involving cameras of different models for training a data-driven system opens side-channel information on model-specific features which acts as the interference for exact device identification.
2. We investigate the appropriate way of dataset construction for learning discriminative device-level fingerprints. We demonstrate the importance of involving only devices of the same model to train CNNs to rule out the effect of interferential model-specific features in the images.

The remainder of the paper is structured as follows. Section 2 presents the proposed training strategy to enhance exact device identification performance. Experimental results and discussions are given in Sect. 3. Finally, conclusions are drawn in Sect. 4.

2   Data-Driven Model and Training Strategy for Source Identification

We demonstrate the impact of model-specific features on exact device identification by studying the behaviour of CNN on datasets constructed employing a different set of cameras. For the evaluation of the impact of interferential model-related features, we perform source camera identification in two phases as depicted in the pipeline in Fig. 1. In the first phase, we build a feature extractor (baseline) that learns to extract source information from the images taken with known set of cameras (closed-set). In the second phase, the feature extractor that has previously learned to extract source information is used to extract features from images captured with a new set of cameras (open-set). Further, the extracted features are used to train a classifier to perform source camera identification. In this section, we briefly describe the used methods and their training strategies.

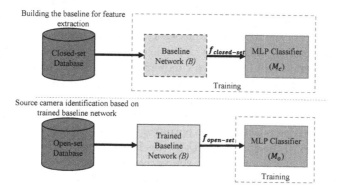

Fig. 1. Evaluation pipeline for source camera identification.

2.1   Baseline Network for Source Camera Identification

The deep learning techniques have shown excellent performance in source camera identification. One of the major inferences from the literature studies is that the depth of the CNN is a crucial parameter [10,28] that significantly affects the performance of the source camera identification task. To improve the performance, the architecture of CNN needs to go deeper. However, after a certain number of layers, the standard scaling strategy does not improve performance. It begins to have a negative impact by reducing CNN's performance. The issue of performance degradation is addressed by a deep residual network (ResNet) [9] by introducing skip/shortcut connections. It facilitates learning richer feature representation by extracting low-level and high-level features simultaneously. Source camera identification, like many other computer vision tasks that have benefited greatly from very deep models, works well in a deeper network. Inspired by the success of ResNet in computer vision, image forensic researchers developed deep learning frameworks based on ResNet to identify the source camera model [2,3,20]. The ResNet model has many variants such as ResNet18, ResNet32, ResNet50, and ResNet101, each with a different number of layers. With the increase in the number of layers, the ResNet model can integrate features from several levels, which improves the discriminative capability of the model. Also, we have empirically found that the ResNet101 variant achieves improved performance over other variants of the ResNet model and other state-of-the-art CNNs such as AlexNet and VGG-16. Thus, we employ the ResNet101 as the baseline (B) to extract features from images for source camera identification.

The previous works on source camera identification using ResNet [2, 3, 20] mainly focused on the features learned by the last fully connected (FC) layer to classify the images into their source categories. It is essential to extract the features from a layer that demonstrates a good capability in distinguishing between different devices. We use features extracted from the Global Average Pooling (GAP) layer of the ResNet101 model which results in extracting a $1 \times 1 \times 2048$ dimensional feature map from each image. The use of features extracted from the GAP layer has the following significant advantages over deep features extracted from the FC layer of the ResNet101 model. 1) The GAP layer reduces the dimension of the feature map by taking the average of each feature map produced by the previous layer. It can be used to summarize the presence of a feature in the image, thus it is more robust to the spatial translation of the input image. It means that no matter where the required feature is present in the feature map, it will still be captured by the GAP layer. 2) Specifically, in the GAP layer, there are no trainable parameters to optimize which avoids the overfitting of the ResNet101 model to the training data at this layer. Thus, the features extracted at this layer aid in enhancing the source camera identification performance. Moreover, it was empirically verified that on average the features extracted from the GAP layer improved the classification accuracy by 3% compared to the features extracted from the last FC layer. The feature map extracted from the GAP layer serves as the source information, which is further used to identify the source camera of images using a Multi-Layer Perceptron (MLP) classifier.

To trace back the source camera of the image, we train an MLP classifier (M_c) on the feature vector ($f_{closed-set}$) taken from the GAP layer of the ResNet101 model. The 2048 dimensional feature vector is fed to the input layer of the MLP classifier. The proposed classifier is made up of two dense layers, each having 1024 and 64 neurons, respectively. Each dense layer is followed by a Rectified Linear Unit (ReLu) activation function. We use a dropout layer with a 0.5 probability to avoid overfitting the model to the training data. The activations at this stage are fed into an output dense layer with as many neurons as the number of cameras used for training the classifier followed by the softmax function to predict the probability that the image in question is captured with a specific camera under investigation.

Once the baseline network is trained on a known set of cameras (closed-set), it will be deployed to extract the source information ($f_{open-set}$) from images captured with a new set of cameras (open-set) that are not used to train the baseline (B). Feature extraction is done by a single pass through the images. The classifier (M_o) trained on these features is employed to map the images to the authentic source camera.

2.2   Training Strategy for Source Camera Identification

To evaluate the impact of interfering model-related features on exact device identification we follow two training protocols/strategies. Both protocols are associated with a way of constructing the dataset for training the baseline network to learn feature extraction. In the first protocol, we construct the dataset by involving devices of the same brand and model. Whereas, in the second protocol, we consider cameras of different brands and models to create the dataset.

In the first protocol, because the images used to train the baseline are captured with devices of the same brand and model, it forces the data-driven model to learn the device-specific features and eliminates the threat of learning interferential model-specific features. The second protocol, which involves cameras from different brands and models, provides the data-driven system with the freedom of learning model-related features from images to distinguish between the camera models under consideration for training. We hypothesize that learning such model-specific features acts as interference for distinguishing different devices of the same model. The trained baseline (B) is employed to extract the source information from a new set of cameras in the open-set scenario. To analyze the effect of model-specific features on exact device identification, we evaluate the performance of the baseline network trained on two aforementioned protocols on various sets of cameras in the open-set scenario. Training the baseline network involves hyperparameter tuning to improve the generalization capability and classification accuracy. To accomplish this we split the data (images taken from a known set of cameras) into the training and testing set. The baseline network is then trained on training data using different sets of hyper-parameters. Finally, the hyperparameters for which the baseline provides the highest accuracy on the test set are selected. To identify the appropriate way to construct the dataset for exact source device identification, we analyze the behaviour of the baseline trained on two different protocols on a new set of data which consists of images captured with cameras not used to train the baseline. We split these open-set data into the training and testing sets and employ the trained baseline as the feature extractor to extract source information from the training images. Finally, the MLP classifier (M_o) is trained on features extracted by the trained baseline network to map the test images to their source cameras.

3   Experimental Results and Discussion

3.1   Experimental Setup

To evaluate the proposed training strategies for source identification, we consider the original images from the VISION dataset [22], Warwick Image Forensic Dataset [18], Daxing dataset [23], and the custom-built dataset. For the generation of the custom-built dataset, we have captured the images of various scenes at the maximum resolution available with default camera settings. Details of the camera model, the number of devices, number of images, cameras used for training the baseline, and cameras used for source identification in the open-set scenario are given in Table 1. Given that the number of suspect cameras belonging to the same brand and model in a real-world forensic investigation is usually less, we consider a smaller number of devices for the evaluation to mimic the real-world forensic scenario. For the evaluation, 75% of images from each device are used for training, and the remaining 25% of images are used for the testing process. We split each image into two equal-sized patches to obtain a larger dataset as the number of images for each camera is limited. Each image patch is downsized to 224 × 224 to align with the input requirement of the baseline network. The baseline network and the MLP classifier are trained for 20 and 1500 epochs, respectively. The categorical cross-entropy loss function with the Adam optimizer is used to obtain the optimum set of parameters. We set the mini-batch size and the learning rate to 12 and 0.001, respectively. Experiments are performed in MATLAB2021a using NVIDIA GeForce GTX 1080 GPU.

Table 1. Dataset details

Dataset	Camera model	No. of devices	No. of images
Cameras used to train the baseline network (closed-set cameras)			
Daxing [23]	Vivo X9	3	1444
	Xiaomi 4A	5	2304
Custom-built	Asus Zenfone Max Pro M1	2	1004
	Redmi Note 5 Pro	2	1016
	Redmi Note-3	3	1334
Warwick [18]	Fujifilm X-A10	2	806
Cameras used to evaluate the impact of training strategies on source identification (open-set cameras)			
VISION [22]	iPhone 5c	3	1523
	iPhone 4s	2	761
	iPhone 5	2	856
	Samsung Galaxy S3 Mini	2	710
	OnePlus A3000	1	574
	OnePlus A3003	1	472
	Huawei P8	1	532
	Huawei Honor 5c	1	542

3.2 Building the Baseline for Feature Extraction Based on Two Training Protocols

To analyze the impact of side-channel model-specific features on exact device identification performance we train the baseline using different training strategies as discussed in Sect. 2.2. We conduct a series of experiments to identify the best training strategy which can better distinguish between different devices of the same brand and model.

For the evaluation of our first training protocol, we build the baseline network by training separately on images taken with (i) three devices of the Vivo X9 model and (ii) five devices of the Xiaomi 4A model. Our protocol evaluation starts by first training the ResNet101 model on training images taken with closed-set cameras then training the MLP classifier (M_c) to trace back the source cameras in the closed-set. We use classification/identification accuracy as the evaluation metric to summarize the achieved results. Table 2 reports the classification accuracy achieved on the testing set by the MLP classifier (M_c) in closed-set scenario. It can be observed from the results that the baseline trained on devices of the same model is able to effectively map the images to their respective source cameras, which demonstrates the good ability of the data-driven model in capturing the source information.

Table 2. Performance achieved based on two training protocols in closed-set scenario.

Experiment	Camera used	Identification accuracy (%)
1 (Devices-1)	3 Vivo X9	97.02
2 (Devices-2)	5 Xiaomi 4A	94.57
3 (Models-1)	Asus Zenfone Max Pro M1, Vivo X9, Xiaomi 4A	99.42
4 (Models-2)	Warwick + Custom-built	92.53

The baseline trained on different devices of the same model based on our first training protocol has shown excellent performance on individual camera device identification. In the second training protocol, we train the baseline on images taken with (i) a Asus Zenfone Max Pro M1, a Vivo X9 and a Xiaomi 4A device, and (ii) Warwick + Custom-built dataset: two devices each from Fujifilm X-A10, Redmi Note 5 pro, Asus Zenfone Max Pro A10, and three devices of Redmi Note 3 model. The performance achieved on the test set in the closed-set scenario in the second protocol setting is reported in Table 2. The experiments named 'Devices-1' and 'Devices-2' involves training of baseline using devices of the same model. Whereas, 'Models-1' and 'Models-2' are experiments carried out by employing the baseline trained on devices of different brands and models. Compared to the results of first training strategy (Experiments: Devices-1 and Devices-2), the identification accuracy achieved by the second training strategy drops for the case of baseline trained on images taken from Warwick and custom-built dataset (Experiment: Models-2). This is because the average number of models used to train the baseline network is more than the average number of devices of the same model. It allows model-specific features to slip into the source information extracted by the data-driven model causing adverse effect in distinguishing devices of the same model. Therefore, we conjecture that involving only devices of the same model to train CNNs rules out the effect of interferential brand/model-specific features in the images. We provide empirical evidence for this conjecture in Sect. 3.3 through the evaluation of the performance of the baseline network trained separately on the datasets constructed based on two protocols on open-set source camera identification.

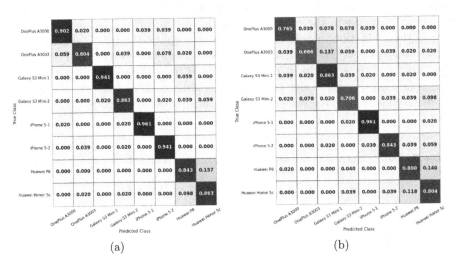

Fig. 2. Normalized confusion matrix obtained for VISION-8 open-set cameras by exploiting the feature extractor trained on (a) three Vivo X9, and (b) Warwick + Daxing datasets.

3.3 Analysis of the Effect of Side-Channel Information on Exact Device Identification in the Open-Set Scenario

In Table 3, we compare the identification accuracies achieved by the baseline network trained separately based on two training strategies to demonstrate the impact of side-channel information on the source camera identification task in the open-set scenario. It is evident from the results that the baseline network trained on images from cameras of different models does not perform as efficiently as the baseline network trained on images from different devices of the same model. This low performance for the baseline trained on cameras from the different models can be justified by the leaking side-channel information on model-specific features, which potentially leads to misclassification. In Figs. 2a and 2b we present the normalized confusion matrices obtained for the original images in the VISION-8 open-set cameras by exploiting the baseline trained on (i) three Vivo X9 (Devices-1), and (ii) Warwick + Daxing (Models-2) datasets, respectively. By comparing the confusion matrices, we observe that the ability on identifying the individual devices of the same model is affected by considering cameras from different models to train the feature extractor. For example, we can see that the exact device identification performance drops for the two iPhone 5c devices and two Samsung Galaxy S3 Mini devices. The results show that involving different camera models to train the data-driven model has a big impact on the identification accuracy. Thus, it is necessary to consider only camera devices of the same model while constructing the dataset for learning discriminative device-level features, which eliminates the threat of leaking side-channel information on model-specific features into the evaluation.

Table 3. Performance of baseline network trained on different datasets in open-set scenario in terms of classification accuracy (%) (* VISION-8 involves: 2 iPhone 5, 2 Samsung Galaxy S3 Mini, OnePlus A3000, OnePlus A3003, Huawei P8, Huawei Honor 5c cameras)

Device/Model Identification	Cameras used for open-set evaluation	Baseline network trained on different datasets (training protocols)			
		Devices-1	Devices-2	Models-1	Models-2
Device Identification	3 iPhone 5c	**92.81**	**93.14**	89.54	90.85
	2 iPhone 4s	**94.89**	**93.18**	89.77	90.91
	2 iPhone 5	**99.02**	**99.02**	97.05	97.55
	2 Samsung Galaxy S3 Mini (SG S3 Mini)	**92.76**	**92.11**	90.79	89.47
Model Identification	iPhone 4s, iPhone 5, iPhone 5c	**89.77**	**90.53**	87.39	86.36
	OnePlus A3000, OnePlus A3003	**94.49**	**94.92**	92.37	92.37
	SG S3 Mini, SG S3, SG S5, SG S4 Mini	**91.91**	**91.91**	87.99	86.52
	3 iPhone 5c, 2 iPhone 4s, 2 iPhone 5	**85.88**	**85.39**	77.92	78.57
	Vision-8*	**88.97**	**87.25**	79.66	80.15

To visualize the class separability we use the t-distributed Stochastic Neighbor Embedding (t-SNE) on the 2048-dimensional features extracted from the GAP layer of the baseline network. We show the results obtained on two devices of the iPhone 4s model in Fig. 3. We can see that spread of features extracted for two iPhone 4s devices by the baseline trained on devices of the same model is less compared to that extracted by the baseline trained on devices of different models. Further, we measure the discriminative capability of the data-driven model in terms of class separability based on a distance measure. To measure the distance between the classes, we find the centroid for features extracted for two iPhone 4s devices, then measure the distance between the class centroids using the Euclidean distance metric. We obtained the Euclidean distance of 15.95 and 15.92 by considering the features extracted by the baseline trained based on Devices-1 and Devices-2, respectively. For the case of baseline trained on Models-1 and Models-2, we achieved Euclidean distances of 11.93 and 11.43, respectively. Thus, we can notice that higher separability between the camera devices can be achieved by involving only devices of the same model for exact device identification.

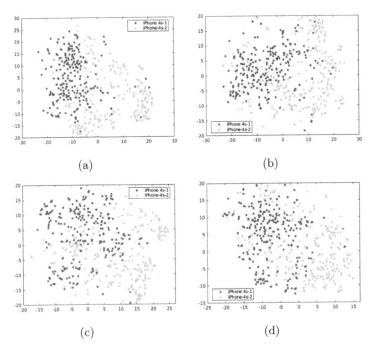

Fig. 3. Results obtained with t-SNE by employing baseline network trained on: (a) Devices-1 (b) Devices-2 (c) Models-1 and (d) Models-2 demonstrating the separation between two devices of iPhone 4s model.

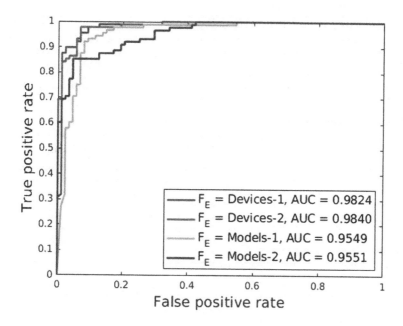

Fig. 4. ROC for baseline trained on different datasets.

A more comprehensive picture of the discriminative capability of the source information extracted by the data-driven model trained on datasets constructed based on two protocols is illustrated in Fig. 4 by plotting Receiver Operating Characteristic (ROC) curves for the iPhone 4s model. The CNN trained on different devices of the same model surpassed the CNN trained on different brands and models by a large margin, with an area under the curve of above 0.98. The discriminative power of the data-driven system is adversely affected by training on devices of different brands and models which greatly hinders their classification capability. This clearly shows that features extracted by training the CNN on different camera brands/models are not appealing for distinguishing different devices of the same model. Thus, it is important to involve only devices of the same model to train the CNN-based source camera identification systems. Doing so prevents the threat of opening side-channel information on model-specific features, which may lead to misclassification.

4   Conclusion

In this work, we propose an effective training strategy for improving the discriminative capability of the data-driven system to better identify the individual camera devices of the same model. Although existing data-driven based approaches have led to a breakthrough in the image forensics, distinguishing different devices of the same model is challenging. We show that the data-driven system trained on different camera models for exact device identification are adversely affected due to the interferential model-specific features which greatly hinders their classification capability. Furthermore, to identify the best way of constructing the dataset for the exact device identification, we analyzed the behaviour of the data-driven system by exploiting the feature extractor trained on different devices of the same model and devices of different models. The results appear to degrade when the data-driven system trained on different camera models is used to perform individual device identification. These observations demonstrate the potential chance of learning interfering model-specific features and emphasize the importance of involving only devices of the same model to make CNN focus on device-specific features which contribute to enhancing the individual device identification performance.

References

1. Bondi, L., Baroffio, L., Güera, D., Bestagini, P., Delp, E.J., Tubaro, S.: First steps toward camera model identification with convolutional neural networks. IEEE Signal Process. Lett. **24**(3), 259–263 (2016)
2. Chen, Y., Huang, Y., Ding, X.: Camera model identification with residual neural network. In: 2017 IEEE International Conference on Image Processing (ICIP), pp. 4337–4341. IEEE (2017)
3. Ding, X., Chen, Y., Tang, Z., Huang, Y.: Camera identification based on domain knowledge-driven deep multi-task learning. IEEE Access **7**, 25878–25890 (2019)
4. Dirik, A.E., Karaküçük, A.: Forensic use of photo response non-uniformity of imaging sensors and a counter method. Opt. Express **22**(1), 470–482 (2014)
5. Dirik, A.E., Sencar, H.T., Memon, N.: Analysis of seam-carving-based anonymization of images against PRNU noise pattern-based source attribution. IEEE Trans. Inf. Forensics Secur. **9**(12), 2277–2290 (2014)
6. Freire-Obregón, D., Narducci, F., Barra, S., Castrillón-Santana, M.: Deep learning for source camera identification on mobile devices. Pattern Recogn. Lett. **126**, 86–91 (2019)
7. Goljan, M., Fridrich, J., Filler, T.: Large scale test of sensor fingerprint camera identification. In: Media Forensics and Security, vol. 7254, p. 72540I. International Society for Optics and Photonics (2009)
8. Hadwiger, B., Riess, C.: The Forchheim image database for camera identification in the wild. In: Del Bimbo, A., et al. (eds.) ICPR 2021. LNCS, vol. 12666, pp. 500–515. Springer, Cham (2021). https://doi.org/10.1007/978-3-030-68780-9_40
9. He, K., Zhang, X., Ren, S., Sun, J.: Deep residual learning for image recognition. In: Proceedings of the IEEE Conference on Computer Vision and Pattern Recognition, pp. 770–778 (2016)
10. Huang, N., He, J., Zhu, N., Xuan, X., Liu, G., Chang, C.: Identification of the source camera of images based on convolutional neural network. Digit. Investig. **26**, 72–80 (2018)
11. Karaküçük, A., Dirik, A.E.: Adaptive photo-response non-uniformity noise removal against image source attribution. Digit. Investig. **12**, 66–76 (2015)
12. Akshatha, K.R., Karunakar, A.K., Anitha, H., Raghavendra, U., Shetty, D.: Digital camera identification using PRNU: a feature based approach. Digit. Investig. **19**, 69–77 (2016)
13. Li, C.-T.: Source camera identification using enhanced sensor pattern noise. IEEE Trans. Inf. Forensics Secur. **5**(2), 280–287 (2010)

14. Li, C.-T., Chang, C.-Y., Li, Y.: On the repudiability of device identification and image integrity verification using sensor pattern noise. In: Weerasinghe, D. (ed.) ISDF 2009. LNICST, vol. 41, pp. 19–25. Springer, Heidelberg (2010). https://doi.org/10.1007/978-3-642-11530-1_3

15. Lin, X., Li, C.-T.: Enhancing sensor pattern noise via filtering distortion removal. IEEE Signal Process. Lett. **23**(3), 381–385 (2016)

16. Lukas, J., Fridrich, J., Goljan, M.: Digital camera identification from sensor pattern noise. IEEE Trans. Inf. Forensics Secur. **1**(2), 205–214 (2006)

17. Manisha, A.K., Li, C.-T.: Identification of source social network of digital images using deep neural network. Pattern Recogn. Lett. **150**, 17–25 (2021)

18. Quan, Y., Li, C.-T., Zhou, Y., Li, L.: Warwick image forensics dataset for device fingerprinting in multimedia forensics. In: 2020 IEEE International Conference on Multimedia and Expo (ICME), pp. 1–6. IEEE (2020)

19. Samaras, S., Mygdalis, V., Pitas, I.: Robustness in blind camera identification. In: 2016 23rd International Conference on Pattern Recognition (ICPR), pp. 3874–3879. IEEE (2016)

20. Sameer, V.U., Dali, I., Naskar, R.: A deep learning based digital forensic solution to blind source identification of Facebook images. In: Ganapathy, V., Jaeger, T., Shyamasundar, R.K. (eds.) ICISS 2018. LNCS, vol. 11281, pp. 291–303. Springer, Cham (2018). https://doi.org/10.1007/978-3-030-05171-6_15

21. Sameer, V.U., Naskar, R.: Deep siamese network for limited labels classification in source camera identification. Multimedia Tools Appl. **79**(37), 28079–28104 (2020)

22. Shullani, D., Fontani, M., Iuliani, M., Al Shaya, O., Piva, A.: Vision: a video and image dataset for source identification. EURASIP J. Inf. Secur. **2017**(1), 1–16 (2017)

23. Tian, H., Xiao, Y., Cao, G., Zhang, Y., Xu, Z., Zhao, Y.: Daxing smartphone identification dataset. IEEE Access **7**, 101046–101053 (2019)

24. Tuama, A., Comby, F., Chaumont, M.: Camera model identification with the use of deep convolutional neural networks. In: 2016 IEEE International Workshop on Information Forensics and Security (WIFS), pp. 1–6. IEEE (2016)

25. Wang, B., Yin, J., Tan, S., Li, Y., Li, M.: Source camera model identification based on convolutional neural networks with local binary patterns coding. Signal Process. Image Commun. **68**, 162–168 (2018)

26. Lin, X., Li, C.-T.: Preprocessing reference sensor pattern noise via spectrum equalization. IEEE Trans. Inf. Forensics Secur. **11**(1), 126–140 (2015)

27. Yang, P., Ni, R., Zhao, Y., Zhao, W.: Source camera identification based on content-adaptive fusion residual networks. Pattern Recogn. Lett. **119**, 195–204 (2019)

28. Yao, H., Qiao, T., Xu, M., Zheng, N.: Robust multi-classifier for camera model identification based on convolution neural network. IEEE Access **6**, 24973–24982 (2018)

Improving Detection of Unprecedented Anti-forensics Attacks on Sensor Pattern Noises Through Generative Adversarial Networks

Yijun Quan[1][(✉)] and Chang-Tsun Li[2]

[1] University of Warwick, Coventry CV4 7AL, UK
yijun.quan@warwick.ac.uk
[2] School of Info Technology, Deakin University, Geelong 3125, Australia
changtsun.li@deakin.edu.au

Abstract. Sensor Pattern Noise (SPN) based methods have been widely applied in multimedia forensics. With SPN being a noise-like signal in an image, anti-forensic attacks can be performed by applying different manipulations to attenuate or remove the SPN and mislead the investigators. Thus, forensic investigators should identify the images subject to such manipulations before applying SPN-based methods. Despite neural network-based classifiers having shown their strength in detecting specific anti-forensics attacks, such a classifier may not generalise well for other manipulations. Given that various manipulations can attenuate or remove SPNs and a classifier's training set may only include certain types of manipulations, a classifier may encounter images subject to attacks unprecedented to it and unable to distinguish them from the pristine ones. To address this problem, we propose a training strategy using Generative Adversarial Networks (GAN). This strategy shifts the classifier's excessive emphasis on the manipulation-specific features with the resultant classifier generalising better for unprecedented anti-forensics attacks.

Keywords: Sensor Pattern Noise · Anti-forensics attack · Generative adversarial networks

1 Introduction

With the pervasiveness of digital images, related information security issues attract much attention from the digital forensics community. To prevent digital images from malicious usage, researchers have been developing image forensic methods like image source camera identification [10], image forgery detection [16] and source-oriented image clustering [11]. Sensor Pattern Noise (SPN) has been an effective tool for these topics. Arising due to the non-uniform response from the image sensors to light, each sensor leaves a distinctive pattern noise on images [14]. This pattern noise can work as the fingerprint of a camera. As a result, SPN-based methods acquire massive popularity among the digital forensic community.

© Springer Nature Switzerland AG 2023
J.-J. Rousseau and B. Kapralos (Eds.): ICPR 2022 Workshops, LNCS 13646, pp. 46–56, 2023.
https://doi.org/10.1007/978-3-031-37745-7_4

Despite the success and popularity of SPN in multimedia forensics, being a noise-like signal makes it vulnerable to different anti-forensics attacks. Residing in the high-frequency domain, the SPN can be easily attenuated or removed even by simple manipulations, including Gaussian blurring and medium filtering, etc. When we perform SPN-based forensic methods on the images subject to attacks, not only will extra computational costs be required, forensic investigators may also be misled to make wrong conclusions. Using source-oriented clustering [13] as an example, this task usually requires the computation of the pairwise correlations between the SPNs extracted from the images. The computation complexity is $\mathcal{O}(n^2)$ with respect to the number of images. Thus, including any images with SPN absent or attacked would significantly increase the computational cost while not providing any useful information. Furthermore, these flawed images should be viewed as outliers in any cluster. With some existing algorithms being particularly sensitive to outliers [11,15], these images could notably downgrade the clustering performance. Therefore, identifying the images subject to anti-forensics attacks before applying the SPN-based methods would be beneficial for subsequent forensic investigations.

Neural network-based methods have been widely applied in various fields of computer science. Neural networks' superior ability to extract non-trivial features compared to the hand-crafted one boosts the popularity of neural networks. It has been shown in [3] that a neural network could not only function in the same manner as the residual-based features used to detect the traces of different anti-forensics attacks but also outperforms them. Thus, we can treat the task of detecting images subject to anti-forensics attacks as an image classification problem with neural networks. A neural network-based classifier can be trained by feeding both pristine and attacked images to the network. However, given a training set of finite size, it may only cover images subject to certain types of attacks. Due to such a limitation, this can divert the goal of the neural network-based classifier. A neural network model, trained with a dataset like this, may perform well in terms of extracting features related to these manipulations. However, when the network is applied to images attacked by unprecedented manipulations, the network's performance cannot be guaranteed. This is because the network put too much focus on the predominant features corresponding to the manipulations presented in the training set. As a result, the network could miss the semantics of the ultimate goal: detecting whether an image is pristine or not.

To address this problem, in this work, we propose a novel training strategy by using Generative Adversarial Networks (GAN) for classifier generalisation to allow the detection of unprecedented attacks. Existing GAN-based methods in the field of SPN related forensics are mainly used to hide the traces of anti-forensics attacks. These methods process the images subject to anti-forensic attacks to fake the 'pristineness' by training the generator directly with the pristine images to fool the discriminator in the GAN framework, e.g., Kim *et al.* [9] compute the pixelwise $L1$ loss between the generated image and its pristine version. Different from these methods, our proposed method uses the GAN framework, not to fool the discriminator, but to train the classifier as the discriminator in the GAN framework to make it generalise better to unprecedented attacks. The generator is trained without direct knowledge of the pristine images. In this way, the generator can only add *superficial* 'pristineness' to the image. The reason we consider such 'pristineness' as superficial is that no matter how closely the generated image may look like the pristine images in general as seen by the discriminator, as long as the image does not preserve its original SPN, it cannot be considered as pristine from the forensic perspective. Given the SPN is random noise and its strength in each image is dependent on the device-specific parameter settings [16], without direct knowledge of the pristine version, this would limit the generator's ability to learn the differences in the statistical distribution of the noises in different images and make the generator focus more on the features related to the attacks presented in the original training set. Due to such a design, through the adversarial process, the discriminator would shift its excessive attention to the attack-related features to the semantics of detecting whether an image's SPN is pristine or not. As the discriminator's focus shifts, the generator may change accordingly through the adversarial process. Thus, to further limit the ability of the generator to add the superficial 'pristiness' only, instead of aiming for a generator that can fool the discriminator completely, we moderate the generator's training process by setting an intermediate goal. In this way, we are not trying to generate pristine images from the images subject to anti-forensics attacks. Instead, we generate 'lightly attacked' images to help the discriminator build a better understanding of the attacked images.

2   Related Work

Ever since the earliest SPN-based image forensic method [14] being proposed by Lukas *et al.*, studies have been carried out on the corresponding anti-forensics attacks. The noise-like nature of this camera fingerprint makes it vulnerable to various manipulations. Generally, these anti-forensics manipulations can be categorized into two groups: (1) by introducing pixel-level misalignment and (2) suppression of SPN. In this work, we focus on the latter group. It is acknowledged in [14] that aggressive denoising filters could suppress the SPNs and prevent SPN-based source camera identification. Sengupta *et al.* [18] use a median filter to anonymize the images. In [19], Villalba *et al.* suppress the SPNs by using a combination of the wavelet transform and Wiener filter. In general, these works attack SPNs by suppressing the high-frequency components of the images.

With the emergence of these anti-forensics attacks, subsequent counter anti-forensics methods are developed to detect these attacks. Different hand-crafted features are designed to detect manipulations like median filtering and wavelet-based image compression [8,20]. In contrast to fabricating features specifically corresponding to a type of attacks, several works [2,5,12] construct universal feature sets which are capable of identifying multiple manipulations. With the rise of neural networks, inspired by the use of residual image extracted through high-pass filtering in [2,12], Bayar and Stamm [1] proposed a manipulation detection method using a constrained Convolutional Neural Network (CNN) architecture with the first convolutional layer forced to perform high-pass filtering. Cozzolino *et al.* further investigate the relationship between residual-based descriptors and CNN in [3]. They found that there is no real contraposition between the residual-based features and CNNs, even for unconstrained CNN architectures. Besides, it is demonstrated that their proposed CNN architecture manages to detect various manipulations accurately, including Gaussian blurring, median filtering and JPEG compression. A similar CNN architecture capable of detecting multiple manipulations is presented in [21].

Though both the aforementioned hand-crafted and CNN extracted features can be used to describe different manipulations on images, they require the prior knowledge of these manipulations presented in the training data. For example, despite the CNN architecture from [21] can perform as a multi-class classifier to identify different manipulations, it requires a subset of images for each potential manipulation in the training process. In other words, these methods are essentially searching for the best features describing each manipulation but not for the ones to excel in the binary classification of differentiating whether an image's SPN is pristine or not. Thus, when these methods encounter images attacked by some unprecedented manipulations, their performance in identifying images with SPN attacked could be compromised. Thus, in this work, we propose a novel training strategy using GAN to improve the classification performance for the binary task of differentiating pristine images and the ones subject to attacks.

GAN is first proposed by Goodfellow *et al.* in [6]. Composed of a pair of networks, namely a generator and a discriminator, the generator can capture the statistical properties of the real samples and improve the generated samples through the adversarial process against the discriminator. Correspondingly, the discriminator will learn the difference between the real and generated samples, forcing the generator to improve. Kim *et al.* use GAN in [9] to hide the trace of median filtering by learning the statistical characteristics of the pristine images. In this work, despite generator being used to learn the difference between the pristine images and the images subject to attacks from the training set, the learnt features are used to help the discriminator to generalize better on images subject to unprecedented attacks. We shall show the method in details in the next section.

3   Proposed Method

The goal of this work is to design a training framework to make a classifier generalize better on images subject to SPN-related anti-forensics attacks, even if the attacks are unprecedented from the training set. To achieve this goal, we train the classifier with a GAN framework, which consists of two networks, namely a discriminator, $\mathcal{D}$, and a generator $\mathcal{G}$. We consider the scenario when we have two sets of image patches, one set, $\mathcal{P}$, with pristine images and the other, $\mathcal{F}$, with images undergone certain types of anti-forensics manipulations. $\mathcal{P}$ and $\mathcal{F}$ have the same number of image patches. SPNs reside in the high-frequency bands of the images. Thus, regardless of the type of manipulations, any effective attacks on SPNs need to change the high-frequency components of the images. It is

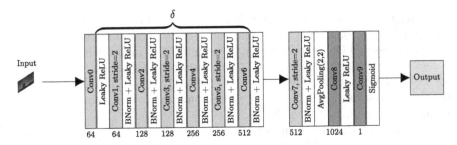

Fig. 1. The network structure of the proposed classifier, which is working as the discriminator, $\mathcal{D}$, in the proposed GAN framework. All the convolutional layers shown in blue have kernel size of 3×3. The convolutional layers shown in yellow have kernel size of 1×1. The number below each convolutional layer represents the number of the output channels from the layers. The layers included in the bracket are the feature extraction layers of the network, marked as δ. The output of the network is a real number in the range of $[0, 1]$.

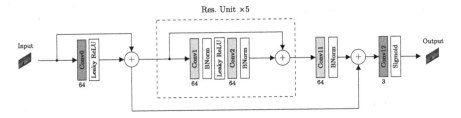

Fig. 2. The structure of the proposed generator, $\mathcal{G}$, in the GAN framework. The generator follows the main concept of ResNet [7] with multiple residual units. The repetitive units are highlighted in the dashed rectangle. The convolutional layers shown in green color have a kernel size of 9×9 while the layers shown in blue have a kernel size of 3×3. The network takes an image as input and output an image of the same size.

reasonable to assume that the traces of attacks could be found by studying the high-frequency residuals of the images. As mentioned in [3], CNN can perform in the same manner as the residual-based descriptors. With this in mind, we build a classifier following a CNN structure (Fig. 2).

The structure of the proposed binary classifier, which also works as the discriminator, $\mathcal{D}$, in the GAN framework, is shown in Fig. 1. The structure is mostly convolutional without any Max pooling or fully-connected layers. We use Leaky ReLUs for the activation layers to prevent vanishing gradients. To above designs are in place to improve the stability of the network during the GAN training process. With the Sigmoid function at the end, the network takes an image patch as input and outputs a single number in the range of $[0, 1]$. The output can be considered as a measurement of the similarity between the input image patch and pristine images. We first train the classifier $\mathcal{D}$ with the pristine and attacked images from $\mathcal{P}$ and $\mathcal{F}$ only. Given an input image patch p_i, we label it with l_i:

$$l_i = \begin{cases} 1, \text{if } p_i \in \mathcal{P}, \\ 0, \text{Otherwise} \end{cases} \tag{1}$$

We define the loss for the binary classification, $\mathcal{L}_{\text{binary}}$, for each output $\mathcal{D}(p_i)$ as:

$$\mathcal{L}_{\text{binary}}(\mathcal{D}(p_i)) = |\mathcal{D}(p_i) - l_i| \tag{2}$$

A binary classifier can be trained by minimising the loss over inputs from $\mathcal{P}$ and $\mathcal{F}$ using the Stochastic Gradient Descent (SGD). We call the classifier trained with this binary data as $\mathcal{D}^*$. As we mentioned earlier, this binary classifier $\mathcal{D}^*$ may focus on the predominant features related to the specific manipulations presented in the training set and would not generalize well for other manipulations. Thus, we introduce the GAN framework to address this problem. We will tune the discriminator $\mathcal{D}$ using images generated from a generator $\mathcal{G}$. Unlike the work in [9] generating images with reference to the pristine images to learn their statistical properties, we want the generated images to have superficial 'pristine-ness' and possess some statistical properties of the images in $\mathcal{F}$, which can help the classifier better understand the attacked images. Our generator G generates images with reference to the manipulated images from $\mathcal{F}$. Using a manipulated image patch p_i from $\mathcal{F}$ as input, the generated image patch $\mathcal{G}(p_i)$ should pose some visual similarity with p_i but differs from p_i in terms of those manipulation-specific features learnt from $\mathcal{D}^*$. Thus, for the generator $\mathcal{G}$, we define its loss as follows:

$$\mathcal{L}_{\mathcal{G}}(\mathcal{G}(p_i)) = \mathcal{L}_{\text{Visual}}(\mathcal{G}(p_i), p_i) - \mathcal{L}_{\text{Feature}}(\mathcal{G}(p_i), p_i) + \mathcal{L}_{\text{Adversarial}}(\mathcal{D}(\mathcal{G}(p_i))) \tag{3}$$

$\mathcal{L}_{\text{Visual}}(\mathcal{G}(p_i), p_i)$ measures the visual difference between the generated patch $\mathcal{G}(p_i)$ and the manipulated patch p_i, which is defined as:

$$\mathcal{L}_{\text{Visual}} = \alpha \cdot |L_2(\mathcal{G}(p_i), p_i) - \Lambda| + \beta \cdot L_2(\text{vgg}(\mathcal{G}(p_i)), \text{vgg}(p_i)) \tag{4}$$

where $L_2(\cdot)$ measures the L_2 distance between two tensors and $\text{vgg}(\cdot)$ is the feature extraction layers from a Visual Geometry Group (VGG)16-net pre-trained on ImageNet [4]. α and β are two weight coefficients and Λ is a relaxation term. The term at the front in Eq. (4) mainly measures the difference between the input and the generated image patch. This can put a constraint on the generated image and make the generated image keep some statistical properties of the manipulated image. However, as we allow the generated image to have some superficial 'pristineness' and be slightly different from the input image, we introduce a small relaxation Λ. The latter term in Eq. (4) measures the perceptual difference between the two image patches. The patches are compared in the feature space of a VGG16-net. This term ensures the generated patches share the perceptual similarity with the input patches.

The term $\mathcal{L}_{\text{Feature}}(\mathcal{G}(p_i), p_i)$ measures the difference between the two patches in the feature space of $\mathcal{D}^*$:

$$\mathcal{L}_{\text{Feature}}(\mathcal{G}(p_i), p_i) = \gamma \cdot L_2(\delta^*(\mathcal{G}(p_i)), \delta^*(p_i)) \tag{5}$$

where γ is another weight coefficient and $\delta^*(\cdot)$ stands for the feature extraction layers (the part in bracket in Fig. 1) of $\mathcal{D}^*$. As the predominant features extracted by $\mathcal{D}^*$ are more likely to be manipulation specific, which might not perform well on the binary classification of deciding whether an image's SPN is pristine or not, we want to feed 'attacked' images without these predominant features to tune the classifier. The negative sign before this term in Eq. (3) encourages the generated image to be different from the input image in terms of these predominant features. The adversarial loss is defined as:

$$\mathcal{L}_{\text{Adversarial}}(\mathcal{D}(\mathcal{G}(p_i))) = \eta \cdot |U - \mathcal{D}(\mathcal{G}(p_i))| \tag{6}$$

Again, η is a weight coefficient. With the definition of labels given in Eq. (1), a traditional GAN framework will immediately set U to 1. In this way, the generator $\mathcal{G}$ will optimize its weight to maximize the chance of having the generated images to be labelled as pristine by the discriminator. However, our goal is not to train a generator which can fool the discriminator completely. We want the discriminator $\mathcal{D}$ to be driven by the generator through the adversarial process to explore different distinctive features for the pristine images and focus less on the predominate features corresponding to specific manipulations. On the other hand, neither it means we should set U to 0. By doing that, there will be no adversarial process. Thus, we want to keep a moderate adversarial process: the generator should be powerful enough to drive the discriminator to explore more features, which can better differentiate the pristine and attacked images; but the generator should not be too powerful such that the generated images will lose all these features. So U is set to a number between 0 and 1 to moderate the adversarial process.

With the loss function for the generator defined, we follow the same definition for labelling and the loss for the discriminator as the ones defined for the original classifier using Eqs. (1) and (2). We fix the weights for the feature extraction layers in $\mathcal{D}$ as δ^* and train the rest of the discriminator with images from $\mathcal{P}$, $\mathcal{F}$ and generated images with a number ratio of 50% : 25% : 25%. With this ratio, it allows equal number of pristine and attacked images to be fed to the discriminator. This ensures that no bias towards one class label is introduced due to the imbalanced number of training images for different labels. We keep using images from $\mathcal{F}$ for training to allow the updated discriminator maintaining its performance in differentiating images from $\mathcal{P}$ and $\mathcal{F}$. We fix the feature extraction layers' weights assuming that the feature extraction performance of $\mathcal{D}^*$ is powerful enough that it has already discovered the features which can differentiate the pristine and attacked images. This is a reasonable assumption considering the deep structure of the discriminator and the features differentiating pristine and attacked images are helpful for the binary classification between images from $\mathcal{P}$ and $\mathcal{F}$. Thus, $\mathcal{D}^*$ has the ability and the incentive to discover features. By locking the feature extraction layers' weights, it prevents the deep structure of the discriminator from being too powerful and cuts the adversarial process and thus, helps to maintain a more stable GAN training process. We will show experiments to prove the effectiveness of the proposed framework.

4   Experiments

To test the effectiveness of the proposed framework, we run experiments on images from the Warwick Image Forensics Dataset [17]. We use images from 8 different cameras and each camera accounts for 200 images. We partitioned the images into patches of size 256×256 pixels and divided them into training and testing sets with a ratio of 90% : 10% randomly. This provides us more than 450,000 image patches for training. On the training images, we keep the original images as $\mathcal{P}$ and generate $\mathcal{F}$ by applying strong Gaussian blurring using a Gaussian kernel with a standard deviation of 8 on all images. Such a strong blurring is effective in removing the SPNs in the images. However, this also leaves obvious visual differences between the attacked and the pristine images. Thus, the neural network-based classifier could easily learn the features associated with this visual effect and differentiate these two types of images. We trained the proposed classifier on the training images for 5 epochs and obtained the weights for $\mathcal{D}^*$. We used the SGD algorithm as the optimizer with a learning rate of 0.04. The training images are loaded in batches with a batch size of 16. Unsurprisingly, this network achieves high accuracy in differentiating the strong Gaussian blurred and pristine images. However, when we applied this network on images attacked by other manipulations or even just using a Gaussian kernel but with a smaller standard deviation, the classification performance becomes much worse.

We applied three types of manipulations on the pristine images to form 3 sets, one with weaker Gaussian blurring using a kernel with a standard deviation of 3, one with Median Filter which has a kernel size of 7×7 and the last one with BM3D denoising. Then, we used $\mathcal{D}^*$ to classify the images. As $\mathcal{D}^*$ outputs a single number which can be viewed as a measure of similarity, we can adjust the threshold for this similarity to generate detection results with different levels of True Positive (TP, attacked images labelled as attacked) rates under different False Positive (FP, pristine images labelled as attacked) rates. As we want to use this classifier to filter attacked images from pristine images when we apply SPN-based methods on a large number of candidate images, we would like to have a small FP rate such that we can keep as many pristine images as possible. Thus, for this test, we only focus on the results when FP rate is below 1%. The Receiver Operating Characteristic (ROC) curves for $\mathcal{D}^*$ on the three test sets are shown in Fig. 3(a). The classifier has TP rate lower than 5% for images manipulated by median filter and BM3D. While the set with the weak Gaussian blurring is performing better than the other two as this manipulation shares more similarities with the images in the training set, the TP rate is still below 10% throughout the range. It proves the neural network-based classifier can be overfitting to the features specifically related to the strong Gaussian blurring.

We applied the proposed framework on $\mathcal{P}$ and $\mathcal{F}$ to tune $\mathcal{D}$. The weight parameters α, β, γ and η are set to 1, 3×10^{-3}, 0.01 and 0.01, respectively. We trained the networks under the GAN framework for 10 epochs. SGD optimizer is used for both the discriminator and the generator with the learning rate set to 0.02 for the generator and 0.01 for the discriminator. The ROC curves for the tuned classifier on the detection of the 3 manipulations are shown in Fig. 3(b). The proposed framework can achieve TP rate as high as 38.1% with FP rate lower than 1% for the weak Gaussian blurring despite all the attacked images in the training set are manipulated by a much strong Gaussian blurring. Even for the BM3D denoised images, which do not show strong local blurring artifacts, the tuned classifier can detect them better than the original classifier can do for the weaker Gaussian blurring. This shows the effectiveness of the proposed framework of shifting the classifier's excessive emphasis on manipulation-specific features to the more generalised features shared by images with their SPNs attacked. With the much better patch-level accuracies at low false positive rates, the improved classifier can detect the anti-forensics attacks at the image-level more accurately.

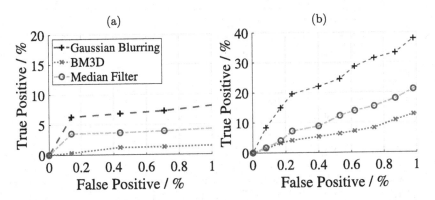

Fig. 3. ROC curves for the classification results on images attacked by three different manipulations detected by (a) $\mathcal{D}^*$, (b) classifier trained under the proposed GAN framework.

5   Conclusion

Existing neural network-based anti-forensics attack detectors have shown superior ability in detecting specific manipulations on images. However, when they are used for the binary classification of deciding whether an image's SPN is attacked or not, their performance could be compromised due to their excessive emphasis on manipulation-specific features. In this work, we proposed a novel strategy to tune such a detector, which is in the form of a binary classifier. By training it as the discriminator in a GAN framework, this makes the classifier generalise better to images subject to unprecedented attacks. Despite the limitation of the original training set which might only contains images subject to a certain type of attacks, the generated images in the GAN framework can shift the classifier's excessive focus on those manipulation-specific features to the ones which can generalise better for the binary classification. The experimental results show that the proposed training scheme could improve the probability of detecting attacks on PRNUs from manipulations not included in the training set while keeping the false positive low for the pristine images.

References

1. Bayar, B., Stamm, M.C.: A deep learning approach to universal image manipulation detection using a new convolutional layer. In: Proceedings of the 4th ACM Workshop on Information Hiding and Multimedia Security, pp. 5–10. IH and MMSec 2016, Association for Computing Machinery, New York, NY, USA (2016)
2. Cao, H., Kot, A.C.: Manipulation detection on image patches using fusionboost. IEEE Trans. Inf. Forensics Secur. **7**(3), 992–1002 (2012)
3. Cozzolino, D., Poggi, G., Verdoliva, L.: Recasting residual-based local descriptors as convolutional neural networks: an application to image forgery detection. In: Proceedings of the 5th ACM Workshop on Information Hiding and Multimedia Security, pp. 159–164 (2017)
4. Deng, J., Dong, W., Socher, R., Li, L., Li, K., Li, F.F.: Imagenet: a large-scale hierarchical image database. In: 2009 IEEE Conference on Computer Vision and Pattern Recognition, pp. 248–255 (2009)
5. Fan, W., Wang, K., Cayre, F.: General-purpose image forensics using patch likelihood under image statistical models. In: 2015 IEEE International Workshop on Information Forensics and Security (WIFS), pp. 1–6 (2015)
6. Goodfellow, I.J., et al.: Generative adversarial networks (2014)
7. He, K., Zhang, X., Ren, S., Sun, J.: Deep residual learning for image recognition. In: Proceedings of the IEEE Conference on Computer Vision and Pattern Recognition, pp. 770–778 (2016)
8. Kang, X., Stamm, M.C., Peng, A., Liu, K.J.R.: Robust median filtering forensics using an autoregressive model. IEEE Trans. Inf. Forensics Secur. **8**(9), 1456–1468 (2013)
9. Kim, D., Jang, H., Mun, S., Choi, S., Lee, H.: Median filtered image restoration and anti-forensics using adversarial networks. IEEE Signal Process. Lett. **25**(2), 278–282 (2018)
10. Li, C.T.: Source camera identification using enhanced sensor pattern noise. IEEE Trans. Inf. Forensics Secur. **5**(2), 280–287 (2010)
11. Li, C.T., Lin, X.: A fast source-oriented image clustering method for digital forensics. EURASIP J. Image Video Process. Special Issues Image Video Forensics Soc. Med. Anal. **1**, 69–84 (2017)

12. Li, H., Luo, W., Qiu, X., Huang, J.: Identification of various image operations using residual-based features. IEEE Trans. Circuits Syst. Video Technol. **28**(1), 31–45 (2018)

13. Lin, X., Li, C.T.: Large-scale image clustering based on camera fingerprints. IEEE Trans. Inf. Forensics Secur. **12**(4), 793–808 (2017)

14. Lukas, J., Fridrich, J., Goljan, M.: Digital camera identification from sensor pattern noise. IEEE Trans. Inf. Forensics Secur. **1**(2), 205–214 (2006)

15. Phan, Q., Boato, G., De Natale, F.G.B.: Accurate and scalable image clustering based on sparse representation of camera fingerprint. IEEE Trans. Inf. Forensics Secur. **14**(7), 1902–1916 (2019)

16. Quan, Y., Li, C.T.: On addressing the impact of ISO speed upon PRNU and forgery detection. IEEE Trans. Inf. Forensics Secur. **16**, 190–202 (2021)

17. Quan, Y., Li, C.T., Zhou, Y., Li, L.: Warwick image forensics dataset for device fingerprinting in multimedia forensics. In: 2020 IEEE International Conference on Multimedia and Expo (ICME), pp. 1–6. IEEE (2020)

18. Sengupta, P., Sameer, V.U., Naskar, R., Kalaimannan, E.: Source anonymization of digital images: a counter-forensic attack on PRNU based source identification techniques. In: Proceedings of the Conference on Digital Forensics, Security and Law, pp. 95–105. Association of Digital Forensics, Security and Law (2017)

19. Villalba, L.J.G., Orozco, A.L.S., Corripio, J.R., Hernandez-Castro, J.: A PRNU-based counter-forensic method to manipulate smartphone image source identification techniques. Futur. Gener. Comput. Syst. **76**, 418–427 (2017)

20. Wang, M., Chen, Z., Fan, W., Xiong, Z.: Countering anti-forensics to wavelet-based compression. In: 2014 IEEE International Conference on Image Processing (ICIP), pp. 5382–5386 (2014)

21. Yu, J., Zhan, Y., Yang, J., Kang, X.: A multi-purpose image counter-anti-forensic method using convolutional neural networks. In: Shi, Y.Q., Kim, H.J., Perez-Gonzalez, F., Liu, F. (eds.) IWDW 2016. LNCS, vol. 10082, pp. 3–15. Springer, Cham (2017). https://doi.org/10.1007/978-3-319-53465-7_1

Document Forgery Detection in the Context of Double JPEG Compression

Théo Taburet[1]([✉])[ID], Kais Rouis[1][ID], Mickaël Coustaty[1][ID], Petra Gomez Krämer[1][ID], Nicolas Sidère[1][ID], Saddok Kébairi[2], and Vincent Poulain d'Andecy[2]

[1] L3i Laboratory, La Rochelle Université, La Rochelle, France
{theo.taburet,kais.rouis,mickael.coustaty,petragomez.kramer,
nicolas.sidere}@univ-lr.fr
[2] Yooz, Aimargues, France
{saddok.kebairi,vincentpoulain.dandecy}@getyooz.com

Abstract. In this paper, we propose a strategy to train a CNN to detect document manipulations in JPEG documents under data scarcity scenario. As it comes to scanned PDF documents, it is common that the document consists of a JPEG image encapsulated into a PDF. Indeed, if the document before tampering was a JPEG image, its manipulation will lead to double compression artefacts within the resulting tampered JPEG image. In contrast to related methods that are based on handcrafted histograms of DCT coefficients, we propose a double compression detection method using a one-hot encoding of the DCT coefficients of JPEG images. We can use accordingly a CNN model to compute co-occurrence matrices and avoid handcrafted features such as histograms. Using simulated frauds on Perlin noise, we train our network and then test it on textual images against a state-of-the-art CNN algorithm trained on natural images. Our approach has shown an encouraging generalization on both the database used in the paper and on a stream of synthetic frauds on real documents used in the company Yooz.

1 Introduction

Over the last few decades, we have seen an upsurge in the use of digital documents to store invoices, contracts and financial documents. In fact, the majority of the documents stored as images are saved in JPEG format, making the forensics over JPEG images a pertinent task that requires appropriate technical considerations. In parallel with the growth of digital document exchanges, the rapid advancement of the image manipulation tools allows the users to tamper the digital documents without apparent visual distortions, which has paved the way to facilitate tampering operations. Hence a robust detection of double compressed JPEG images helps for instance to detect whether a document is directly captured from a primary scanning process, or it has been re-compressed to perform a possible manipulation.

The highly privileged information such as personal data could be a subject of a security issue. In this vein, it is a critical task to confirm the integrity of sensitive information to avoid taking advantage over another entity or organization. Numerous approaches have been particularly proposed to handle the case of document images:

© Springer Nature Switzerland AG 2023
J.-J. Rousseau and B. Kapralos (Eds.): ICPR 2022 Workshops, LNCS 13646, pp. 57–69, 2023.
https://doi.org/10.1007/978-3-031-37745-7_5

- Optical watermarks [15] carrying an authentication pattern along with specific features such as designed inks or coatings are among the most popular.
- Verifiable fields checking (2D-Doc, MRZ). Recently, the 2D-DOC system has become more familiar to authenticate the 'Electronic Health Certificates' documents. The tampering is easily detectable since the content of the QR-code corresponds to the user personal data.
- Copy Detection Pattern [9] (CDP) methods which are based on printing digital patterns designed to be sensitive to direct duplication. The counterfeits are detected with respect to the information loss generated by a Print-and-Scan process.

Actually, the above methods help answer some of the forensics questions. Nevertheless, the digital document authenticity problem is still relevant to prevent scammers from operating effectively. In this paper we will address the detection of fraud in documents stored as images under the prism of double JPEG compression and the associated artifacts, assuming that the original documents are encapsulated in a PDF and have been scanned and recorded in JPEG format.

First, we would clearly point out the gap between the real-scene image domain and the document image domain. It is evident that accurate discriminative features, that could be used for instance to detect possible forgeries, greatly depends on the visual complexity of the image content. In other words, processing images with textured blocks and a variety of curved objects is fairly different from processing images with textual content over a white and smooth background.

Most of tampering detection methods in the state-of-the-art proposed technical solutions particularly to solve the JPEG double compression issues for real images. Some benchmark tampering datasets are publicly available and contribute to conduct extended experiments. On the contrary, in our case, the first struggle to deal with is the lack of data as tampered document images. The second issue concerns the characteristics of a document representing textual information within most of image regions. We are indeed facing low entropy and much less frequencies (frequency domain analysis) compared to real images' data.

Moreover, the need for high detection performances for a wide range of document classes, requires in fact an appropriate deep-learning model as feature extractor (generalization task). Here we have another major issue as the deep convolutional operations on data samples characterized by low entropy, could easily lead to an overfit scenarios related to the gradient exploding among the layers' weights. In this sense, a pre-processing step can be involved to ensure a good functioning of deep model learning stage.

The contributions can be summarized as follows:

1. Suitable methodology to overcome the lack of tampered document images datasets.
2. Adaptive Convolutional Neural Network (CNN) architecture that is able to learn on synthetic images and to generalize on document images.
3. Relevant proof of the afforded technical concepts.

The rest of the paper is organized as follows. In Sect. 2, we present the backgroundconcepts about the JPEG format and the used notations in the different sections.

We introduce in Sect. 3 the related works and we provide a discussion about the corresponding limitations. Section 4 describes the CNN-based proposed method and the pre-processing step carried out for a better convergence of our neural network. Experiments in Sect. 5 show the performances of our method and finally, some conclusions are drawn in the last section.

2 Background and Concepts

To clearly introduce our topic, we first introduce an overview of Spatial forgery impact on JPEG coefficients

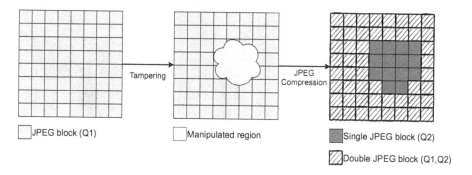

Fig. 1. Considered image manipulation case.

In a fraud scenario, a scammer could use an image editing software to locally modify a JPEG image and subsequently save it using the JPEG format. As a result, some parts of the image will undergo a double compression. Figure 1 illustrates the behaviour of single and double JPEG compressed blocks within a manipulated image. The genuine image exhibits properties of a single compression using a quantization matrix Q_1. The alteration of the decompressed image takes place in the spatial domain. In this way, some of the 8×8 DCT coefficients remain intact, but after saving the altered image as a JPEG using a different quantization matrix Q_2, they exhibit double compression artifacts (from Q_1 and Q_2). However, the blocks that have been manipulated in the spatial domain have actually the features of a single compressed JPEG image with the Q_2 quantization matrix.

The lossy compression JPEG format is likely to remove subtle traces of the original image while leaving undesirable traces. In fact, several approaches have been proposed to explore these traces for the tampering detection task.

3 Related Works and Discussion

3.1 Early Detection for JPEG Double Compression

An early detection approach implies the extraction of handcrafted features [4,6,11,12] from DCT coefficients to distinguish between single and double JPEG compressed images. Most of these methods are based on the DCT coefficient histograms. The double compression impact on the distribution of the coefficients is called the "double-quantization artifact".

For integrity checking of natural images, the distribution analysis of the DCT coefficients has been examined under different angles:

- Popescu et al. proposed to quantify statistical correlations that result from specific forms of digital tampering and devise detection schemes to reveal these correlations [14].
- In [7], Fu et al. concluded that Benford's rule holds for JPEG coefficients.
- Chen et al. demonstrated in [5] that the periodic patterns appear in the spatial and frequency domains and proposed to handle the image detection based on this concept.

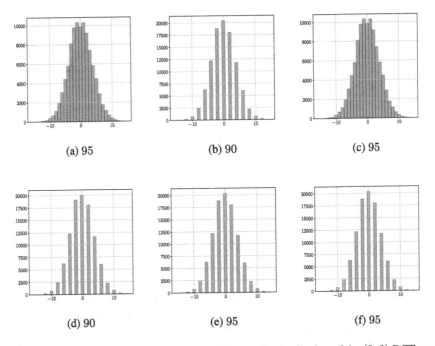

Fig. 2. Illustration of the double compression artifact on the distribution of the $(3, 2)$ DCT coefficients after inverse quantization (during decompression). (a, b, c) are single compressed images at QF 95, 90 and 95, respectively. (d, e, f) are their double compressed version at QF 90, 95 and 95, respectively.

Figure 2 shows an example of double compression artifacts for $(k, l) = (3, 2)$:

- Figures 2 (a), (b) and (c) are bargraphs of the single quantized histogram at the frequency $(3, 2)$ of an uncompressed image for quality factors $QF_1 = 95$, $QF_1 = 90$ and $QF_1 = 95$, respectively.

– Figures 2 (d), (e) and (f) highlight the twice-quantized histograms over two quality factors $(QF_1 = 95, QF_2 = 90)$, $(QF_1 = 90, QF_2 = 95)$ and $(QF_1 = 95, QF_2 = 95)$, respectively.

From Fig. 2 (c), we can see that when an image is subject to a double JPEG compression with $QF_1 \leqslant QF_2$, the histogram of the double-quantized DCT coefficient can exhibit a certain periodic pattern of peaks and troughs. Contrarily, when $QF_1 > QF_2$, although the DCT coefficient histogram may represent a periodic fluctuation, it is difficult to detect the underlying effect as the distribution of bins in this situation is very similar to the distribution of bins in a simple compression (Figs. 2 (b) and (e)).

3.2 Double JPEG Detection Using CNN

Some CNN-based architectures have been proposed to address the double compression issues. In contrast to classical hands-crafted features based approaches [3, 13, 17], some CNN model could be used to distinguish between histogram features (after extracting DCT coefficients) which were inserted into the network. Two recent references proposed to use a one-hot encoding [10, 21] which is at the basis of our approach.

However, due to the very limited use of these quality factors, this approach is not very useful on JPEG documents.

One should bear in mind that few references considered the JPEG document images which are very challenging compared to real images, starting from the lack of sufficient available data with appropriately generated frauds. More precisely, there are no available real-case tampered documents datasets to train a deep CNN model. The problem that we are trying to solve does not only raise the point of an adequate network architecture for which the state-of-the-art is already well introduced, but rather the question of training this network without any forged document examples. We propose indeed a two-fold methodology, first to resolve the struggle of missing data and then to detect image forgeries in JPEG compressed textual images. Data scarcity will be overcome by using synthetic data, and a CNN-based detection is proposed so the model input will be a *binary one-hot representation* [19] of the JPEG coefficients for each processed image.

4   Proposed Method

As previously specified in Sect. 3, we intend to focus in this paper on the fraud detection while ignoring the spatial domain analysis (pixels) of the JPEG text images. In order to process the JPEG coefficients, we first carry out a pre-processing step to ensure a better convergence of our neural network.

4.1 Notations

Matrices are written in uppercase ($\mathbf{A}$) and vectors of scalar or random variables in lowercase boldface font ($\mathbf{a}$). $\mathbf{A}^t$ is the matrix transposition and the element-wise multiplication and division are denoted by $\odot$ and $\oslash$, respectively. The Kronecker product is denoted by $\otimes$, and the operation $\boxplus$ stands for staking along a third dimension. Thus if $\mathbf{A}$ and $\mathbf{B}$ are $m \times n$ matrices, we obtain a $m \times n \times 2$ tensor.

The operator $[.]$ corresponds to the rounding of $x \in \mathbb{R}$ to the nearest integer. The clipping operation of x to $b \in \mathbb{R}$ is denoted by $x^{\perp b}$. The remainder of the euclidean division is computed as $c = a \% b$ using $a \in \mathbb{R}$ and $b \in \mathbb{N}$.

4.2 Binary One-Hot Encoding

We introduce in the following the pre-processing step using a binary one-hot encoding. The main objective is to conduct a CNN-based binary classification method. Let $\mathbf{C}$ be a matrix of size $H \times W$ and T is a given integer. $\mathbf{N}$ is composed of the matrix coefficients $\mathbf{C}$ after computing their absolute value and being clipped to T. Hence we define OH as the One-hot encoding operator:

$$\text{OH} : \mathbb{Z}^{H \times W} \times \mathbb{N} \to \{0, 1\}^{H \times W \times (T+1)}$$

$$(\mathbf{C}, T) \mapsto \overset{T}{\underset{t=0}{\boxplus}} \left(|c_{i,j}|^{\perp T} = t \right)_{i,j < H,W}$$

As an example, Fig. 3 illustrates the effect of the OneHot-encoding on an array of integers. At the output of this operation, the array is composed of three channels. Each channel indicates by 1 the positions of the 0, 1 and 2 values in the input array, respectively. In [19], the authors demonstrated that this technique allows the CNN to compute co-occurrences matrices after a convolution operation.

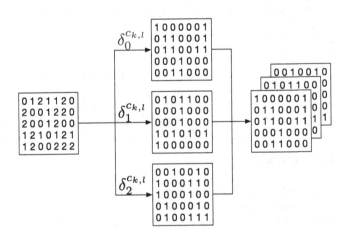

Fig. 3. One-hot encoding over an array with $T = 2$.

Note that the clipping operation is needed for memory restrictions. The value of T should have a relatively small value for the same purpose. To this end, $T = 5$ is accordingly used in our work. The absolute values are further computed to populate a little more the bins of the 2D-histograms which will be thereafter estimated. In our case the matrix dimensions are set to $(H, W) = (128, 128)$.

Using such a one-hot encoding method, it is possible to insert additional information in along with the JPEG coefficients. During our experiments, we propose to investigate two strategies:

- The first strategy *"OH-JPEG"* consists of a one-hot encoding of the JPEG coefficients based only on the input array. Let $\mathbf{I} \in \{0,1\}^{128 \times 128 \times (T+1)}$ be the input tensor of the neural network:

$$\mathbf{I} = \mathrm{OH}(\mathbf{C}, T).\tag{1}$$

- The second strategy *"OH-JPEG + PQL (Parity Quantization Layer)"* is an extension of the first one, where we add information on the parity of the coefficients of the quantization matrix. At this point, we have $\mathbf{I} \in \{0,1\}^{128 \times 128 \times (T+2)}$ and $\mathbf{Q}$ is the quantization matrix $\mathbf{C}$. We denote by $\mathbf{1}_{16 \times 16}$ the 16×16 all-ones matrix:

$$\mathbf{I} = (\mathrm{OH}(\mathbf{C}, T) \boxplus (\mathbf{1}_{16 \times 16} \otimes \mathbf{Q} \% 2)).\tag{2}$$

Thus, the parity of the quantization matrix coefficient associated with each JPEG coefficient is indicated in the input tensor. Note that the use of $\mathbf{1}_{16 \times 16} \otimes \mathbf{Q}$ is mandatory to repeat the quantization matrix in order to fill out a 128×128 matrix:

$$\mathbf{1}_{16 \times 16} \otimes \mathbf{Q} = \begin{bmatrix} \mathbf{Q} & \cdots & \mathbf{Q} \\ \vdots & \ddots & \vdots \\ \mathbf{Q} & \cdots & \mathbf{Q} \end{bmatrix} \in \mathbb{Z}^{128 \times 128}.$$

In order to have a fair comparison between the two strategies in terms of dimensionality, we assume $T = 5$ for *"OH-JPEG"* and $T = 4$ for *"OH-JPEG + PQL"*. Therefore, we conclude a binary classification network to handle the data structure.

4.3   Network Architecture

Figure 4 shows the overall architecture of the proposed OneHot-CNN. The network input tensor has a size of $128 \times 128 \times \tilde{T}$ ($\tilde{T}$ is an integer). The network has two branches which are fed with the same input tensor:

- The first one uses a 32-channels 2D-convolutional layer using 3×3 kernels aiming at learning *intra-block correlations*.
- The second branch uses a 32-channels layer of 8-dilated [20] 2D-convolutional operations with 3×3 kernels. The aim here is to extract features over DCT coefficients of the same frequency in order to capture *inter-block correlations*.

The output of these two branches is then concatenated and undergoes sequentially:

- 64-channels of 2D-convolutions with 3×3 kernels + Batch-Normalization + ReLU activation,
- an adaptive average pooling to output a $64 \times 2 \times 2$ vector,
- a fully connected layer with 8 neurons + ReLU activation,
- a fully connected layer with 2 neurons,
- and finally a Logsoftmax to output the scores of the two classes ("genuine" and "tampered").

To train this network we do not have access to a reliable labelled image database, so we have created an alternative methodology to demonstrate our method's performance.

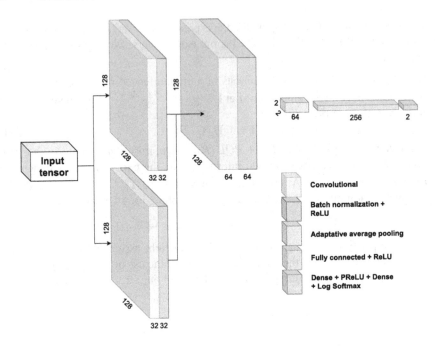

Fig. 4. Diagram of the proposed OneHot-CNN architecture.

4.4 Addressing the Lack of Fraud Examples

Due to their sensitive nature, there are very few public document fraud datasets that can meet our needs, i.e., sufficient samples of labeled document images that can be used to train accurately a deep model.

To the best of our knowledge, the only suitable dataset is FindIt [1]. The main problem is that the original JPEG images (not tampered) have been saved with the same quantization matrix $\mathbf{Q}_{\text{genuine}}$. For the tampered images, we observe the same problem with $\mathbf{Q}_{\text{genuine}} \neq \mathbf{Q}_{\text{tampered}}$ making the detection very easy in our case.

In order to meet our image needs, we propose here to generate artificially the frauds to generate a set of training images in such a way that these images exhibit in the DCT domain some artifacts likely to be generated during an image manipulation. We try then to carry out an a *prior* learning phase where the semantics of the image do not matter, and only the statistics on the JPEG coefficients are considered. In the case of small datasets or lack of data, the use of phantom data can be granted. Our intention is to provide enough data relative to the implementation of a deep-learning scheme [2][?].

In our experiments, we generate images (three examples are shown in Fig. 5) to constitute the train dataset using a Perlin noise[1] aiming to obtain full spatial resolution images without JPEG compression.

---

[1] Perlin noise is a procedural texture primitive, it is a gradient noise used to improve the realism of the CGI.

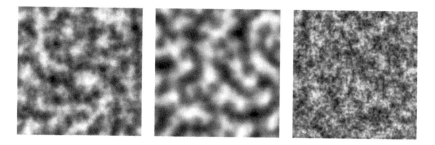

Fig. 5. 128 × 128 sample images produced using Perlin noise.

In Fig. 6, we illustrate how from a spatial image, a synthetical fraud is generated. From the Perlin noise we obtain an 8-bit image from which we generate two JPEG versions:

– compressed only at QF_2,
– compressed at QF_1 then QF_2.

By doing so, one can create a composite JPEG image that is supposed to mimic the effects of a "well tampered" JPEG file at QF_1 in the spatial domain and saved at QF_2. The idea behind this proposal is that the composite image contains the same semantics as the original image. Ergo, the exploitation of spatial correlation seems to be unrealistic as it is more likely to be preserved.

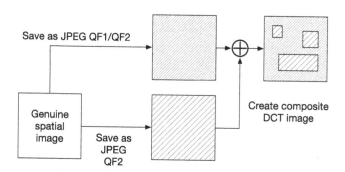

Fig. 6. Creation of a simulated fraud on an image. The composite image designated as "spoofed" contains between 0% and 50% of the original image content compressed at QF_2. The other blocks containing the original content are compressed twice (at QF_1 then at QF_2).

5   Experiments

In order to inspect the possibility of training a neural network to detect double compression in a document from noise images, we have generated a set of training samples including images from various compression factors, whether for the generation of "genuine" or "tampered" inputs. Furthermore, to highlight the advantages or weaknesses of our approach, we aim to provide a realistic assessment of the generalization accuracy of our network based on a cross table.

5.1 Results

During the training and validation phases, the datasets are made up of 128×128 monochromatic phantom images (formed from Perlin noise):

- 20000 images for the training set,
- 5000 images for the validation set.
- 20000 images for the testing set.

For each set the genuine/tampered classes are balanced with mixed quality parameters. The different quantization tables are used (corresponding to those obtained from Python Imaging Library (PIL) [16] for $QF_{50}, QF_{55}, \ldots, QF_{100}$).

The performances in terms of accuracy are reported in the table where each cell corresponds to an estimate of the accuracy on a subset of images such as :

- Genuine are saved at QF_1,
- Tampered images are from QF_1 images saved at QF_2 with original QF_1 blocks (Table 2).

Table 1. Accuracy $Acc(\%)$ for **OH-JPEG** on Perlin testing set.

$Acc(\%)$	QF_1					
QF_2	75	80	85	90	95	100
75	50.0	94.0	100.0	99.0	51.0	50.0
80	98.5	50.0	99.5	96.5	64.0	50.5
85	99.0	100.0	50.0	99.0	51.0	50.0
90	99.5	100.0	100.0	50.0	92.0	50.5
95	100.0	98.0	100.0	100.0	50.0	49.5
100	99.5	99.0	98.5	98.5	100.0	59.5

5.2 State of the Art Relevance

In order to qualify the viability of our approaches we have submitted them to a series of tests:

- Accuracy estimation of each method on the test dataset (Perlin noise),
- Accuracy estimation using 5000 cropped 128×128 FindIt [1] images of tampered or genuine areas.

We can see from Table 1 that when faced with new images, approach 2 allows us to detach ourselves from the random guesses. We can specify here that the FindIt data are not very usable here: they are often images containing very little content, this comes from the crop function which is not perfected. We can also note that method "OH-JPEG + PQL" allows to treat combinations of quality factors that are challenging for the other approaches. In Table 4, for each combination of quality factors, the gains in accuracy on the test base (Perlin noise) are displayed (Table 3).

Table 2. Accuracy $Acc(\%)$ for **OH-JPEG + PQL** on Perlin testing set.

$Acc(\%)$	QF_1					
QF_2	75	80	85	90	95	100
75	50.0	88.5	100.0	98.0	52.0	50.0
80	99.5	50.0	100.0	95.5	65.0	51.0
85	99.5	99.5	50.0	99.5	50.5	50.0
90	99.5	98.5	100.0	50.0	98.5	50.0
95	99.5	98.5	100.0	100.0	50.0	49.5
100	99.0	99.0	99.5	100.0	100.0	61.0

Table 3. Average accuracy $Acc(\%)$ for **DJPEG, OH-JPEG** and **OH-JPEG+PQL** on FindIt and Perlin testing sets.

$Acc(\%)$	Methods		
Datasets	DJPEG	OH-JPEG	OH-JPEG+PQL
Perlin	68.40	**84.24**	83.91
FindIt	54.40	47.25	**61.95**

Table 4. Accuracy gain or loss for **OH-JPEG + PQL** vs **DJPEG**. on Perlin testing set.

$Acc(\%)$	QF_1					
QF_2	75	80	85	90	95	100
75	−0.01	**16.4**	**11.49**	**15.82**	−30.14	**2.6**
80	**20.9**	−0.16	**27.07**	**10.68**	−12.38	**13.24**
85	**26.6**	**22.08**	-0.23	**22.44**	−12.32	**9.38**
90	**28.15**	**25.**	**16.9**	**0.01**	**3.46**	**23.69**
95	**26.32**	**10.23**	**9.79**	**25.**	**0.6**	**23.82**
100	**23.99**	**10.7**	**10.08**	−1.5	**4.17**	**10.48**

6 Discussion and Conclusions

We investigated the double compression detection task in documents saved as JPEG images. Our proposed technique provided promising results taking into account several issues, such as the lack of tampered samples and the visual characteristics of the documents. For our future work we are considering three possibilities:

- to further enhance the generalization of our network by constructing a larger fraud dataset of genuine and tampered JPEG documents,
- to investigate GAN generated documents fraud [18],
- to add the rounding error study to our toolbox, based on the fact that industrial scanners use adaptive segmentation [8] to achieve a less aggressive compression on the text and more apparent artifacts on the background, we have observed an

interesting phenomenon with regard to the JPEG rounding errors that we would also like to use.

Acknowledgments. This work is supported by the Region Nouvelle Aquitaine under the grant number 2019-1R50120 (CRASD project) and AAPR2020-2019-8496610 (CRASD2 project) and by the LabCom IDEAS under the grant number ANR-18-LCV3-0008.

References

1. Artaud, C., Sidère, N., Doucet, A., Ogier, J.M., Yooz, V.P.D.: Find it! fraud detection contest report. In: 2018 24th International Conference on Pattern Recognition (ICPR), pp. 13–18. IEEE (2018)
2. Bae, H.J., et al.: A Perlin noise-based augmentation strategy for deep learning with small data samples of HRCT images. Sci. Rep. **8**(1), 1–7 (2018)
3. Barni, M., et al.: Aligned and non-aligned double jpeg detection using convolutional neural networks. J. Vis. Commun. Image Represent. **49**, 153–163 (2017)
4. Bianchi, T., Piva, A.: Analysis of non-aligned double jpeg artifacts for the localization of image forgeries. In: 2011 IEEE International Workshop on Information Forensics and Security, pp. 1–6. IEEE (2011)
5. Chen, Y.L., Hsu, C.T.: Detecting recompression of JPEG images via periodicity analysis of compression artifacts for tampering detection. IEEE Trans. Inf. Forensics Secur. **6**(2), 396–406 (2011)
6. Farid, H.: Exposing digital forgeries from JPEG ghosts. IEEE Trans. Inf. Forensics Secur. **4**(1), 154–160 (2009)
7. Fu, D., Shi, Y.Q., Su, W.: A generalized Bedford's law for JPEG coefficients and its applications in image forensics. In: Security, Steganography, and Watermarking of Multimedia Contents IX. vol. 6505, p. 65051L. International Society for Optics and Photonics (2007)
8. Huang, J.: Segmentation-based hybrid compression scheme for scanned documents (May 20 2008), US Patent 7,376,265
9. Khermaza, E., Tkachenko, I., Picard, J.: Can copy detection patterns be copied? evaluating the performance of attacks and highlighting the role of the detector. In: 2021 IEEE International Workshop on Information Forensics and Security (WIFS), pp. 1–6. IEEE (2021)
10. Kwon, M.J., Yu, I.J., Nam, S.H., Lee, H.K.: Cat-net: Compression artifact tracing network for detection and localization of image splicing. In: Proceedings of the IEEE/CVF Winter Conference on Applications of Computer Vision, pp. 375–384 (2021)
11. Li, B., Shi, Y.Q., Huang, J.: Detecting doubly compressed jpeg images by using mode based first digit features. In: 2008 IEEE 10th Workshop on Multimedia Signal Processing, pp. 730–735. IEEE (2008)
12. Lin, Z., He, J., Tang, X., Tang, C.K.: Fast, automatic and fine-grained tampered JPEG image detection via DCT coefficient analysis. Pattern Recogn. **42**(11), 2492–2501 (2009)
13. Park, J., Cho, D., Ahn, W., Lee, H.-K.: Double JPEG detection in mixed JPEG quality factors using deep convolutional neural network. In: Ferrari, V., Hebert, M., Sminchisescu, C., Weiss, Y. (eds.) ECCV 2018. LNCS, vol. 11209, pp. 656–672. Springer, Cham (2018). https://doi.org/10.1007/978-3-030-01228-1_39
14. Popescu, A.C., Farid, H.: Statistical tools for digital forensics. In: Fridrich, J. (ed.) IH 2004. LNCS, vol. 3200, pp. 128–147. Springer, Heidelberg (2004). https://doi.org/10.1007/978-3-540-30114-1_10
15. van Renesse, R.L.: Paper based document security-a review. In: European Conference on Security and Detection, 1997. ECOS 1997, pp. 75–80. IET (1997)

16. Umesh, P.: Image processing in python. CSI Commun. **23**, 1–25 (2012)
17. Wang, Q., Zhang, R.: Double JPEG compression forensics based on a convolutional neural network. EURASIP J. Inf. Secur. **2016**(1), 1–12 (2016)
18. Wu, L., et al.: Editing text in the wild. In: Proceedings of the 27th ACM International Conference on Multimedia, pp. 1500–1508 (2019)
19. Yousfi, Y., Fridrich, J.: An intriguing struggle of CNNs in JPEG steganalysis and the onehot solution. IEEE Signal Process. Lett. **27**, 830–834 (2020)
20. Yu, F., Koltun, V.: Multi-scale context aggregation by dilated convolutions. arXiv preprint arXiv:1511.07122 (2015)
21. Yu, I.J., Nam, S.H., Ahn, W., Kwon, M.J., Lee, H.K.: Manipulation classification for JPEG images using multi-domain features. IEEE Access **8**, 210837–210854 (2020)

Making Generated Images Hard to Spot: A Transferable Attack on Synthetic Image Detectors

Xinwei Zhao and Matthew C. Stamm

Drexel University, Philadelphia, PA 19104, USA
{xz355,mcs382}@drexel.edu

Abstract. Visually realistic GAN-generated images have recently emerged as an important misinformation threat. Research has shown that these synthetic images contain forensic traces that are readily identifiable by forensic detectors. Unfortunately, these detectors are built upon neural networks, which are vulnerable to recently developed adversarial attacks. In this paper, we propose a new anti-forensic attack capable of fooling GAN-generated image detectors. Our attack uses an adversarially trained generator to synthesize traces that these detectors associate with real images. Furthermore, we propose a technique to train our attack so that it can achieve transferability, i.e. it can fool unknown CNNs that it was not explicitly trained against. We evaluate our attack through an extensive set of experiments, where we show that our attack can fool eight state-of-the-art detection CNNs with synthetic images created using seven different GANs, and outperform other alternative attacks.

Keywords: GAN-based attacks · Forensic detectors · Anti-forensics

1 Introduction

Recent technological advances have enabled the creation of synthetic images that are visually realistic. Generative adversarial networks (GANs) [17] in particular have driven this development. Several GANs have been proposed that are capable of synthetically generating images of both objects and human faces that are convincingly real to human observers [6,10,12,22–25,39]. Unfortunately, these synthetic image generation

---

This material is based on research sponsored by DARPA and Air Force Research Laboratory (AFRL) under agreement number HR0011-20-C-0126. The U.S. Government is authorized to reproduce and distribute reprints for Governmental purposes notwithstanding any copyright notation thereon. The views and conclusions contained herein are those of the authors and should not be interpreted as necessarily representing the official policies or endorsements, either expressed or implied, of DARPA and Air Force Research Laboratory (AFRL) or the U.S. Government. This material is based upon work supported by the National Science Foundation under Grant No. 1553610. Any opinions, findings, and conclusions or recommendations expressed in this material are those of the authors and do not necessarily reflect the views of the National Science Foundation.

© Springer Nature Switzerland AG 2023
J.-J. Rousseau and B. Kapralos (Eds.): ICPR 2022 Workshops, LNCS 13646, pp. 70–84, 2023.
https://doi.org/10.1007/978-3-031-37745-7_6

techniques can be used for malicious purposes, such as the creation of fake personas to be used as part of misinformation campaigns.

To combat this threat, researchers have developed many techniques to detect GAN-generated images [15,32,34,42,47] and to attribute them to the specific GAN used to create them [30,31,44]. At the same time, adversarial examples have arisen as a new threat to classifiers built from neural networks [7,18,27,28,38,40]. These represent important threats to the forensic community because they can be used as an anti-forensic attack against forensic detectors [2,8,19]. Recent work from the forensic community, however, suggests that these attacks may not achieve transferability, i.e. they may be unable to attack classifiers other than those they were directly trained against [1,48].

For an anti-forensic attack to be successful, it must (1) fool a victim classifier and (2) maintain high visual quality within the attacked image. Furthermore, it is highly desirable for an attack to (3) transfer to victim classifiers not seen during training and (4) be easily deployable in practical scenarios, i.e. it should work on images of any size, not require specific knowledge of the image window analyzed by a forensic CNN, deploy quickly and efficiently, etc.

In this paper, we propose a new attack that is capable of fooling forensic synthetic image detectors into thinking that GAN-generated images are in fact real images. This attack achieves each of the four goals described above, including a significant degree of transferability, which enables it to attack victim classifiers that are unseen during training. Instead of crafting adversarial examples that exploit flaws in forensic detectors, our attack uses an anti-forensic generator to synthesize forensic traces associated with real images. We propose GAN-based approaches for training our anti-forensic generator for both white-box scenarios and zero-knowledge scenarios. Once the anti-forensic generator is trained, it can be used to attack images of arbitrary size without requiring re-training or additional tuning to the image under attack.

The main contributions of this work are as follows:

- We propose a new generative anti-forensic attack that is able to fool CNN-based synthetic image detctors. Our attack operates by synthesizing forensic traces associated with real images while introducing no perceptible distortions into an attacked image.
- We propose an ensemble loss training strategy that enables our attack to achieve transferability in zero-knowledge scenarios.
- We demonstrate the effectiveness of our attack against many state-of-the-art forensic CNNs, using synthetic images from a wide variety of different GANs.
- We show that our proposed attack achieves in a higher attack success rate, image quality, and transferability than other alternative attacks, including other adversarial example and GAN-based attacks.

2   Related Work

Here we briefly review related work on detecting GAN-generated images and adversarial attacks.

GAN-Generated Image Detectors: To defend against the misinformation threat posed by synthetic media, significant research has been done to create GAN-generated image detection algorithms [15,29,32,34,42,44,47]. Previous research has shown that GANs leave behind forensic traces that are distinguishable from real images. These forensic traces left by GANs can be utilized to detect GAN-generated images. Some approaches operate in a data driven manner [15,29,42], while other approaches utilize semantic information [32] or hand-crafted features [34]. Additionally, forensic techniques are also developed to identify which GAN was used to generate an image [30,44,47].

Adversarial Attacks on Forensic Classifiers: At the same time, adversarial attacks on neural networks have emerged as an important threat [18,45]. These attacks can be adapted to attack forensic classifiers [2]. Roughly speaking, we can group these attacks into two different families: adversarial-example-based attacks and GAN-based attacks.

Adversarial example attacks operate by creating additive image perturbations that cause a victim classifier to misclassify the image. Several techniques have been proposed to create these perturbations, including L-BFGS [40], FGSM and iterative-FG [18,27], JSMA [38], CW [7], PGD [28]. Attacks based on adversarial examples have been used to forensic algorithms, including camera model identification algorithms [19] and deepfake detectors [8]. Research by Barni et al. has shown, however, that adversarial example attacks do not transfer well to other forensic classifiers [1].

Previous research has also shown that GANs can be utilized to construct attacks that falsify forensic traces. GANs were used by Chen et al. to falsify camera model fingerprints [9] and by Cozzolino et al. to falsify device fingerprints [14]. Kim et. al used a GAN to remove forensic traces left by median filtering [26]. However, research has shown that the GAN-based anti-forensic attacks also have trouble in transferring [48].

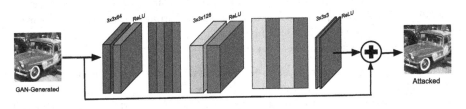

Fig. 1. Architecture of the proposed anti-forensic generator.

3   Proposed Attack

Our attack is designed to modify a GAN-generated image I so that a forensic CNN will instead classify it as a 'real' image. This forensic CNN is alternately referred to as the victim classifier, and is trained to differentiate between real and GAN-generated images.

Our attack operates by passing the GAN-generated image through a pre-trained anti-forensic generator G in order to falsify its forensic traces. The anti-forensic generator is designed to remove forensic traces associated with GAN-generated images and synthesize traces associated with 'real' images. As a result, a victim classifier will classify the attacked GAN-generated image $G(I)$ as a real one. Furthermore, the anti-forensic generator designed to make no changes to the image's contents and to introduce no visually perceptible distortions into the attacked image. This will prevent a human from visually identifying that an image was attacked.

The anti-forensic generator in our attack learns to synthesize 'real' forensic traces through adversarial training. It is trained as part of a GAN in which the discriminator is replaced by a forensic classifier (or set of classifiers) that has been pre-trained to learn the distribution of forensic features associated with real and GAN-generated images.

Different strategies are used to train the anti-forensic generator depending on whether the attack is launched in a white-box or zero-knowledge scenario. In the white-box scenario, our attack aims to synthesize forensic features with the distribution learned by the victim classifier, even if they deviate from the ideal feature distribution of real images. In the zero-knowledge scenario, our attack aims to learn the distribution of forensic features of real images. However it avoids synthesizing features in regions where different classifiers may make different decisions. Instead, it aims to synthesize features that any classifier will likely associate with a real image.

3.1 Proposed Anti-Forensic Generator Architecture

The proposed anti-forensic generator consists of a sequence of convolutional layers followed by ReLU activations [33] shown in Fig. 1. The first three convolutional layers use 64 filters, the middle three convolutional layers use 128 filters, and the final convolutional layer uses three filters to reduce the 128 feature maps to a three color channel image. The output of the generator is the summation of the input of the generator and the output of the last activated convolutional layer. The skip connection is designed to give the generator a better initialization for producing high visual quality attacked images. All convolutional layers use 3×3 filter with stride 1. The small filter size allows the generator to synthesize forensic traces in small areas. We avoid using any pooling layers to ensure that the output of the generator is of the same size as the input of the generator. Therefore, the proposed anti-forensic generator can be applied to images of arbitrary sizes, and does not need to be trained for images of different sizes individually. This characteristic makes the deployment of the proposed anti-forensic generator efficient and quick.

3.2 Anti-Forensic Generator Training

When adversarially training the anti-forensic generator G, we formulate a loss function to ensure that a attacked image can both fool a victim classifier and maintain high visual quality. This loss function $\mathcal{L}_G$ consists of the weighted sum of two terms: the perceptual loss $\mathcal{L}_p$ and classification loss $\mathcal{L}_c$

$$\mathcal{L}_G = \alpha \mathcal{L}_p + \mathcal{L}_c, \tag{1}$$

where α is used to balance the trade-off between the visual quality and performance of the attack.

Perceptual Loss: This term is used to minimize distortions introduced by the anti-forensic generator and control the visual quality of the attacked image. We define this term as the mean absolute difference between the GAN-generated image I (i.e. the input of the generator) and the attacked image produced by the generator $G(I)$, such that

$$\mathcal{L}_p = \tfrac{1}{N} \| I - G(I) \|_1, \tag{2}$$

where N is the number of pixels in I and $G(I)$.

Classification Loss: This term is used to measure if the attacked images produced by the anti-forensic generator can fool the CNN detector used for training. It allows the generator to learn forensic traces learned by the CNN detector. The classification loss is provided by the victim classifier for white-box attacks, and is provided by an ensemble of classifiers chosen by the attacker for zero-knowledge attacks.

White-Box Attack Training: In the white-box scenario, the attacker has direct access to the forensic CNN under attack. Hence, the anti-forensic generator can be directly trained against the victim classifier. In this case, we define the classification loss $\mathcal{L}_c$ as the softmax cross-entropy between the CNN detector's output of attacked images and the real class,

$$\mathcal{L}_c = - \sum_k t_k \log \left(C(G(I))_k \right), \tag{3}$$

where $C(\cdot)$ is the victim classifier and t_k is the kth entry of ideal softmax vector with a 1 for the real class and a 0 for the fake class. Defining the classification loss in this manner incentivizes the anti-forensic generator to learn the victim classifier's model of forensic features from real images.

Zero-Knowledge Attack Training: In the zero-knowledge scenario, the attacker has no access to the victim classifier that they wish to attack, nor do they know its architecture. This differs from the black box scenario in which the attacker can probe the victim classifier through an API, then observe the victim classifier's input-output relationship. Instead, the attacker must rely entirely on the transferability of their attack to fool the victim CNN.

To achieve transferability, we propose adversarially training against an ensemble of forensic classifiers created by the attacker. Here, the classification loss $\mathcal{L}_c$ is formulated as the weights sum of individual classification loss pertaining to each CNN detector in the ensemble,

$$\mathcal{L}_c = \sum_{s=1}^{S} \beta^{(s)} \mathcal{L}_c^{(s)}, \tag{4}$$

where S is the number of CNN detectors in the ensemble, $\mathcal{L}_c^{(s)}$ corresponds to individual classification loss of the sth CNN detector calculated using Eq. 3, $\beta^{(s)}$ corresponds to the weight of sth individual classification loss.

Each classifier in the ensemble learns to partition the forensic feature space into separate regions for real and GAN-generated images. By defining the classifier loss in this fashion, we incentivize the anti-forensic generator to synthesize forensic features that lie in the intersection of these regions. If a diverse set of classifiers are used to form the ensemble, this intersection will likely lie inside the decision region that other classifiers associate with real images.

4 Experimental Setup

4.1 Datasets

We created two datasets to evaluate our attacks, each containing both real and GAN-generated images. The first dataset contains only images of human faces, while the second contains images of non-human objects.

Human Face Dataset: This dataset consists of real images and GAN-generated images of human faces. The GAN-generated images were created using StyleGAN [24], Style-GAN2 [25], and StarGAN-v2 [12]. StyleGAN and StyleGAN2 generated images were downloaded from publicly available datasets shared by Nvidia Research Lab [35, 36]. The StarGAN-v2 generated images were created using pre-trained StarGAN-v2 generator shared at [11]. The real images were downloaded from FFHQ dataset [25] and CelebA-HQ dataset [22]. In total, the human face dataset contains $66,000$ real images with $44,000$ from FFHQ and $22,000$ from CelebA-HQ; $126,000$ GAN-generated images drawn equally from StyleGAN, StyleGAN2, and StarGAN-v2.

Next, we partitioned the data into two disjoint training sets, the *D-set* and the *A-set*, as well as an evaluation set *Eval-set*. The *D-set* was used to train the victim forensic CNN detectors. It contains $60,000$ GAN-generated images drawn equally from StyleGAN, StyleGAN2 and StarGAN-v2; and $60,000$ real images with $40,000$ from FFHQ and $20,000$ from CelebA-HQ. The *A-set* was used to train the proposed attack. Since training the proposed attack only requires GAN-generated images, *A-set* contains $60,000$ GAN-generated images drawn equally from StyleGAN, StyleGAN2 and StarGAN-v2.

We benchmarked the baseline performance of the victim forensic CNN detectors and evaluated the performance of our proposed attack against these CNNs using a common evaluation set, *Eval-set*. The *Eval-set* contains $6,000$ GAN-generated images drawn equally from StyleGAN, StyleGAN2 and StarGAN-v2; and $6,000$ real images with $4,000$ from FFHQ and $2,000$ from CelebA-HQ.

Object Dataset: This dataset contains real images and GAN-generated images of objects. The object dataset is a subset of publicly available ForenSynths dataset [42]. The ForenSynths dataset was created to demonstrate that CNNs could learn general forensic traces of synthesized images. Therefore CNNs trained on generated images produced by one GAN method can detect generated images produced by other generative models. The training set of ForenSynths dataset contains only ProGAN generated images of objects and real images from LSUN dataset [43]. The testing set of Foren-Synths dataset contains varying numbers of generated images produced by different generative methods.

From the training set of the ForenSynths dataset, we created two disjoint training sets: *D-set* for training victim CNN detectors and *A-set* for training the proposed attack. *D-set* contains $50,000$ randomly selected ProGAN generated images and $50,000$ randomly selected real images. *A-set* contains $50,000$ randomly selected ProGAN generated images.

We benchmarked the baseline performance of victim forensic CNN detectors and evaluated the performance of our proposed attack against these CNNs using a common evaluation set, *Eval-set*. *Eval-set* contains $4,000$ real images from LSUN, and all the generated images of objects created by six different GAN methods from the testing set of ForenSynths dataset, which consists of 26,300 images comprised of 4,000 images from ProGAN [22], 1,300 from CycleGAN [49], 6,000 from StyleGAN [24], 8,000 from StyleGAN2 [25], 2,000 from BigGAN [6], and 5,000 from GauGAN [39].

4.2   Victim Forensic CNN Detectors

Before training and evaluating the proposed attack, we trained and benchmarked the performance of forensic CNNs on detecting GAN-generated images. These forensic CNNs were trained as binary classifiers to differentiate between real images and GAN-generated images. We used eight state-of-the-art CNN models trained as GAN-generated image detectors, Xception [13], ResNet-50 [20], DenseNet [21], MIS-LNet [3], PHNet [5], SRNet [4], Image CNN [46], and CamID CNN [41]. We trained each forensic CNN individually using the *D-set* of the human face dataset and the object dataset. This yielded 16 CNN detectors in total and formed the set of victim classifiers we attacked in this paper.

The classification accuracies of victim CNN detectors on both datasets are shown in Table 1. On average, the average classification accuracy is 95.94% on the human face dataset and 99.14% on the object dataset.

Table 1. Classification accuracies of victim CNN detectors achieved on the human face dataset and the object dataset.

CNNs	Human Face Dataset	Object Dataset
Xception	99.67%	99.75%
ResNet-50	78.26%	99.14%
DenseNet	96.39%	97.04%
MISLNet	99.93%	99.15%
PHNet	95.15%	99.73%
SRNet	99.50%	99.78%
Image CNN	99.49%	99.10%
CamID CNN	99.16%	99.46%
Avg.	**95.94%**	**99.14%**

4.3   White-Box Attack

The first set of experiments was designed to evaluate the effectiveness of our proposed attack in the white-box scenario. Here, we assume the attacker has access to the victim classifier and can train directly against it.

For each victim CNN detector trained on the human face dataset and the object dataset, we trained an individual anti-forensic generator to attack it. To evaluate the performance of the anti-forensic generator, we used the generator to attack each GAN-generated image in the *Eval-set*, saving the attacked images to disk as PNG files. This is to ensure the pixel values of attacked images reside in the range from 0 to 255. Next, we calculated the attack success rate by using the victim CNN detector to classify the attacked images. To evaluate the visual quality of attacked images, we calculated the mean PSNR between the GAN-generated images and the attacked images.

The anti-forensic generators presented in this paper were trained from scratch for 32 epochs with a learning rate of 0.0001. Weights were initialized using Xavier initializer [16] and biases were initialized as 0's, and were optimized using stochastic gradient descent. To balance the image quality and attack success rates, α in Eq. 1 was chosen after a grid search range from 1 to 200 with an increment of 20. As a result, α equals to 20 for attacks on the human face dataset and 100 for attacks on the object dataset.

4.4 Zero-Knowledge Attack

This set of experiments was conducted to evaluate the proposed attack in the zero-knowledge scenario. We assume the attacker has no knowledge about the victim CNN detector that the investigator would use to classify images. Particularly, the attacker has no access to the victim CNN detector and cannot observe any input or output of the CNN detector, since the investigator may use a private CNN detector that the attacker by all means cannot have access to. This is a more realistic yet challenging scenario. In the zero-knowledge scenario, we evaluated the transferability of the proposed attack to attack unseen CNN detectors.

To achieve the transferability, we built an ensemble of forensic CNN detectors to train the proposed anti-forensic generator. To mimic the zero-knowledge scenario, each ensemble used to train the attack did not include the victim classifier. We assume that if the attacker has no knowledge of the victim classifier's architecture, the attacker will use all available CNNs in their ensemble to strengthen their attack. Due to limited GPU memory, Xception was excluded from the training ensemble in our experiments. We trained zero-knowledge attacks using same hyperparameters and other settings as white-box attacks.

5   Experimental Results and Discussion

5.1   White-Box Attack Results

Table 2 shows the performance achieved by white-box attacks on both datasets. Results are presented for our proposed attack, as well as other existing GAN-based and adversarial example based attacks. Here, the attack success rate (ASR) corresponds to the mean ASR achieved over synthetic images from all GAN generators for a particular victim CNN. Similarly, the PSNR in this table is defined as the mean PSNR between the original and attacked image.

Proposed Attack Performance: The performance of our proposed attack is shown along the rightmost columns of Table 2. On average, our proposed attack achieved an attack success rate of 93.66% against detectors trained on the Human Face Dataset while maintaining an average PSNR of 48.95. Similarly, our proposed attack achieved an ASR of 91.62% against detectors trained on the Object dataset while maintaining an average PSNR of 53.21. Example images created by the proposed attack are shown in Fig. 2. From this figure, we can see that our attack introduces no visually identifiable artifacts.

Table 2. Mean attack success rates and mean image quality achieved for white-box attacks.

Human Face Dataset

	Residual Gen. [26]		MISLGAN [9]		CW [7]		FGSM [18]		PGD [28]		Proposed	
CNNs	ASR%	PSNR	ASR%	PSNR	ASR%	PSNR	ASR%	PSNR	ASR%	PSNR	ASR%	PSNR
Xception	98.43	29.01	66.68	32.24	98.48	47.29	54.17	44.20	100.00	47.32	100.00	45.52
ResNet-50	42.73	28.82	66.05	34.64	40.91	38.78	37.50	40.01	57.20	35.13	81.23	35.97
DenseNet	99.37	29.72	99.97	35.11	94.32	50.36	87.50	44.16	98.86	51.31	97.08	54.28
MISLNet	98.18	29.82	97.93	34.50	95.46	50.53	52.65	44.26	100.00	51.17	99.40	51.28
PHNet	96.83	30.21	99.68	34.84	98.86	51.05	97.73	51.14	99.24	51.22	94.94	41.85
SRNet	97.53	29.46	94.28	33.09	95.83	49.84	81.87	51.14	100.00	51.22	88.05	50.97
ImageCNN	66.67	29.21	80.50	34.36	100.00	49.54	0.00	44.47	94.70	49.04	94.31	53.64
CamID CNN	99.80	28.89	42.23	33.30	94.69	49.25	0.38	44.16	92.88	51.15	94.25	58.10
Avg.	87.44	29.39	80.92	34.01	89.82	48.33	51.47	45.44	92.86	48.44	**93.66**	**48.95**

Object Dataset

	Residual Gen.		MISLGAN		CW		FGSM		PGD		Proposed	
CNNs	ASR%	PSNR	ASR%	PSNR	ASR%	PSNR	ASR%	PSNR	ASR%	PSNR	ASR%	PSNR
Xception	99.63	39.73	94.83	32.09	66.67	50.31	74.82	51.19	67.42	51.15	99.52	52.59
ResNet-50	94.61	38.51	88.46	31.50	89.85	49.58	74.79	51.16	86.36	51.17	95.24	55.41
DenseNet	95.22	37.52	95.15	31.22	81.23	50.80	79.93	51.15	81.81	51.16	91.16	50.22
MISLNet	83.53	40.49	99.12	31.75	64.02	51.08	65.91	51.26	71.21	51.16	92.70	50.97
PHNet	96.46	40.22	83.07	31.00	82.20	50.93	81.82	51.15	83.71	51.15	98.02	51.99
SRNet	82.06	37.36	94.06	31.68	61.35	46.61	0.00	51.16	72.35	51.15	82.87	56.41
ImageCNN	63.42	38.66	81.09	33.43	67.05	50.95	69.70	51.46	69.32	51.15	80.57	55.32
CamID CNN	80.39	39.02	75.69	31.37	60.61	49.01	59.09	51.34	57.20	51.15	93.05	52.77
Avg.	86.95	38.94	88.93	31.76	71.62	49.91	63.19	51.23	73.67	51.16	**91.64**	**53.21**

Table 3. Mean attack success rates and mean image quality achieved for zero-knowledge attacks.

	Human Face Dataset								Object Dataset							
	CW		FGSM		PGD		Proposed		CW		FGSM		PGD		Proposed	
CNNs	ASR%	PSNR	ASR%	PSNR	ASR%	PSNR	ASR%	PSNR	ASR%	PSNR	ASR%	PSNR	ASR%	PSNR	ASR%	PSNR
Xception	19.75	39.58	17.58	40.07	0.54	38.89	91.07	37.93	45.70	40.95	41.67	40.12	82.19	39.06	96.63	39.95
ResNet-50	19.53	39.99	20.18	40.07	18.13	38.15	24.35	42.90	70.20	41.09	50.43	40.13	54.60	39.06	80.45	41.75
DenseNet	12.72	39.97	4.06	40.07	4.87	38.92	87.30	38.79	68.74	41.17	52.71	40.13	60.87	38.34	95.19	40.46
MISLNet	0.50	39.91	0.00	40.06	0.05	38.89	39.80	38.14	43.37	41.63	52.92	40.11	64.88	39.06	25.04	41.39
PHNet	4.22	40.18	0.08	40.07	14.61	38.98	91.62	41.69	51.46	41.38	41.67	40.13	52.16	39.09	97.48	42.18
SRNet	11.91	39.72	16.45	40.07	1.08	38.98	88.78	40.16	11.73	41.25	16.45	40.13	0.00	39.09	8.49	39.95
ImageCNN	11.09	39.55	11.69	40.03	14.77	38.87	86.73	41.27	39.34	41.20	52.97	40.02	75.92	39.06	60.38	41.03
CamID CNN	0.05	39.84	0.00	40.07	10.82	38.92	91.17	42.77	52.70	40.82	53.57	40.09	85.15	39.13	99.06	43.43
Avg.	9.97	39.84	8.85	40.06	6.47	38.84	**75.10**	**40.46**	52.70	41.19	45.30	40.11	59.75	38.99	**70.30**	**41.27**

These results indicate that our attack can successfully fool a wide variety of CNNs with different architectures trained to detect synthetic images. In each case, our attack maintained a very high image quality, indicating that our attack is not detectable to the human eye. Additionally, these results show that our attack can make synthetic images created by a wide variety of GANs appear to be real. We note that for attacks on the object dataset, our proposed attack was trained using only ProGAN generated images. Despite this, our attack can still reliably fool all detectors used in this experiment. These results show that our attack can be used on synthetic images made by GANs that our attack was not explicitly trained with.

Finally, we note that our proposed attack outperforms all other adversarial and GAN-based attacks. These results were significantly more pronounced on the Object Dataset, where our attack achieved an ASR that was 17% higher than then best performing adversarial example attack (PGD). These results are discussed in greater detail below.

Comparison With Adversarial Example Attacks: We compared our proposed attack with three well-known adversarial example attacks: Carlini-Wagner (CW) [7], Fast Gradient Sign Method (FGSM) [18], and Projected Gradient Descent (PGD) [28]. We used the CleverHans toolbox [37] to launch these attacks, then saved attacked images as PNGs. We note that due to computational limitations, adversarial example attacks were evaluated using a representative subset of the *Eval-set*. This is because adversarial example attacks must be individually trained for each image that they attack. For these experiments, our *Eval-set* for each adversarial example attack corresponded to 6,240 images for the Human Face Dataset and 12,480 images for the Object Dataset.

From Table 2, we can see that at the same image quality our attack outperformed adversarial example attacks. On the Human Face Dataset, our attack achieved an attack success rate of 93.66%. By contrast, the CW attack achieved an ASR of 89.82%, FGSM achieved an ASR of 51.47%, and PGD achieved an ASR of 92.86%. These results were more pronounced on the Object Dataset. Our attack achieved an average ASR of 91.64%, while CW achieved an ASR of 71.62%, FGSM achieved an ASR of 63.19%, and PGD achieved an ASR of 73.67%. These results show that even in white-box scenarios, our attack yields important performance advantages over adversarial example attacks.

We note that in these experiments, we chose the parameters for each adversarial example attack such that the mean PSNRs of attacked images were similar to those obtained by our attack. This was done for two reasons. The first was to maintain a fair comparison between our attack and these attacks. The second was to maintain acceptable visual quality for anti-forensic applications. It is well-known that a stronger attack typically means more visible perturbations. While this can be acceptable in computer vision algorithms, it is not acceptable for anti-forensic applications. Images with implausible visual distortions such as speckles will be rejected as inauthentic by humans. As a result, anti-forensic attacks have a higher visual quality requirement.

Comparison With Other Anti-Forensic Generators: We also compared our proposed attack to existing GAN-based anti-forensic attacks [9,26]. The results in Table 2 show that our proposed attack can outperform these attacks in terms of both ASR and image quality. On the Human Face Dataset, our attack generator achieved an ASR that was 6.22% than the residual generator [26] and 12.74% higher than MISLGAN [9] while maintaining at least 15dB PSNR higher in image quality. We note that the image qualities achieved by the residual generator and MISLGAN are low enough that visually detectable artifacts and distortion are present. At comparable image qualities, our attack's performance gains are likely to be significantly more pronounced. Similar results were achieved on the Object Dataset, where our attack generator achieved an ASR that was 4.69% than the residual generator [26] and 12.74% higher than MISL-GAN [9] while maintaining at least 15dB PSNR higher in image quality.

Fig. 2. Attacked images produced by the proposed white-box attack.

5.2 Zero-Knowledge Attack Results

Next, we evaluated attack performance in the zero-knowledge scenario, in which the victim CNN is unknown to the attacker and cannot be probed in a black box manner. As a result, the attack's success relies entirely on transferability.

Table 3 shows the performance achieved on both datasets by zero-knowledge attacks. Each entry in the table corresponds to the mean attack success rate (ASR) and mean PSNR achieved by an attack when attacking a particular victim CNN detector. The other anti-forensic GANs were omitted from these experiments due to both space limitations, because our anti-forensic generator outperformed these other generators in white-box results presented in Sect. 5.1, and because these generators introduced visible artifacts into attacked images.

Proposed Attack Performance: The results in Table 3 show that our proposed attack can achieve significant transferability, resulting in strong ASRs even in the zero-knowledge scenario. On the Human Face Dataset, our attack achieved an ASR of 75.10% while maintaining an average PSNR of 40.46. Similarly, our attack achieved an ASR of 70.30% while maintaining an average PSNR of 41.27. These results are particularly important because in many realistic conditions, forensic detectors will be kept private and will not be publicly queriable (e.g. detectors used by governmental and defense agencies, law enforcement, etc.). In these conditions, both white-box and black-box attacks are infeasible.

Images from the Human Face Dataset attacked using our zero-knowledge attack are shown in Fig. 3. From this figure, we can see that our attack maintains high visual quality without introducing perceptible distortions or artifacts.

We note that when compared to the white-box scenario, the performance drop incurred by our attack in the zero-knowledge scenario was largely attributable to a small number of CNNs. For the Human Face Dataset our attack had lower transferablity to both MISLnet and ResNet-50, while on the Object Dataset, our attack had lower transferability to both MISLnet and SRNet. Excluding these CNN, our average ASR is 89.45% on the Human Face Dataset and is 88.20% on the Object Dataset. We note that adversarial example attacks had difficulty attacking these CNNs too. Future studies of this may provide insight into designing CNN architectures that are more resilient to anti-forensic attacks.

StyleGAN   StyleGAN2

GAN
Generated

Attacked

Fig. 3. Attacked images produced by zero-knowledge attack.

Comparison with Adversarial Example Attacks: The zero-knowledge performance of the CW, FGSM and PGD adversarial example attacks are also shown in Table 3. To measure the transferability of an adversarial example attack against a particular victim CNN detector, we launched the attack against every other CNN detectors, then used the victim CNN detector to classify the attacked images. For a fair comparison, we chose the parameters for each adversarial example attack such that the mean PSNRs of attacked images were comparable to PSNRs achieved by our attack.

From Table 3, we can see that adversarial example attacks were broadly unsuccessful on the Human Face Dataset. The most successful attack was the CW attack, achieving an ASR of 9.97%. Adversarial example attacks were more successful on the Object Dataset, but still achieved ASRs significantly lower than our proposed attack.

6   Conclusion

In this paper, we proposed a new attack to fool GAN-generated image detectors. Our attack uses an adversarially trained generator to synthesize forensic traces that these detectors associate with 'real' images. We proposed training protocols to produce both white-box as well as zero-knowledge attacks. The latter protocol, which is based on training against an ensemble of classifiers, enables our attack to achieve transferability to unseen victim classifiers. Through a series of experiments, we demonstrated that our attack does not create perceptible distortions in attacked images, and can fool eight different GAN-generated image detectors. Furthermore, the proposed attack outperforms other alternative attacks in both white-box and zero-knowledge scenarios.

References

1. Barni, M., Kallas, K., Nowroozi, E., Tondi, B.: On the transferability of adversarial examples against CNN-based image forensics. In: 2019 IEEE International Conference on Acoustics, Speech and Signal Processing, pp. 8286–8290 (2019)
2. Barni, M., Stamm, M.C., Tondi, B.: Adversarial multimedia forensics: overview and challenges ahead. In: 2018 26th European Signal Processing Conference (EUSIPCO), pp. 962–966. IEEE (2018)

3. Bayar, B., Stamm, M.C.: Constrained convolutional neural networks: a new approach towards general purpose image manipulation detection. IEEE Trans. Inf. Forensics Secur. **13**(11), 2691–2706 (2018)
4. Boroumand, M., Chen, M., Fridrich, J.: Deep residual network for steganalysis of digital images. IEEE Trans. Inf. Forensics Secur. **14**(5), 1181–1193 (2018)
5. Boroumand, M., Fridrich, J.: Deep learning for detecting processing history of images. Electron. Imaging **30**, 1–9 (2018)
6. Brock, A., Donahue, J., Simonyan, K.: Large scale GAN training for high fidelity natural image synthesis. arXiv preprint arXiv:1809.11096 (2018)
7. Carlini, N., Wagner, D.: Towards evaluating the robustness of neural networks. In: 2017 IEEE Symposium on Security and Privacy, pp. 39–57, May 2017. https://doi.org/10.1109/SP.2017.49
8. Carlini, N., Farid, H.: Evading deepfake-image detectors with white-and black-box attacks. In: Proceedings of the IEEE/CVF Conference on Computer Vision and Pattern Recognition Workshops, pp. 658–659 (2020)
9. Chen, C., Zhao, X., Stamm, M.C.: MisIGAN: an anti-forensic camera model falsification framework using a generative adversarial network. In: 2018 25th IEEE International Conference on Image Processing (ICIP), pp. 535–539. IEEE (2018)
10. Choi, Y., Choi, M., Kim, M., Ha, J.W., Kim, S., Choo, J.: StarGAN: unified generative adversarial networks for multi-domain image-to-image translation. In: Proceedings of the IEEE Conference on Computer Vision and Pattern Recognition (2018)
11. Choi, Y., Uh, Y., Yoo, J., Ha, J.W.: Pre-trained stargan-v2 (2019). https://github.com/clovaai/stargan-v2
12. Choi, Y., Uh, Y., Yoo, J., Ha, J.W.: StarGAN v2: diverse image synthesis for multiple domains. In: Proceedings of the IEEE Conference on Computer Vision and Pattern Recognition (2020)
13. Chollet, F.: Xception: deep learning with depthwise separable convolutions. In: Proceedings of the IEEE Conference on Computer Vision and Pattern Recognition, pp. 1251–1258 (2017)
14. Cozzolino, D., Thies, J., Rössler, A., Nießner, M., Verdoliva, L.: SPOC: Spoofing camera fingerprints. arXiv preprint arXiv:1911.12069 (2019)
15. Cozzolino, D., Thies, J., Rössler, A., Riess, C., Nießner, M., Verdoliva, L.: Forensictransfer: Weakly-supervised domain adaptation for forgery detection. arXiv (2018). https://justusthies.github.io/posts/forensictransfer/
16. Glorot, X., Bengio, Y.: Understanding the difficulty of training deep feedforward neural networks. In: Teh, Y.W., Titterington, M. (eds.) Proceedings of the Thirteenth International Conference on Artificial Intelligence and Statistics. Proceedings of Machine Learning Research, vol. 9, pp. 249–256. PMLR, Chia Laguna Resort, Sardinia, Italy, 13–15 May 2010. https://proceedings.mlr.press/v9/glorot10a.html
17. Goodfellow, et al.: Generative adversarial nets. In: Advances in Neural Information Processing Systems, pp. 2672–2680 (2014)
18. Goodfellow, I.J., Shlens, J., Szegedy, C.: Explaining and harnessing adversarial examples. arXiv preprint arXiv:1412.6572 (2014)
19. Guera, D., Wang, Y., Bondi, L., Bestagini, P., Tubaro, S., Delp, E.J.: A counter-forensic method for CNN-based camera model identification. In: Computer Vision and Pattern Recognition Workshops (CVPRW), pp. 1840–1847. IEEE, July 2017
20. He, K., Zhang, X., Ren, S., Sun, J.: Deep residual learning for image recognition. In: Proceedings of the IEEE Conference on Computer Vision and Pattern Recognition (CVPR), June 2016
21. Huang, G., Liu, Z., Van Der Maaten, L., Weinberger, K.Q.: Densely connected convolutional networks. In: Proceedings of the IEEE Conference on Computer Vision and Pattern Recognition, pp. 4700–4708 (2017)

22. Karras, T., Aila, T., Laine, S., Lehtinen, J.: Progressive growing of GANs for improved quality, stability, and variation. arXiv preprint arXiv:1710.10196 (2017)
23. Karras, T., et al.: Alias-free generative adversarial networks. In: Proceedings of NeurIPS (2021)
24. Karras, T., Laine, S., Aila, T.: A style-based generator architecture for generative adversarial networks. In: Proceedings of the IEEE/CVF Conference on Computer Vision and Pattern Recognition, pp. 4401–4410 (2019)
25. Karras, T., Laine, S., Aittala, M., Hellsten, J., Lehtinen, J., Aila, T.: Analyzing and improving the image quality of StyleGAN. In: Proceedings of CVPR (2020)
26. Kim, D., Jang, H.U., Mun, S.M., Choi, S., Lee, H.K.: Median filtered image restoration and anti-forensics using adversarial networks. IEEE Signal Process. Lett. **25**(2), 278–282 (2017)
27. Kurakin, A., Goodfellow, I., Bengio, S., et al.: Adversarial examples in the physical world (2016)
28. Madry, A., Makelov, A., Schmidt, L., Tsipras, D., Vladu, A.: Towards deep learning models resistant to adversarial attacks. arXiv preprint arXiv:1706.06083 (2017)
29. Marra, F., Gragnaniello, D., Cozzolino, D., Verdoliva, L.: Detection of GAN-generated fake images over social networks. In: 2018 IEEE Conference on Multimedia Information Processing and Retrieval (MIPR), pp. 384–389 (2018). https://doi.org/10.1109/MIPR.2018.00084
30. Marra, F., Gragnaniello, D., Verdoliva, L., Poggi, G.: Do GANs leave artificial fingerprints? In: 2019 IEEE Conference on Multimedia Information Processing and Retrieval (MIPR), pp. 506–511 (2019). https://doi.org/10.1109/MIPR.2019.00103
31. Marra, F., Saltori, C., Boato, G., Verdoliva, L.: Incremental learning for the detection and classification of GAN-generated images. In: 2019 IEEE International Workshop on Information Forensics and Security (WIFS), pp. 1–6 (2019). https://doi.org/10.1109/WIFS47025.2019.9035099
32. McCloskey, S., Albright, M.: Detecting GAN-generated imagery using color cues. arXiv preprint arXiv:1812.08247 (2018)
33. Nair, V., Hinton, G.E.: Rectified linear units improve restricted Boltzmann machines. In: Proceedings of the 27th International Conference on Machine Learning (ICML-2010), pp. 807–814 (2010)
34. Nataraj, L., Mohammed, T.M., Manjunath, B., Chandrasekaran, S., Flenner, A., Bappy, J.H., Roy-Chowdhury, A.K.: Detecting GAN generated fake images using co-occurrence matrices. Electron. Imaging **2019**(5), 1–532 (2019)
35. Nvidia Research Lab: Public database of styleGAN (2019). https://github.com/NVlabs/stylegan
36. Nvidia Research Lab: Public database of styleGAN2 (2019). https://github.com/NVlabs/stylegan2
37. Papernot, N., et al.: Technical report on the cleverhans v2.1.0 adversarial examples library. arXiv preprint arXiv:1610.00768 (2018)
38. Papernot, N., McDaniel, P., Jha, S., Fredrikson, M., Celik, Z.B., Swami, A.: The limitations of deep learning in adversarial settings. In: 2016 IEEE European Symposium on Security and Privacy (EuroS&P), pp. 372–387. IEEE (2016)
39. Park, T., Liu, M.Y., Wang, T.C., Zhu, J.Y.: GauGAN: semantic image synthesis with spatially adaptive normalization. In: ACM SIGGRAPH 2019 Real-Time Live!, pp. 1–1. Association for Computing Machinery (2019)
40. Szegedy, C., et al.: Intriguing properties of neural networks (2014)
41. Tuama, A., Comby, F., Chaumont, M.: Camera model identification with the use of deep convolutional neural networks. In: International Workshop on Information Forensics and Security (WIFS), pp. 1–6. IEEE, December 2016. https://doi.org/10.1109/WIFS.2016.7823908

42. Wang, S.Y., Wang, O., Zhang, R., Owens, A., Efros, A.A.: CNN-generated images are surprisingly easy to spot... for now. In: Proceedings of the IEEE/CVF Conference on Computer Vision and Pattern Recognition, pp. 8695–8704 (2020)
43. Yu, F., Seff, A., Zhang, Y., Song, S., Funkhouser, T., Xiao, J.: LSUN: Construction of a large-scale image dataset using deep learning with humans in the loop (2016)
44. Yu, N., Davis, L., Fritz, M.: Attributing fake images to GANs: Learning and analyzing GAN fingerprints. In: 2019 IEEE/CVF International Conference on Computer Vision (ICCV), pp. 7555–7565 (2019). https://doi.org/10.1109/ICCV.2019.00765
45. Yuan, X., He, P., Zhu, Q., Li, X.: Adversarial examples: attacks and defenses for deep learning. IEEE Trans. Neural Netw. Learn. Syst. **30**(9), 2805–2824 (2019)
46. Zhan, Y., Chen, Y., Zhang, Q., Kang, X.: Image forensics based on transfer learning and convolutional neural network. In: Proceedings of the 5th ACM Workshop on Information Hiding and Multimedia Security, pp. 165–170 (2017). https://doi.org/10.1145/3082031.3083250
47. Zhang, X., Karaman, S., Chang, S.F.: Detecting and simulating artifacts in GAN fake images. In: 2019 IEEE International Workshop on Information Forensics and Security (WIFS), pp. 1–6. IEEE (2019)
48. Zhao, X., Stamm, M.C.: The effect of class definitions on the transferability of adversarial attacks against forensic CNNs. Electron. Imaging **2020**(4), 1–119 (2020)
49. Zhu, J.Y., Park, T., Isola, P., Efros, A.A.: Unpaired image-to-image translation using cycle-consistent adversarial networks. In: Proceedings of the IEEE International Conference on Computer Vision, pp. 2223–2232 (2017)

AI for De-escalation: Autonomous Systems for De-escalating Conflict in Military and Civilian Contexts (AI4D)

AI for De-escalation (AI4D): Autonomous Systems for De-escalating Conflict in Military and Civilian Contexts

Held on Sunday August 21, 2022 at *Palais des Congrès*, Montréal, Canada.

Autonomous systems such as drones are being developed and deployed globally in security and law enforcement roles; currently emerging case studies include the role of drones in the Russia-Ukraine War (24 February 2022), and the integration of AI in police body cams in support of fully-searchable video evidence. Such applications raise a range of ethical, technical and public policy questions in need of urgent address.

As the proposing organizer, I hoped that this transdisciplinary workshop would bring together researchers and practitioners from across engineering, social sciences and the humanities to consider the role of existing, and potential of future, machines in de-escalating Human-Human, and Human-Robot interactions. It started with a simple question: Compared to the pre-AI days, does AI fuel, constrain or remain neutral to escalation in policing and military contexts? Another formulation of this question is to ask whether AI favour the responsible use of force.

Inspired by the term 'machine translation' as the automated process whereby computer programs translate text from one natural language to another, I propose the term 'machine de-escalation' to capture the (currently fictitious) task of automating de-escalation, both human-human and human-machine. Saturated by technologies and made precarious by converging crises, we are living against what our presenter Sanjay Khanna calls, "a background of escalation". If this trend persists, it is reasonable to expect that societies that are most able to achieve responsible use of force by their police and military institutions may become those that enjoy higher levels of trust in their governance, and also may exemplify higher levels of social justice.

Consider the scenario of a verbal altercation between two patrons in a shopping mall. A robot security officer as the one depicted in the paper presented by Enas Tarawneh could be programmed with the latest de-escalation techniques as offered by the latest social psychology to conversationally guide the disputants away from physical violence. And if AI could not quite achieve all that, the robot could minimally distract the humans long enough to allow for a skillful human mediator to arrive on the scene before things escalate too much.

Machine de-escalation has at least three key vulnerabilities. First, we can expect that a machine de-escalation bot (MDB) will not have a perfect score in detecting conflict. It may also not consistently meet any reasonable context-informed threshold of performance. It should be noted that humans also perform inconsistently on the conflict detection task. For example, older adults routinely mislabel teenagers in conversation as fighting, and teenagers are regularly mislabel the bickering that characterizes long-term relationships as mutual dislike. Therefore, we can expect that the AI will get it wrong often enough. Sometimes, it will engage with humans as though they were in conflict when they are not. The AI could also malfunction. In such cases, humans may feel annoyed, frustrated, and victimized as the MDB would likely not be capable to walk things back with the finesse of a human. Depending on the context, humans may even feel angry, defeating the purpose of the MDS. Imagine an MDB systematically misclassifying conversations between women or persons of colour as instances of conflicts. In such cases, the unwarranted intervention from our AI may trigger conflict where there was none, but this time between the humans and the robot.

The second key vulnerability of a MDB is that, being a machine, it could be hacked. That is, it could be made to malfunction on purpose, or at least to function in ways that support a task at odds with de-escalation. The AI could pick fights with humans by making comments on their physical appearance that they will predictably find unflattering, or by making overtly sexist or racist remarks. The machine could even be made to pervert its mission by escalating rather than de-escalating conflict between humans. For example, a hacker could program the MDB to sow discord among humans of identifiably different types, like of different ages or of different skin melanin types and levels. Most perversely, the MDB could be programmed to be duplicitous. It could gain the trust of humans by announcing that it seeks to reduce conflict between humans, all the while using its detailed knowledge of emotion psychology informed techniques to exacerbate things and ensure that escalation of conflict is more rather than less likely!

The third vulnerability of machine de-escalation for discussion is the one we can do the most about: it is that de-escalation remains too infrequently considered in the engineering design and build phase automated use of force technologies. This workshop can be thought of as a piece of advocacy for de-escalation as a core feature, rather than being an add-on or even a bug of these systems.

While only two papers appear in the *Proceedings*, attendees were treated to seven (7) presentations from a diverse set of expertise and action areas, leading to unusually rich and transdisciplinary discussions.

Soldier-engineer Jack Collier presented "Why Soldiers Value De-escalation"
Futurist Sanjay Khanna spoke on Autonomous De-escalation
Doctoral candidate Enas Tarawneh presented a paper titled, "An Infrastructure for Studying the Role of Sentiment in Human-Robot Interaction"
Legal scholar Karen Eltis spoke on "AI De-escalation: The Legal & Policy Issues"
Communications scholar Dara Byrne spoke on "The Future of De-escalation"
Government scientist and AI expert Iraj Mantegh spoke on "Intruder Detection and Classification"
Doctoral candidate Aleksander Trajcevski presented paper titled, "Sensorimotor System Design of Socially Intelligent Robots"

The combination of keynotes, technical paper presentations, and panel discussions, explored current and future technologies, and their legal, ethical and social implications. At every turn, human choice loomed large. Humans build the machines. It is often the same systems that increase quality of life and safety, that can also harm or kill. The workshop reached its aim to expand the conversation and considered the technical, ethical and public policy choices at hand.

Organization

Workshop Chair

Jean-Jacques Rousseau   York University, Canada

Program Committee List

Stephanie Craig   Guelph University, Canada
Dara Byrne   City University of New York (CUNY)
James Elder   York University, Canada

An Infrastructure for Studying the Role of Sentiment in Human-Robot Interaction

Enas Tarawneh[✉], Jean-Jacques Rousseau, Stephanie G. Craig,
Deeksha Chandola, Walleed Khan, Adnan Faizi, and Michael Jenkin

Lassonde School of Engineering, York University, Toronto, Canada
{enas,jnjrousseau}@eecs.yorku.ca, {sgcraig,deekshac,jenkin}@yorku.ca,
{walleedk,adnan500}@my.yorku.ca

Abstract. The need for social robot systems has become even more critical as a result of the ongoing pandemic. Labour shortages in the services sector and public health concerns around infection transmission combine to favour the deployment of autonomous systems in a number of traditional roles including server robots in restaurants, companion robots in long-term care homes and security robots in public spaces, to identify but a few examples. To be successful, social robots must communicate with a wide range of individuals under a wide range of different scenarios. Understanding and reacting to the sentiment being expressed by an individual is key in human-human interaction, especially in critical situations that require de-escalation. This paper takes as a starting point that user sentiment is also critical for the successful deployment of social robot systems. Although much can be learned from experiments performed in simulation, real-world experiments in the development of sentiment-aware social robots requires an infrastructure upon which to explore questions related to the role of sentiment in social robotics. This includes the development of an appropriate robot morphology and user/robot interface. This paper reports early results in the development of sentiment and display technologies as part of the development of a sentiment-informed social robot named Sentrybot, an autonomous robot intended for deployment in the security domain.

Keywords: Sentiment Analysis · Emotion Estimation · Trust in Human-Robot Interaction · Audio Emotion Classification · Textual Emotion Classification · Multi-modal Emotion Classification

1 Introduction

Social robots [1] are robots that are designed to interact with humans in a socially acceptable fashion. The last 20 years have seen significant advances in the development of social robots and recent surveys of the field can be found in [2,3]. Although there is perhaps no universally agreed-upon standard for a definition of social robots (see [4]), a key aspect of social robots as identified in [4] is that social robots are autonomous or semi-autonomous physical bodies that

© Springer Nature Switzerland AG 2023
J.-J. Rousseau and B. Kapralos (Eds.): ICPR 2022 Workshops, LNCS 13646, pp. 89–105, 2023.
https://doi.org/10.1007/978-3-031-37745-7_7

generally possess human- or animal-like qualities. In particular, these embodied agents perceive and respond to environmental cues, engage in social interactions, communicate, cooperate, learn, make decisions and perform actions. All these abilities become 'social' in as much as they are enacted by robots and evaluated by humans according to the community's goals and social norms."[1]. In this paper, we report on an infrastructure of technologies aimed at supporting the development of emotionally aware robots, a feature that we believe is essential for the fuller realisation of social robotics.

Fig. 1. The Sentrybot showing its avatar interface. The Sentrybot robot is powered by a Dingo robot base and an onboard laptop provides other onboard support. The vast majority of computing is provided by off-board and cloud-based systems.

Social acceptance of autonomous robots is an open question. In the domain of autonomous security robots (ASR) there have been limited efforts to understand the factors that influence trust and acceptance of these devices. [5], for example, used static images of robots engaged in interactions with humans of different ages and gender to study this question. They found that robot manners were a significant factor in terms of the threat that the participants perceived in the robot's interaction. More real-world experiments are needed to validate findings

---

[1] [4] p. 11.

from simulations. While studies (e.g., [6]) using video of an ASR interacting with individuals as stimuli are useful in assessing the acceptability of having a robot deploy non-lethal weapons, static photos, canned videos and video game simulations can only be suggestive of what to expect in the real world. Asking complex questions related to trust in human robot interactions requires an actual system upon which to validate laboratory results.

Sentrybot is a robot security guard that provides physical security to a facility and interacts with visitors as it monitors the environment and reports on anomalies. The long term solution for sentrybot is to use its interaction mechanisms to aid in the de-escalation of situations that, if left unchecked, might lead to open conflict. Achieving de-escalation of conflict situations is a complex task because de-escalation is a collaborative exercise where effective emotional communication and assessment is essential [7–10]. [10] further suggests that one pivotal strategy in de-esclation is physical expressions of empathy. Being both emotionally present and actively engaged (e.g. engaging in frequent one-on-one conversations) can help promote trust and respect, in order to prevent escalation or successfully de-escalate a situation [11]. The robot should detect the sentiment of the human user, and express sentiments. That is to maintain emotional calm, listening and using acceptable verbal communication which are common de-esclation tactics [7–10]. De-escalation involving an autonomous robot implies the development of adaptive automated systems that do not merely require the user to adapt to them but machines that can also adapt to the human [12]. This means developing systems that are not blind to the emotions associated with a visitor's actions and speech, but instead can estimate user sentiment in near real-time and adapt the robot's interactions in response to changing user sentiment. By generating personalized responses, the system works to establish trust that, in turn, increases the effectiveness of the robot to de-escalate conflict situations between the user and the robot. This is a special application of the more general need for emotionally aware robots. The realisation of emotionally aware systems would be of great benefit to applications across a wide range of domains, from scenarios in the services sector to personal companion applications.

This paper describes work to date on Sentrybot, an infrastructure designed to support research in the use of a social robot to engage visitors at some fixed facility, and in particular to support research into tools and techniques that measure and integrate the sentiment of the visitor in the robot's interaction to aid de-escalation.

2   Robot Infrastructure

Figure 1 shows the Sentrybot robot in action with one of its avatar faces being displayed. As the goal is to build an infrastructure that supports a range of different experiments including exploring how robot morphology and visual persona impacts trust in human robot interaction, the robot itself is mostly a hollow shell and relies on a Clearpath Dingo [13] for mobility. (The Dingo is housed within the bottom 15cm of the robot. The vast majority of the visible portion of the

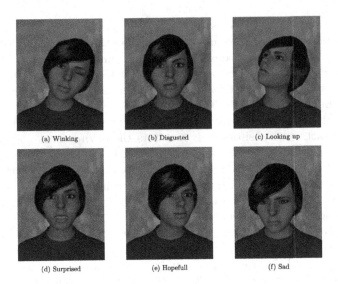

(a) Winking (b) Disgusted (c) Looking up

(d) Surprised (e) Hopefull (f) Sad

Fig. 2. Sample avatar faces. The avatar relies on a 3d rendering engine to render a puppet driven by a lip-syncing module. Different faces (both human and non-human) can be simulated as can different apparent emotional states.

robot is a hollow 3D printed shell designed to provide a particular robot morphology.) The Dingo base provides an omnidirectional robot base self-contained for power and which provides wireless offboard communication for teleoperation and higher level control.) All other on-board processing is performed via a laptop housed within the robot's shell. This laptop also provides the video display and audio input/output for the robot. As much as possible, Sentrybot relies on this laptop and offboard and cloud-based computing.

2.1 Navigation

As the focus of the project is to explore different strategies for human-robot interaction, we leverage standard approaches for robot navigation, localization and mapping. The robot is equipped with a front-facing LIDAR and we assume a previously-captured map of the environment. Adaptive Monte Carlo Localization (AMCL) [14] is used to localize the robot with respect to the map. Standard ROS navigation functions [15] are used to plan the robot's path within the test environment. The Sentrybot robot is also simulated within Gazebo along with simulated LIDAR measurements.

2.2 Speech-based Interaction

The primary input modality of Sentrybot is audio/speech. Audio is captured on the robot using a microphone capable of capturing speech at a 1–3m distance from the robot as shown in Fig. 1. Audio is transmitted off-board for further processing. As speech-to-text processing has access to both high-performance local as well as cloud-based computational resources, both local speech recognition (e.g., by Pocketsphinx [17]) as well as more sophisticated, cloud-based mechanism (e.g., Google cloud speech API [18], IBM speech to text [19], Microsoft Bing voice recognition [20], Wit.ai [21] and Houndify API [22]) are available. More local processing generally provides a reduced processing latency while more remote processing generally provides a more robust speech to text process. When transducing text to speech, again the bulk of the processing is performed off-board prior to being integrated with the avatar display (described below) and then transmitted to the robot for generation.

2.3   Avatar Display

The avatar framework used in this study is based on the Extensible Cloud-based Avatar described in [16]. This avatar is a puppetry toolkit with support for ROS (Robot Operating System). Figure 3 illustrates the basic structure of the Avatar System. When responding to a human interaction, the response text is given to the avatar system for integration in the avatar display. Rather than transmitting straight English text, the text to be rendered by the avatar is placed within a

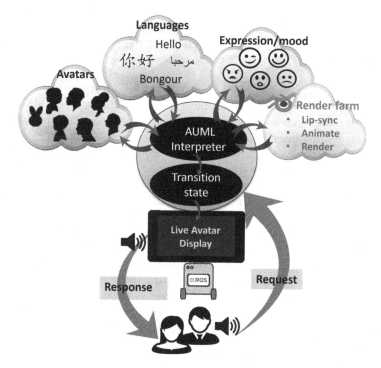

Fig. 3. Structure of the Avatar System. The avatar uses a collection of rigged 3d avatar models to provide the display. Knowledge of a set of different languages provided through cloud-based services provides support mapping textual utterances to lip motions, and general appearance of the avatar is provided via sentiment-tuned expressions. An idle loop structure provides animation instructions when the avatar is not rendering an utterance. See [16] and the text for details.

structured framework that provides rendering hints for both audio generation and avatar sentiment rendering through the Avatar Utterance Markup Language (AUML), a formal language for avatar utterances. This language is represented in XML; it defines a set of rules for encoding a desired output using a textual data format. Every utterance includes the avatar's detailed description, language, spoken words, expression associated with sub phrases and emotion. Figure 2 shows example avatar expressions and emotions. Our rendering mechanism, as described in [23], blends the audio with animated lip syncing and emotional facial expressions. It then produces an animated display segment to be smoothly integrated using the idle loop display as described below.

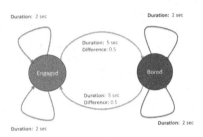

Fig. 4. A demonstration of the display graph where the avatar transitions between different states. See [24] and text for more details.

Rather than providing a static image of the avatar between utterances, a sophisticated idle loop process animates the avatar between utterances and helps to obscure rendering latency introduced by off-board rendering. A graph of idle video segments is constructed, where video segments are associated with edges and nodes represent seamless transitions from one video clip to another. When not generating utterances the avatar conducts a random walk through this graph to simulate a non-engaged but nevertheless animated speaker. We structure the waiting states to simulate emotion or mood, by labelling edges with the emotional state associated with that edge and then during the walk choose in a probabilistic manner the loop edge that is consistent with that edge. Figure 4 illustrates the **Bored** and **Engaged** nodes associated with two idle loops. The utterances are patched into the idle loop structure only at the **Engaged** node. When bored, the avatar loops through the bored portion of the graph (by setting the weights of the bored loop to match a bored persona), and when engaged, the avatar loops through the engaged portion of the graph. When rendering utterances, the utterance is animated and connected to the display graph. The avatar then transmits the utterance in the graph and displays the utterance. This allows for a smooth transition when uttering the response.

Rendering the avatar takes place off-board the robot using a cloud platform. We have leveraged commercial cloud platforms for rendering, but we currently use a local cloud platform made of a number of compute engines with multi core CPUs, a GPU, and sufficient RAM and disk space to support animation rendering. Our compute engines are headless Ubuntu servers and use the Blender rendering engine [25]. In order to enable accelerated rendering each instance is provided with VirtualGL [26], a software to forward off-screen rendering requests to the GPU for hardware acceleration. The rendering workload is distributed across the rendering engines using a task allocation process that is aware of the time horizon required for each part of the animation to be ready for display. See [24] for details of this process.

The blender engines lip-syncs the spoken words in the utterance with the video and audio to provide a realistic utterance. The text is used to animate the lips by utilizing a dictionary of phonemes. We use this list of sounds in the utterance to plot the sequence of lip-syncing events. In order to obtain the expected duration of utterances we trained our system on the duration of every word in a dictionary using the text-to-speech engine.

3   Sentiment Analysis

Figure 5 summarizes the basic structure of the sentiment-aware HRI framework deployed in Sentrybot. Details of the avatar-based rendering and audio input and output processes are described above. Here we consider the process of understanding the sentiment being expressed by the user. The following section considers how this information is integrated into audio responses and the appearance of the avatar.

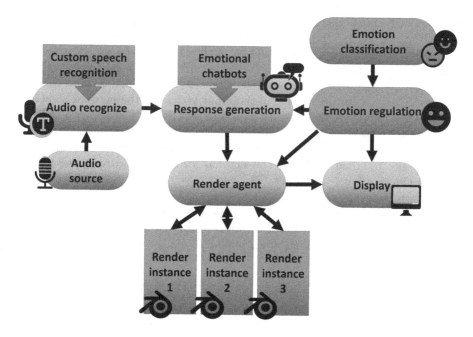

Fig. 5. Sentrybot's sentiment-aware HRI Framework

There are many possible mechanisms for estimating speaker sentiment, including vision-based (e.g., [27–29]), text-based (e.g., [30,30–33]), audio signal-based (e.g., [34–37]), and there have even been efforts to explore multi-modal techniques (e.g., [38–40]). There is a large and active literature in this domain, see [41] for a review. Within the Sentrybot project, work has concentrated on text-based and audio signal-based approaches and their integration. The audio-signal based approach operates on the raw audio signal associated with the speaker. The text-based approach operates at the sentence-level where an emotion category is assigned for each individual input sentence. Both models are trained and tested using the *Interactive Emotional Dyadic Motion Capture* (IEMOCAP) [42] dataset. The dataset consists of approximately 12 h of audio-visual data, including video, speech, motion capture of face, and text transcriptions. The IEMOCAP dataset provides ten labelled emotions. In order to simplify the integration of different cues to sentiment, we characterize the sentiment of the user, and the robot's response by considering seven commonly-used emotion categories (Sadness, Excitement, Anger, Neutral, Happy, Fear, and Surprised) for model training.

3.1 Audio-based Emotion Classification

One of the most fundamental methods of interaction between humans is speech. This is progressively being integrated into the realm of computer applications. Speech contains a vast amount of sentiment data. This data is both explicit [38] (i.e., the semantic meaning of the words) and implicit (i.e., frequency, volume, energy density, etc.) used by the speaker. The audio-based sentiment classification performed here is inspired by [43]. Features from the audio signal over a short temporal window are processed through a neural network (NN) to map to a one-hot sentiment vector. Here the input audio signal is represented by: 13 *Mel-Frequency Cepstral Coefficients*, 13 *Chroma features*, and 8 *Time-Spectral* features. These 34 features make up the input vector for the network structure shown in Fig. 6a. These features are passed into two LSTM layers with 512 and 256 neurons, respectively. The final LSTM layer is connected to a dense layer with 512 neurons. Using a ReLU activation function, the output from this layer is passed into the final dense layer, which has a total of 7 neurons, one neuron for each emotion label in our set. The output from this is then passed into a Softmax function, in order to output a confidence score for each emotion. The Adam optimizer was found to improve the accuracy of the model. After limiting the dataset to the aforementioned emotions, the final model was trained with 5,678 samples, and a testing accuracy of 63.8%.

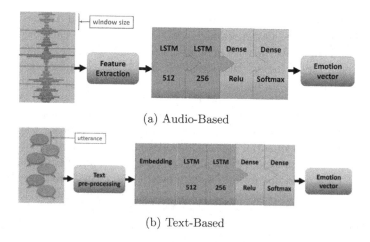

(a) Audio-Based

(b) Text-Based

Fig. 6. Emotion Classification

In similar systems (e.g., [34,38,43–45]), data is typically processed in batches of prerecorded audio files. The Sentrybot system generates live sentiment estimations by using a circular buffer containing 10 non-overlapping windows, each elapsing 0.5 s. Live audio is collected and loaded into the last window of this buffer. As new data enters the system, the buffer is queued for estimation generation. The model is then able to make estimations with a latency of approximately 3 s on average as highlighted in Fig. 6a.

3.2   Text-based Emotion Classification

There exists a vast literature on emotion detection from text due to the huge availability of online data in the form of dialogues, short texts, messages and social media posts. Text-based emotion classification works at three levels: word-level, phrase-level and at sentence-level and by extracting features from the input text. [46] presents a recent survey on text-based emotion detection. This survey highlights the main approaches used for emotion detection in text such as rule-based, hybrid approaches and most commonly and widely implemented machine learning methods. Many researchers uses machine learning models (e.g. [32,47–49]) to classify the emotions expressed in text into different emotions categories. Work by [50] utilized a Long-Short Term Memory (LSTM)-based model for text based emotion classification using two features based on an emotional word vector and semantic word vector of the input text. This approach improves the detection accuracy as compared to earlier CNN-based methods. [49] reviewed transformer based approaches such as Generative Pre-Training (GPT), Bidirectional Encoder Representations from Transformers (BERT), XLNet, Robustly Optimized BERT (RoBERTa), and DistilBERT that are used in text based emotion classification. [51] adopted a pre-trained BERT model to classify emotions in each utterance of two common datasets, Friends and EmotionPush. [33] use a BERT-based model trained on a large, manually annotated dataset using 58k Reddit comments called GoEmotions labelled for 27 emotion categories. To better understand the conversation's general emotion and the user specific emotion, [52] proposed a model named DialogueRNN that is based on a recurrent neural network to extract emotions based on three factors: the speaker, the preceding context in the conversation, and the preceding emotion behind the conversation. DialogueGCN more advanced variant of this approach is proposed by [53]. This framework is based on a graph convolutional network that includes a speaker level and sequential context encoder and emotion classifier. [54] proposed a method for emotion detection in conversation using the different aspects of common sense including events, mental events and casual relations. Based on these elements the model learns the interactions between speakers.

For Sentrybot, we used two stacked LSTM layer models to perform text based emotion classification. Following [55] the model is initialised with Glove word vector embeddings of dimension 300. The complete text based emotion classification is summarized in Fig. 6b. The model takes as input the aggregated text and is trained according to the class labels. The maximum sequence length for each utterance is 500. The model architecture is inspired by [43]. The first LSTM layer has 512 units followed by 256 units for the second LSTM layer. The dense layer has 512 hidden units with Relu as the activation function. Finally, the output is fed to the final dense layer with 7 neurons followed by a Softmax activation function to classify the text data as one of the chosen emotion classes (Sadness, Excitement, Anger, Neutral, Happy, Fear, and Surprised). Using this multi-class emotion classification we obtain a macro average F1 accuracy score of 0.55. The testing accuracy achieved is 58%.

3.3   Multi-modal Emotion Classification

With the unimodal models described above, and building upon previous audio-textual sentiment classification approaches (e.g., [38, 40]), we have developed a real-time multi-modal emotion classification approach. Each unimodal classifier is treated as an independent pipeline and the final outputs are concatenated. The audio pipeline is a trained audio-only model, as described in the Sect. 3.1. The text sentiment pipeline starts by taking input from the speech-to-text conversion, described in Sect. 3.2. As the full text is received it is fed into the text-based classification model which then classifies the text as one of the emotion classes. In the combined model, we concatenate the final layers from the two model to perform feature fusion. After this we also added a dense layer with 256 neurons followed by a softmax layer to compute the final output class probability. Based on the output, the emotion class is selected and an emotion sensitive chatbot is triggered for response generation. With the benefit of these models working independently, estimations take approximately five seconds from the moment audio is given as an input.

4   Emotional Response Generation

Taking human emotions into account during human-robot interactions can aid in successfully integrating socially assistive robots within society [56]. Humans use emotional intelligence to adapt their behaviour in interactions. Humans also have their own unique aggregated persona that others take into account when generating their conceptual and emotional reaction during natural conversations [57]. [58] proposed a novel chatbot for psychiatric counseling service. The chatbot generates personalized counseling response by sensing the emotional flow in the continuous conversations. Another recent work proposed by [59] works towards generating emotionally context and semantically consistent responses. They proposed the Emotion Capture Chat Machine (ECCM) which has a encoder-decoder architecture to capture the emotional signal and semantic signal to generate emotionally coherent responses.

Emotional chatbots (specifically trained to target emotionally-charged conversation utterances) may allow for positive emotional shifts in conversations. In this work, we created chatbots optimised to respond to utterances associated with specific emotion labels by utilizing customized chatbots for different emotional states. They were implemented using Python ChatterBots [60]. ChatterBot uses machine learning algorithms and a number of logic adapters (e.g. best match, time, specific response, etc) to select a response to a given utterance. Each one of our Chatterbots was trained with a set of acceptable social encounters that generates an appropriate response based on the emotional classification of a given utterance within a conversational context. The emotional label of the user utterance is determined by our multi-modal emotion classifier. The chatbot responses are selected based on the text of the user utterance, the emotional label of that utterance and the set of identified keywords in the utterance at a given time. We currently use an emotion regulator that uses hard coded mappings to map the emotion label of a user's utterance to an appropriate responsive avatar emotion state. The chatbot response utterance and the selected appropriate avatar emotion are used to generate an animated emotional avatar display.

The emotional response generation process is illustrated in Fig. 7. We are currently working on enhancing our response generation: by (*i*) training a model that identifies conversational emotional patterns that best promotes happy, neutral and excited emotions in the coming utterances; (*ii*) using the selected chatbot utterance, a prediction of the user's next future emotion and a representation of the user's emotional history as input to enhance emotion regulation.

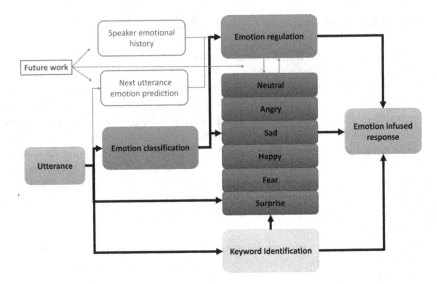

Fig. 7. Emotional Response Generation

5 Ongoing Work

This work describes an infrastructure for social human-robot interaction that aids in conducting studies on building trust between humans and robots and the generation of emotionally aware interactions. Our infrastructure, when engaging in conversation, estimates human emotions using an (*audio-text*) multi-modal classifier. We train chatbots to respond to an utterance with a given emotion. These chatbots generate socially acceptable responses that promote happy, neutral or excited emotions. This type of infrastructure, that allows for more positive experiences, may be particularly useful in security robots or robots that may encounter situations that require de-escalation. However, pleasant human robot interactions may be desired in many other applications (e.g., education, retail, medical).

We built the infrastructure detailed in this paper to support ongoing research in social robot-interaction in the security application domain. Like all social robots, our robot takes for granted that human users will trust the system enough to interact with it. In addition to the technical achievements noted above, our ongoing work is guided by a transdisciplinary approach that takes a broader perspective on trust in robots. It seeks to contribute to the current understanding of the factors influencing humans' perception and trust of robots, which may influence their desire to interact with robots in the future.

Ongoing work starts with the preliminary observation that trust is built on repeated interactions, where the user perception of consistency in system responses matters. It also seems that, if humans do not trust a robot, the task of de-escalation becomes all but impossible [10,11]. Currently, the factors we are reviewing as candidates for drivers of user include demographic (e.g., age, gender, racial background) and psychological (e.g., personality type, trust in conspiracy theories) variables.

It also appears that robots in different domains may require different levels of trust from users, perhaps linked to the levels of vulnerability that the user is being asked to tolerate [61]. For example, server robots at a restaurant appear to perform tasks at the lower end of the user trust scale, while companion robots or those engaged in therapy appear to perform tasks at the higher end of required user trust. Robots in the security domain appear to be between these points of trust.

That repeated interactions increase trust is premised on user willingness to engage in the first place. This raises questions of whether the perceived gender, race and personality of the robot at a distance impacts user expectations of its trustworthiness and friendliness. This is especially important when selecting the appropriate avatar for a specific job in a given domain. When isolating the robot itself as a physical object, its morphology, that is its shape and size, there may be features that also impact the user willingness to both engage and predispose the user to trust (or not) robot actions based on the robot's perceived reasonableness and intelligence [62]. These morphology traits include level of anthropomorphism, height and volume of the robot's utterances.

Our transdisciplinary approach to emotionally-aware autonomous systems is grounded in a marriage of engineering, social science and the humanities. Its aim is the development of systems capable of socially-useful performances across industries and domains. By merging the technical and human considerations at the stage of design, we expect to increase the likelihood of faster deployment and wider acceptance of social robotics in the service of human-centered concerns.

Acknowledgments. The development of the infrastructure detailed in this paper was funded by the Innovation for Defence Excellence and Security (IDEaS) program of the Department of National Defence of the Government of Canada, in support of the Canadian Armed Forces. The support of the NSERC Canadian Robotics Network is gratefully acknowledged. The authors are solely responsible for the content of this publication and thank Helio Perroni Filho for his helpful comments and suggestions.

References

1. Braezeal, C., Scassellati, B.: How to build robots that makes friends and influence people. In: IEEE/RSJ IROS. Kyongju, Korea (1999)
2. Daily, S.B., et al.: Affective computing: historical foundations, current applications, and future trends. In: Jeon, M. (ed.) Emotions and Affect in Human Factors and Human-Computer Interaction, pp. 213–231. Academic Press, San Diego (2017)
3. Henschel, A., Laban, G., Cross, E.S.: What makes a robot social? a review of social robots from science fiction to a home or hospital near you. Cogn. Robot. **2**, 9–19 (2021)
4. Sarrica, M., Brondi, S., Fortunati, L.: How many facets does a "social robot" have? a review of scientific and popular definitions online. Inf. Techol. People **33**, 1–21 (2020)
5. Inbar, O., Meyer, J.: Manners matter: trust in robotic peacekeepers. In: Proceedings of the Human Factors and Ergonomics Society Annual Meeting, vol. 59, pp. 185–189 (2016)
6. Lyons, J.B., Vo, T., Wynne, K.T., Majoney, S., Nam, C.S., Gallimore, D.: Trusting autonomous security robots: the role of reliability and stated social intent. J. Hum. Factors Ergon. Soc. **63**(4), 603–618 (2020)

7. Mavandadi, V., Bieling, P.J., Madsen, V.: Effective ingredients of verbal de-escalation: validating an English modified version of the 'de-escalating aggressive behaviour scale. J. Psychiatr. Ment. Health Nurs. **23**(6–7), 357–368 (2016)

8. Hallett, N., Dickens, G.L.: De-escalation of aggressive behaviour in healthcare settings: concept analysis. Int. J. Nurs. Stud. **75**, 10–20 (2017)

9. Mavandadi, V., Bieling, P.J., Madsen, V.: Effective ingredients of verbal de-escalation: validating an English modified version of the 'de-escalating aggressive behaviour scale. J. Psychiatr. Ment. Health Nurs. **23**(6–7), 357–68 (2016)

10. Rabenschlag, F., Cassidy, C., Steinauer, R.: Nursing perspectives: reflecting history and informal coercion in de-escalation strategies. Front. Psychiatry **10**, 231 (2019)

11. Goodman, H., Papastavrou Brooks, C., Price, O., Barley, E.A.: Barriers and facilitators to the effective de-escalation of conflict behaviours in forensic high-secure settings: a qualitative study. Int. J. Men. Health Syst. **14**, 1–16 (2020)

12. Toichoa Eyam, A., Mohammed, W.M., Martinez Lastra, J.L.: Emotion-driven analysis and control of human-robot interactions in collaborative applications. Sensors **21**, 4626 (2021)

13. Clearpath Robotics, R.: Dingo indoor mobile robot. https://clearpathrobotics.com/dingo-indoor-mobile-robot/

14. Das, S.: Robot localization in a mapped environment using adaptive monte carlo algorithm. Int. J. Sci. Eng. Res. **9**, 10 (2018)

15. Yang, X.: Slam and navigation of indoor robot based on ROS and LIDAR. J. Phys. **1748**, 1 (2021)

16. Altarawneh, Enas, Jenkin, Michael, Scott MacKenzie, I..: An extensible cloud based avatar: implementation and evaluation. In: Brooks, Anthony Lewis, Brahman, Sheryl, Kapralos, Bill, Nakajima, Amy, Tyerman, Jane, Jain, Lakhmi C.. (eds.) Recent Advances in Technologies for Inclusive Well-Being. ISRL, vol. 196, pp. 503–522. Springer, Cham (2021). https://doi.org/10.1007/978-3-030-59608-8_27

17. Huggins-Daines, D., Kumar, M., Chan, A., Black, A., Ravishankar, M., Rudnicky, A.: Pocketsphinx: a free, real-time continuous speech recognition system for handheld devices. In: 2006 IEEE International Conference on Acoustics Speed and Signal Processing Proceedings, May 2006

18. Ravulavaru, A.: Google Cloud AI Services Quick Start Guide: Build Intelligent Applications with Google Cloud AI Services. Packt Publishing, Birmingham (2018)

19. Packowski, S., Lakhana, A.: Using IBM WATSON cloud services to build natural language processing solutions to leverage chat tools. In: Proceedings of the 27th Annual International Conference on Computer Science and Software Engineering (CASCON), Markham, Ontario, Canada, pp. 211–218 (2017)

20. Larsen, L.: Learning Microsoft Cognitive Services: Use Cognitive Services APIs to Add AI Capabilities to Your Applications, 3rd edn. Packt Publishing, Birmingham (2018)

21. Biswas, M., Wit.ai and Dialogflow. Apress, Berkeley, CA, pp. 67–100 (2018). https://doi.org/10.1007/978-1-4842-3754-0_3

22. Aronsson, J., Lu, P., Strüber, D., Berger, T.: A maturity assessment framework for conversational AI development platforms. New York, NY, USA, Association for Computing Machinery, pp. 1736–1745 (2021). https://doi.org/10.1145/3412841.3442046

23. Altarawneh, E., jenkin, M.: System and method for rendering of an animated avatar, U.S. Patent 10 580 187B2, 7 March 2020

24. Altarawneh, E., Jenkin, M.: Leveraging cloud-based tools to talk with robots. In: Proceedings of 16th International Conference On Informatics in Control, Automation and Robotics (ICINCO), July 2019

25. Valenza, E.: Blender Cycles: Materials and Textures Cookbook, Third Edition, 3rd ed. Packt Publishing, Birmingham (2015)
26. Paradis, D.J., Segee, B.: Remote rendering and rendering in virtual machines. In. International Conference on Computational Science and Computational Intelligence (CSCI), vol. 2016, pp. 218–221 (2016)
27. Doshi, U., Barot, V., Gavhane, S.: Emotion detection and sentiment analysis of static images. In: IEEE International Conference on Convergence to Digital World, Mumbai, India (2000)
28. Rajesh, K.M., Naveenkumar, M.: A robust method for face recognition and face emotion detection system using support vector machines. In: 2016 International Conference on Electrical, Electronics, Communication, Computer and Optimization Techniques (ICEECCOT), pp. 1–5 (2016)
29. Reney, D., Tripathi, N.: An efficient method to face and emotion detection In: Fifth International Conference on Communication Systems and Network Technologies, vol. 2015, pp. 493–497 (2015)
30. Li, W., Xu, H.: Text-based emotion classification using emotion cause extraction. Expert Syst. Appl. **41**(4), 1742–1749 (2014)
31. Agrawal, A., An, A.: Unsupervised emotion detection from text using semantic and syntactic relations. In: 2012 IEEE/WIC/ACM International Conferences on Web Intelligence and Intelligent Agent Technology, vol. 1. pp. 346–353. IEEE (2012)
32. Abdi, A., Shamsuddin, S.M., Hasan, S., Piran, J.: Deep learning-based sentiment classification of evaluative text based on multi-feature fusion. Inf. Process. Manag. **56**(4), 1245–1259 (2019)
33. Demszky, D., Movshovitz-Attias, D., Ko, J., Cowen, A., Nemade, G., Ravi, S.: Goemotions: a dataset of fine-grained emotions, arXiv preprint arXiv:2005.00547 (2020)
34. Fersini, E., Messina, E., Arosio, G., Archetti, F.: Audio-based emotion recognition in judicial domain: a multilayer support vector machines approach. In: Perner, P. (ed.) MLDM 2009. LNCS (LNAI), vol. 5632, pp. 594–602. Springer, Heidelberg (2009). https://doi.org/10.1007/978-3-642-03070-3_45
35. Lalitha, S., Geyasruti, D., Narayanan, R., Shravani, M.: Emotion detection using MFCC and cepstrum features. Procedia Comput. Sci. **70**, 29–35 (2015)
36. Sayedelahl, A., Fewzee, P., Kamel, M.S., Karray, F.: Audio-based emotion recognition from natural conversations based on co-occurrence matrix and frequency domain energy distribution features. In: D'Mello, S., Graesser, A., Schuller, B., Martin, J.-C. (eds.) ACII 2011. LNCS, vol. 6975, pp. 407–414. Springer, Heidelberg (2011). https://doi.org/10.1007/978-3-642-24571-8_52
37. Chernykh, V., Sterling, G., Prihodko, P.: Emotion recognition from speech with recurrent neural networks, CoRR, vol. abs/1701.08071 (2017)
38. Cai, L., Hu, Y., Dong, J., Zhou, S.: Audio-textual emotion recognition based on improved neural networks. Math. Prob. Eng. **2019**, 1–9 (2019). https://www.hindawi.com/journals/mpe/2019/2593036/
39. Ren, M., Nie, W., Liu, A., Su, Y.: Multi-modal correlated network for emotion recognition in speech. Vis. Inf. **3**(3), 150–155 (2019)
40. Sebe, N., Cohen, I., Huang, T.S.: Multimodal emotion recognition. In: Handbook of Pattern Recognition and Computer Vision. World Scientific, pp. 387–409 (2005)
41. Soleymani, M., Garcia, D., Jou, B., Schuller, B., Chang, S.-F., Pantic, M.: A survey of multimodal sentiment analysis. Image Vis. Comput. **65**, 3–14 (2017)
42. Busso, C., et al.: IEMOCAP: interactive emotional dyadic motion capture database. Lang. Resour. Eval. **42**(4), 335–359 (2008)

43. Tripathi, S., Beigi, H.S.M.: Multi-modal emotion recognition on IEMOCAP dataset using deep learning, CoRR, vol. abs/1804.05788 (2018). http://arxiv.org/abs/1804.05788

44. Chernykh, V., Prihodko, P.: Emotion recognition from speech with recurrent neural networks (2018)

45. Poria, S., Majumder, N., Hazarika, D., Cambria, E., Hussain, A., Gelbukh, A.: Multimodal sentiment analysis: addressing key issues and setting up the baselines. IEEE Intell. Syst. **33**, 17–25 (2018)

46. Acheampong, F.A., Wenyu, C., Nunoo-Mensah, H.: Text-based emotion detection: advances, challenges, and opportunities. Eng. Rep. **2**(7), e12189 (2020)

47. Xu, D., Tian, Z., Lai, R., Kong, X., Tan, Z., Shi, W.: Deep learning based emotion analysis of microblog texts. Inf. Fusion **64**, 1–11 (2020)

48. Rashid, U., Iqbal, M.W., Skiandar, M.A., Raiz, M.Q., Naqvi, M.R., Shahzad, S.K.: Emotion detection of contextual text using deep learning. In: 2020 4th International Symposium on Multidisciplinary Studies and Innovative Technologies (ISMSIT), pp. 1–5. IEEE (2020)

49. Acheampong, F.A., Nunoo-Mensah, H., Chen, W.: Transformer models for text-based emotion detection: a review of BERT-based approaches. Artif. Intell. Rev. **54**(8), 5789–5829 (2021). https://doi.org/10.1007/s10462-021-09958-2

50. Su, M.-H., Wu, C.-H., Huang, K.-Y., Hong, Q.-B.: Lstm-based text emotion recognition using semantic and emotional word vectors. In: First Asian Conference on Affective Computing and Intelligent Interaction (ACII Asia), vol. 2018, pp. 1–6 (2018)

51. Luo, L., Wang, Y.: Emotionx-hsu: adopting pre-trained BERT for emotion classification, CoRR, vol. abs/1907.09669 (2019)

52. Majumder, N., Poria, S., Hazarika, D., Mihalcea, R., Gelbukh, A., Cambria, E.: Dialoguernn: an attentive RNN for emotion detection in conversations. In: AAAI, pp. 6818–6825 (2019)

53. Ghosal, D., Majumder, N., Poria, S., Chhaya, N., Gelbukh, A.: DialogueGCN: a graph convolutional neural network for emotion recognition in conversation. In: Proceedings of the 2019 Conference on Empirical Methods in Natural Language Processing and the 9th International Joint Conference on Natural Language Processing (EMNLP-IJCNLP), Hong Kong, China, Association for Computational Linguistics, pp. 154–164. November 2019

54. Ghosal, D., Majumder, N., Gelbukh, A., Mihalcea, R., Poria, S.: COSMIC: commonsense knowledge for emotion identification in conversations. In: Findings of the Association for Computational Linguistics: EMNLP 2020, Association for Computational Linguistics, pp. 2470–2481, November 2020

55. Pennington, J., Socher, R., Manning, C.: GloVe: global vectors for word representation. In: Proceedings of the 2014 Conference on Empirical Methods in Natural Language Processing (EMNLP), Doha, Qatar, Association for Computational Linguistics, pp. 1532–1543, October 2014. https://aclanthology.org/D14-1162

56. Spezialetti, M., Placidi, G., Rossi, S.: Emotion recognition for human-robot interaction: recent advances and future perspectives. Front. Robot. AI **7**, 532279 (2020)

57. Ishiguro, H., Ono, T., Imai, M., Maeda, T., Kanda, T., Nakatsu, R.: Robovie: an interactive humanoid robot. Int. J. Ind. Robot **28**(6), 498–504 (2001)

58. Tian, Z., et al.: Emotion-aware multimodal pre-training for image-grounded emotional response generation. In: International Conference on Database Systems for Advanced Applications, pp. 3–19, vol. 13247. Springer, Cham (2022). https://doi.org/10.1007/978-3-031-00129-1_1

59. Mao, Y., Cai, F., Guo, Y., Chen, H.: Incorporating emotion for response generation in multi-turn dialogues. Appl. Intell. **52**(7), 7218–7229 (2022)
60. Cox, G.: Chatterbot. https://pypi.org/project/ChatterBot/
61. Malle, B.F., Ullman, D.: A multi-dimensional conception and measure of human-robot trust. In: Nam, C.S., Lyons, J.B. (eds.) Trust in Human-Robot Interaction: Research and Applications, Elsevier, pp. 3–2 (2021)
62. Schaefer, K.E., Sanders, T.L., Yordon, R.E., Billings, D.R., Hancock, P.: Classification of robot form: factors predicting perceived trustworthiness. In: Proceedings of the Human Factors and Ergonomics Society 56th Annual Meeting, Nam, C.S., Lyons, J.B., (eds.), pp. 1548–1552 (2012)

Sensorimotor System Design of Socially Intelligent Robots

Aleksander Trajcevski[✉], Helio Perroni Filho, Nizwa Javed,
Tasneem Naheyan, Kartikeya Bhargava, and James H. Elder

Department of Electrical Engineering and Computer Science, Centre for AI &
Society, York University, Toronto, ON M3J 1P3, Canada
{atrajcev,helio,nizwaj,tnaheyan,kkb,jelder}@yorku.ca
https://www.elderlab.yorku.ca/

Abstract. We describe and demonstrate a sensorimotor architecture for
social robots, highlighting in particular the value of attentive sensing for
acquisition of more detailed information about people in the far field,
and how this can inform the robot's behaviour.

Keywords: attentive sensing · social robotics · computer vision ·
dynamic scene analysis · sensorimotor architecture

1 Introduction

Social robots tasks generally involve approaching and interacting with individuals of interest while avoiding collisions or conflicts with other humans in the field, all of which requires that the robot be broadly socially aware and able to estimate human intentions and goals. These requirements suggest a very wide (ideally panoramic) sensory field-of-view (FOV) to avoid blind spots, i.e., directions in which the robot is unaware of human occupancy or activity. At the same time, identifying individuals and understanding intent in the far field generally requires high spatial acuity, to support face or expression recognition or estimation of gaze direction, for example. For a fixed sensor pixel resolution, this generates a **resolution-FOV tradeoff**: Expansion of the FOV to support wide-field awareness leads to a reduction in acuity needed for interpretation, especially in the far field. In this paper, we describe a sensorimotor system that addresses this trade-off using attentive sensor technology.

2 Related Work

The human visual system provides a very wide binocular FOV (more than 180 deg horizontally), providing broad situational awareness. Acquisition of visual detail is supported by a high-resolution fovea in the central 1–2 deg of the visual field, coupled with a fast and accurate oculomotor plant.

J.-J. Rousseau and B. Kapralos (Eds.): ICPR 2022 Workshops, LNCS 13646, pp. 106–118, 2023.
https://doi.org/10.1007/978-3-031-37745-7_8

Fig. 1. Attentive sensor prototype

Early work on attentive vision systems employed a probabilistic combination of background subtraction, motion and skin colour features to detect humans in low-resolution pre-attentive imagery, generating gaze targets for a high-resolution attentive sensor [5,6,9], with an ultimate aim to support face recognition in the far field [8]. Figure 1 shows a prototype attentive sensor device that was developed in this project. It consists of two identical cameras with horizontal axes lying in the same vertical plane. The lower, pre-attentive camera is fitted with a wide-FOV lens, while the upper, attentive camera is fitted with a narrow FOV lens. The attentive gaze is deflected horizontally and vertically via two mirrors mounted on rotational motors.

A distinction between pre-attentive and attentive processing has more recently been made for robot software design (e.g., [1,3,4]) and for robot sensor chips (e.g., [2]), and attention has been used as a framework for the control of binocular robot eyes (e.g., [7]), but none of this work addresses the resolution-FOV tradeoff.

3   Hardware Platform

Figure 2 shows our experimental robot as well as our target for commercial deployment, the CrossWing Bishop platform. Our experimental robot uses the omnidirectional Clearpath Dingo-O as a base on which is mounted a custom modular frame that houses sensors and an onboard computer.

Our system architecture employs a distributed computing approach. A remote server is used to detect and localize people in the robot's environment

Fig. 2. Left: Experimental robot platform, based on a Clearpath Ding-O base. Right: The CrossWing Bishop platform, our target for commercial deployment.

and sends their locations to an onboard computing platform that handles SLAM and navigation to approach selected individuals.

3.1 Pre-attentive Sensing

Our sensing strategy includes four wide-angle 1280 × 720 pixel Intel RealSense RGBD cameras with nearly 90-deg horizontal FOV. These are mounted near the top of the platform at a height of 1.5 m with horizontal axes at 90 deg intervals, thus collectively providing a nearly seamless panoramic FOV to support SLAM, safe navigation and broad social awareness. (A fifth RealSense camera mounted lower on the frame and tilted down provides sensing for obstacle avoidance in the near field, but will not be discussed further here.) Figure 3 shows example output from two of these pre-attentive sensors.

3.2 Attentive Sensing

The attentive sensor (Fig. 4) is mounted directly above the pre-attentive sensors, at a viewing height of 1.6 m. We employ a Sony Alpha 7C 3840 × 2160 pixel camera, with a Sony E PZ 18–200 mm powered zoom lens fixed at its longest focal length, which yields an 8 deg horizontal FOV. The camera system supports

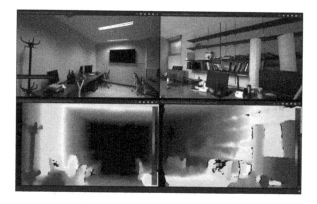

Fig. 3. Example RGB images (top) and depth maps (bottom) from two of our preattentive sensors.

Fig. 4. Attentive sensor design (left) and as built (right).

auto-focus, which is critical to acquiring in-focus images of human activity over a broad range of distances. Note that this attentive sensor provides linear acuity that is roughly 32 times better than our pre-attentive camera system.

The attentive camera body is mounted vertically so that the lens extends upward between the pre-attentive cameras. Gaze is deflected horizontally by a mirror mounted on a vertical motor at a 45 deg angle. Rotation of the motor shifts the azimuth of the attentive FOV, providing attentive resolution in any direction of interest identified by the pre-attentive stream. The mirror and the Sony camera are both controlled from the onboard computer. The four posts that support the mirror-motor assembly do generate small occlusions in the attentive FOV. Interestingly, due to the proximity of these posts to the lens, for larger lens apertures, objects behind the posts still partially image onto the sensor. We therefore believe it may be possible to photometrically calibrate this occlusion out of the attentive image stream - this remains future work.

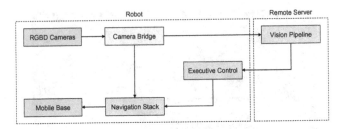

Fig. 5. Overall software system design with modules

4   Software System Design and Navigation

Our software architecture, which is implemented in ROS [10] and Python, is designed with the goal of providing a robot with the capacity to navigate in social scenarios with sufficient awareness of its environment. To perform this social navigation, our architecture consists of three modules: the vision pipeline, executive control, and the navigation stack. These modules interact based on input from the pre-attentive cameras referred to in Sect. 3. The flow of this architecture follows an ordered behaviour of perception, decision, and then action to navigate in a social environment (Fig. 5).

We optimize computational load through a distributed computing architecture, where the executive control and navigation modules are computed on the robot, while the more computationally expensive vision pipeline is performed by a remote server. With this architecture, our robot performs the following scenario:

– The robot begins at an observation point, identifying people on the map.
– Based on observations, make a decision on who to apporach and avoid
– Use attentive sensor to recognize people of interest.
– Approach the person and engage based on use case.
– After engagement, identify new goal of approach or return to observation point.

4.1   Vision Pipeline

The vision pipeline supports the robots social awareness by detecting and localizing people in its environment, to allow the robot to both approach people of interest and to avoid others. Due to the computational demands, our vision pipeline is implemented on a remote server. The vision pipeline begins with the sensory data received as RGBD images from the pre-attentive cameras, detailed in Sect. 3.1. We use our object detector, YoloV3 [11] on the pre-attentive images to derive 2D bounding boxes around people in the field of view. The depth of these 2D bounding boxes is estimated by using the depth images in the corresponding pre-attentive images. We then use the camera's geometry to convert the 3D coordinates from the camera frame to the robot-centric frame, generating a set of ground-plane coordinates. This process (Fig. 6) occurs for each of the cameras which compose the near 360° field of view. We then aggregate all the 3D coordinates from each camera to compose a set of aggregated coordinates for all individuals in the robots field of view (Fig. 7). These aggregated coordinates are used by the robot's navigation stack (Sect. 4.3) for the purpose of approach and avoidance of people in the environment. The attentive sensor, detailed in Sect. 3.2, also uses the aggregated coordinates collected from the wider range pre-attentive cameras to focus on the 3D coordinates by pivoting the mounted mirror in the direction of the individual, allowing the attentive camera to direct to persons of interest and provide the necessary high-resolution imagery. We use DeepSORT ([15, 16]) to implement person tracking in our pre-attentive cameras so the robot is capable of distinguishing people for approach and avoidance over time, and to help with navigating towards people on the move.

We unify our social navigation scenario with our attentive sensor through face recognition. Using deepface ([12, 13]), we perform face recognition on our attentive images by comparing with a known set of face the robot carries. By relating recognized faces with the known set, the robot tracks people of interest when a person is recognized as familiar. This initiates the approach scenario in our prototype by having the robot treat familiar faces as ones who the robot should approach, and this is augmented with the attentive sensor which provides long-range sensing for such face recognition which would otherwise be difficult.

Using this high-resolution image from the attentive camera, we have a number of applications. For our goal of a socially aware robot, we aim to enable face identification and re-identification, the ability to estimate a number of attributes such as age, gender, and ethnicity, and the ability track individuals in the environment.

4.2   Executive Control

The executive control of the robot dictates and updates the policy that robot will follow. These policies describe who to approach through identifying features of interest, approach the individual to carry out the goal dictated, and then to either return to its idle position or updates its policy to approach a new individual of interest (Fig. 8). The implementation of the executive control function uses the ROS [10] package SMACH (State MACHines). This package uses a Python API for creating hierarchical state machines along with the expected ROS middleware of topics, services and actions. The executive control function computes goals from detected person poses detected in the map frames and local frames processed in the navigation stack. It also identifies exclusion zones to avoid repeat approaches to the same person of interest. Figure 9 demonstrates the executive control in action, with the RGB feeds from the four RealSense cameras at the top, the navigation map on the bottom left, and the state machine visualization tool from SMACH in the bottom right.

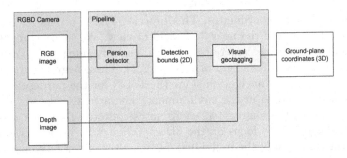

Fig. 6. Visual of pipeline converting RGBD images into 3D ground-plane coordinates.

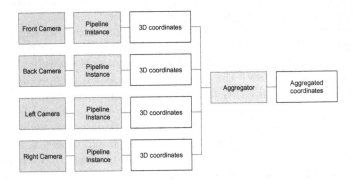

Fig. 7. Visual of each camera pipeline aggregating all the coordinates.

4.3   Navigation Stack

Our navigation stack architecture (Fig. 10) receives sensory data from the pre-attentive cameras and outputs to our SLAM algorithm and the move_base proto-col. The SLAM algorithm we have used is known as real-time appearance based mapping. We use all depth maps from each of our cameras and collapse them vertically to get the depth of the closest objects to develop 2D occupancy maps of the environment. This process is visualized in Fig. 11, where the left side is the pre-attentive feed of the wide angle cameras, and the right side is the corre-sponding depth maps. In the centre we have the 2D occupancy map, where the red lines represent the depth of the closest objects, drawing out the boundaries of the map, similar to LIDAR. These maps provide the move_base protocol and the Trusted Motion Planner with data on positions of the robot itself on the map, and the human traffic around it.

The global_costmap functions as the initial map of the area predetermined with the slam_toolbox, developing a 2D occupancy map of its environment. The global_planner develops a plan to maneuver through the map. The local_costmap updates according to local obstacles on the map. Therefore, the move_base stack,

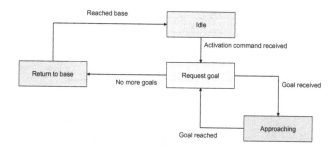

Fig. 8. Executive control state machine

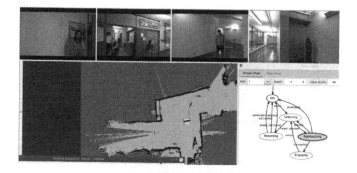

Fig. 9. Demonstration of the executive control in action. RGBD cameras (top), navigation map (left) and state machine visualization tool from SMACH (right). (Color figure online)

generates an optimal path in a global sense, while also generating a costmap derived on the local obstacles. An example of the navigation map can be seen in Fig. 9, with the global map being defined by the grey traversable region and black lines defining the walls in the environment. The local elements of the robot's current position on the map is defined with the yellow cube, and the red arrows mark the location of people on the map. The robot's designated movement can also be seen, with the direct path defined by the blue arrow and straight green line.

The trusted motion planner is based on a non-linear model predictive control algorithm developed by Teatro et al. [14]. This algorithm uses the data provided by the slam_toolbox and the move_base stack, i.e. the map, the position of the robot on the map, a cost_map describing local obstacles to avoid, and an absolute path for the robot to reach it's destination. The trusted motion planner uses this information to generate the actual path the robot will take, seen as the red curve in Fig. 9. Turn rates are optimized to avoid obstacles by penalizing turn rates to avoid local obstacles. Therefore, this control algorithm in the trusted motion planner minimizes the path error between the absolute path and the actual path.

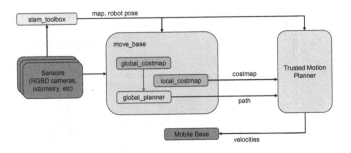

Fig. 10. Navigation architecture

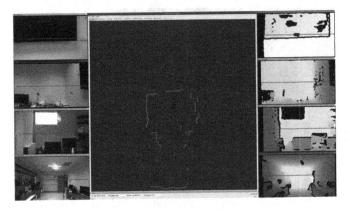

Fig. 11. 2D occupancy map (centre) along with the regular video feed (left) and depth maps (right)

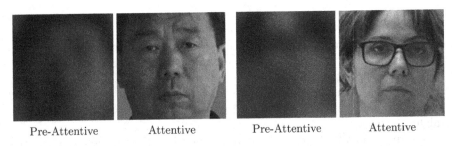

Pre-Attentive   Attentive   Pre-Attentive   Attentive

Fig. 12. Faces at pre-attentive and attentive resolution.

5   Experiments

5.1   Vision-related Experiments

We experimented on the ranges at which our couple camera system is able to perform at. Within 4.5 m, our attentive camera is not necessary for our vision algorithms, as the pre-attentive cameras are capable at performing everything for object detection and face detection even with the lower resolution due to the close range. At greater than 4.5 m, the pre-attentive cameras are still capable and most appropriate for object detection, up to a calculated 118 m. In turn, our attentive camera is used for face detection for ranges from 4.5 m to our expected maximum range of object detection at 118 m, as well as face recognition and attribute estimation due to the high resolution image capture at long range.

5.2   Attentive Sensor Demonstration

In this section, we demonstrate the use of our attentive sensor design to acquire high resolution facial imagery. People detected in the panoramic pre-attentive video form attentive targets, fixated by rotating the mirror to deflect gaze to the azimuth of the corresponding bounding box. Figure 12 shows pre-attentive facial crops from the top of the bounding box of successfully detected people as well as the resulting high-resolution attentive face images. It is clear that the higher attentive resolution provides enormous advantage for facial understanding.

5.3   Social Navigation Demonstration

Next we demonstrate the robot's current capacity to navigate an area by identifying people, selecting a person and then approaching the person selected.

In Fig. 13 we have a view of the navigation stack, executive control function and the RGB feeds of the four cameras. In the first image we see the transition from idle to selecting state and the navigation map it generated from this starting position. It has all individuals in each camera identified, and makes its first selection. This selection process is based on familiar faces that is preloaded on the robot. It transitions out of the selection process and approaches the first person in the approach state. The navigation stack marks a direct path, and begins adjusting the velocities of the mobile base to turn and approach the selected person. The bottom image has the robot in the engagement state. The engaging state indicates a completion of approach, however this state will expand and allow social interaction as needed by the use case. The robot will reselect and re-approach as needed, or more back to the idle position if there is no one else to approach.

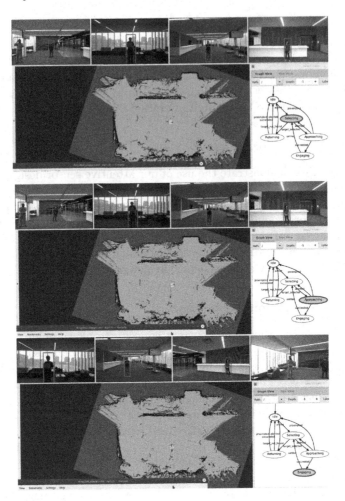

Fig. 13. GUI demonstrating the navigation map, state machine and RGB view of the robot. State machine transitions to each state, from selecting a person (top), approaching (middle), engaging (bottom).

6   Conclusion

In this work we have validated a sensorimotor design for social robotics, demonstrating how attentive sensing can be used to extend the range of social awareness, much in the way humans can make sense of a social scene through a series of strategic saccades. As an example, we have explored a scenario in which a person of interest has been identified and attentive sensing is used in conjunction with person detection to obtain face images of sufficient resolution to positively identify the presence of the person of interest in the scene. This initiates our navigation and tracking strategy which allows us to approach and ultimately interact with the person of interest. Future work will provide more quantitative validation of this attentive sensing strategy.

Acknowledgement. The authors would like to thank Michael Pickering (Cloud Constable) and Tim Teatro (Ontario Tech University) for helpful comments. This research was conducted as part of the SentryNet project led by Prof. Michael Jenkin (York University) and funded by the Canadian IDEaS program.

References

1. Bandera, J., Marfil, R., Palomino, A., Bandera, A., Vázquez-Martín, R.: Visual perception system for a social robot. In: 2010 IEEE Conference on Robotics, Automation and Mechatronics, pp. 243–249 (2010). https://doi.org/10.1109/RAMECH. 2010.5513182
2. Bartolozzi, C., Mandloi, N.K., Indiveri, G.: Attentive motion sensor for mobile robotic applications. In: 2011 IEEE International Symposium of Circuits and Systems (ISCAS), pp. 2813–2816 (2011). https://doi.org/10.1109/ISCAS.2011. 5938190
3. Colombini, E.L., Ribeiro, C.H.C.: An attentive multi-sensor based system for mobile robotics. In: 2012 IEEE International Conference on Systems, Man, and Cybernetics (SMC), pp. 1509–1514 (2012). https://doi.org/10.1109/ICSMC.2012. 6377949
4. Colombini, E.L., da Silva Simões, A., Costa Ribeiro, C.H.: An attentional model for autonomous mobile robots. IEEE Syst. J. **11**(3), 1308–1319 (2017). https:// doi.org/10.1109/JSYST.2015.2499304
5. Elder, J.H., Hou, Y., Prince, S.D., Sizinstev, M.: Pre-attentive face detection for foveated wide-field surveillance. In: Applications of Computer Vision and the IEEE Workshop on Motion and Video Computing, IEEE Workshop on, vol. 1, pp. 439–446. IEEE Computer Society, Los Alamitos, CA, USA (2005). https:// doi.org/10.1109/ACVMOT.2005.95, https://doi.ieeecomputersociety.org/10.1109/ ACVMOT.2005.95
6. Elder, J.H., Prince, S.J.D., Hou, Y., Sizintsev, M., Olevskiy, E.: Pre-attentive and attentive detection of humans in wide-field scenes. Int. J. Comput. Vis. **72**(1), 47–66 (2007). https://doi.org/10.1007/s11263-006-8892-7
7. Madhusanka, B., Jayasekara, A.: Design and development of adaptive vision attentive robot eye for service robot in domestic environment. In: 2016 IEEE International Conference on Information and Automation for Sustainability (ICIAfS), pp. 1–6 (2016). https://doi.org/10.1109/ICIAFS.2016.7946529
8. Prince, S., Elder, J., Hou, Y., Sizinstev, M., Olevsky, E.: Towards face recognition at a distance. In: Crime and Security. The Institution of Engineering and Technology Conference, pp. 570–575 (2006). https://doi.org/10.1049/ic:20060363
9. Prince, S., Elder, J., Hou, Y., Sizintsev, M., Olevskiy, Y.: Statistical cue integration for foveated wide-field surveillance. In: 2005 IEEE Computer Society Conference on Computer Vision and Pattern Recognition (CVPR 2005), vol. 2, pp. 603–610 (2005). https://doi.org/10.1109/CVPR.2005.333
10. Quigley, M., et al.: ROS: an open-source robot operating system. In: ICRA Workshop on Open Source Software (2009)
11. Redmon, J., Farhadi, A.: YOLOv3: an incremental improvement (2018). 10.48550/ARXIV.1804.02767. https://arxiv.org/abs/1804.02767

12. Serengil, S.I., Ozpinar, A.: Lightface: a hybrid deep face recognition framework. In: 2020 Innovations in Intelligent Systems and Applications Conference (ASYU), pp. 23–27. IEEE (2020). https://doi.org/10.1109/ASYU50717.2020.9259802
13. Serengil, S.I., Ozpinar, A.: Hyperextended lightface: a facial attribute analysis framework. In: 2021 International Conference on Engineering and Emerging Technologies (ICEET), pp. 1–4. IEEE (2021). https://doi.org/10.1109/ICEET53442.2021.9659697
14. Teatro, T.A.V., Eklund, J.M., Milman, R.: Nonlinear model predictive control for omnidirectional robot motion planning and tracking with avoidance of moving obstacles. Can. J. Electr. Comput. Eng. **37**(3), 151–156 (2014). https://doi.org/10.1109/CJECE.2014.2328973
15. Wojke, N., Bewley, A.: Deep cosine metric learning for person re-identification. In: 2018 IEEE Winter Conference on Applications of Computer Vision (WACV), pp. 748–756. IEEE (2018). https://doi.org/10.1109/WACV.2018.00087
16. Wojke, N., Bewley, A., Paulus, D.: Simple online and realtime tracking with a deep association metric. In: 2017 IEEE International Conference on Image Processing (ICIP), pp. 3645–3649. IEEE (2017). https://doi.org/10.1109/ICIP.2017.8296962

3rd Workshop on Applied Multimodal Affect Recognition (AMAR)

Workshop on Artificial Intelligence for Multimedia Forensics and Disinformation Detection

Deliberate manipulations of multimedia content for malicious purposes have been a prevailing problem. With the phenomenal leap of AI and deep learning in recent years, realistically forged multimedia data is being used to propagate disinformation and fake news. This phenomenon is impacting social justice at the personal level and major political campaigns and national security at the national level. Moreover, it is affecting the stability of international relationships at the global level. The Workshop on Artificial Intelligence for Multimedia Forensics and Disinformation Detection (AI4MFDD) is intended to disseminate recent developments in AI-enabled multimedia forensics and disinformation detection. Multimedia data carry not only the value of their content but also their value in digital forensics for combating crimes and fraudulent activities, including disinformation.

AI4MFDD 2022 is the first edition of this workshop and was organized in conjunction with the 2022 International Conference on Pattern Recognition. The workshop received over 20 submissions. The top eight papers were selected for a presentation covering a wide range of topics, including deep fake detection, image watermarking, and source camera identification. The participants included researchers from eight countries: the USA, the UK, Australia, Italy, France, Switzerland, Austria, and India.

AI4MFDD 2022 included two keynote speakers: Prof. Anderson Rocha, from the University of Campinas, Brazil, and Dr. Pavel Korshunov, from the IDIAP Research Institute, Switzerland. Prof. Rocha's talk highlighted the main challenges in digital forensics and how AI is helping to tackle them. Dr. Korshunov's talk summarized how deep fakes are created and the difficulties in detecting them by using AI.

The success of this first edition of AI4MFDD set the basis for the organization of future editions.

Victor Sanchez
Chang-Tsun Li

The Effect of Model Compression on Fairness in Facial Expression Recognition

Samuil Stoychev$^{(\boxtimes)}$ and Hatice Gunes(ID)

Department of Computer Science and Technology, University of Cambridge,
Cambridge, UK
ss2719@cantab.ac.uk, hatice.gunes@cl.cam.ac.uk

Abstract. Deep neural networks are computationally expensive which has motivated the development of model compression techniques to reduce the resource consumption. Nevertheless, recent studies have suggested that model compression can have an adverse effect on algorithmic fairness, amplifying existing biases in machine learning models. With this work we aim to extend those studies to the context of facial expression recognition. To do that, we set up a neural network classifier to perform facial expression recognition and implement several model compression techniques on top of it. We then run experiments on two facial expression datasets, namely the Extended Cohn-Kanade Dataset (CK+DB) and the Real-World Affective Faces Database (RAF-DB), to examine the individual and combined effect that compression techniques have on the model size, accuracy and fairness. Our experimental results show that: (i) Compression and quantisation achieve significant reduction in model size with minimal impact on overall accuracy for both CK+ DB and RAF-DB; (ii) in terms of model accuracy, the classifier trained and tested on RAF-DB is more robust to compression compared to the CK+ DB; and (iii) for RAF-DB, the different compression strategies do not increase the gap in predictive performance across the sensitive attributes of gender, race and age which is in contrast with the results on the CK+ DB where compression seems to amplify existing biases for gender.

Keywords: Facial Expression Recognition · Fairness · Model Compression

1 Introduction

Recent years have seen *deep neural networks* (DNNs) achieve state-of-the-art performance on a variety of problems including face recognition [33], cancer detection [22], natural language processing [22], etc. Deep learning has proved particularly effective at extracting meaningful representations from raw data [35]. However, as the predictive performance of deep neural networks has increased, so has the size of deep learning architectures: Modern DNNs can consist of hundreds of millions of parameters [9], making them slow to train and hard

© Springer Nature Switzerland AG 2023
J.-J. Rousseau and B. Kapralos (Eds.): ICPR 2022 Workshops, LNCS 13646, pp. 121–138, 2023.
https://doi.org/10.1007/978-3-031-37745-7_9

to store. Deep learning's growing computational cost has made it hard to deploy deep learning models on resource-constrained devices (e.g. mobile phones, robots, microcontrollers) which often lack the storage, memory or processing power to support large DNNs [19,23,37]. The high resource consumption associated with deep learning models has also been problematic in the light of initiatives such as the "Green-AI" [34,38] movement advocating for a reduction in the carbon emissions and the environmental impact associated with artificial intelligence. This has given rise to the development of *model compression* strategies, which aim to reduce the size of deep learning models. Examples of model compression techniques include *pruning* [47], *quantisation* [19], *weight clustering* [16], etc.

However, a couple of recent studies have suggested that, by reducing the network capacity of the DNNs, model compression can amplify existing biases: Hooker et al. [18] demonstrate that pruning and post-training quantisation can amplify biases when classifying hair colour on CelebA DB. This issue is also raised in a study by Paganini [32] who discusses the effect of pruning on algorithmic fairness.

With this work, we aim to extend the aforementioned studies to the task of *facial expression recognition* (FER) where the model has to classify expressions based on images of human faces. To this end, we train FER models using the CK+ DB and the RAF-DB, and implement three compression strategies (pruning, weight clustering and post-training quantisation) on top of them. We then evaluate and compare the performance of the baseline models against the performance of the compressed models, and analyse the results to address three research questions: **RQ1: *"How effective is model compression for FER?"*** That is, can compression techniques achieve a considerable reduction in the model size, while preserving a high level of predictive accuracy? **RQ2: *"Do model compression techniques amplify biases?"*** Here we seek to verify the claims by Paganini and Hooker et al. across a wider variety of compression techniques and in the context of FER. **RQ3: *"Is the impact on fairness identical across different compression techniques?"*** We investigate whether all compression strategies amplify biases to the same extent.

This study extends the previous works by Paganini and Hooker et al. in three directions:

– **Extending the problem to FER:** We consider the problem of compression's effect on fairness in the context of affective computing, and in particular facial expression recognition. By comparison, the study by Hooker et al. is based on classifying hair colour on CelebA [28], and the study by Paganini considers object recognition and digit classification tasks.
– **Considering a variety of model compression techniques:** Our study involves three compression strategies (pruning, weight clustering and post-training quantisation) - one more by Hooker et al. (who consider pruning and post-training quantisation), and two more by the study by Paganini, which focuses solely on pruning.
– **Considering the combined effect of compression techniques:** The previous studies only examined the individual behaviour of compression tech-

niques. In practice, compression techniques are often combined together to form the so-called *"compression pipelines"* [16], therefore we consider the combinations of pruning with quantisation and weight clustering with quantisation.

2   Background

2.1   Algorithmic Fairness

Nowadays, machine learning algorithms are used to inform or automate decision-making across various fields of high social importance. Machine learning approaches have been used for automating recruitment in large companies [44], assigning credit scores [25,45] and anticipating criminal activity [17] to name a few.

The increasing impact of machine learning on our society has highlighted the importance of *algorithmic fairness*. An algorithm is considered to be fair if its behaviour is not improperly influenced by sensitive attributes (e.g., a person's gender or race) [31]. Nevertheless, recent studies have exposed the propensity of algorithms to be unfair and exhibit dangerous *biases*, potentially *"reinforcing the discriminatory practices in society"* [5]. For example, Amazon's AI recruitment tool has been reported to favour male applicants over female applicants [12]. Apple's credit score has also been shown to systematically disadvantage women [1]. A study by Joy Buolamwini has demonstrated that popular facial analysis services perform disproportionately poorly on dark-skinned females [8].

The increasing awareness of algorithmic biases has given rise to multiple fairness initiatives such the Algorithmic Justice League [20], IBM's AI Fairness 360 [2] and Google's ML Fairness [36]. Research into fairness in FER has also started gaining momentum (e.g., [41]) and Cheong et al. provided an overview and techniques for achieving fairness in facial affect recognition but they do not consider the effects of model compression on fairness [11].

2.2   Model Compression Techniques

Quantisation. Quantisation is a popular compression method which can significantly reduce the size of the model, leading to savings in storage and memory [10]. The key idea behind quantisation is sacrificing precision for efficiency - while most standard DNN implementations represent weights and activations using the `float32` datatype, quantisation allows to represent those values using a smaller data type - normally `float16` or `int8` [27]. Quantisation can either be introduced *during* training (also known as *quantisation-aware training*), or it can be applied to a pre-trained model, which is known as *post-training quantisation* [30]. In our experiments, we consider post-training quantisation to the `int8` type.

Pruning. Weight pruning is another compression strategy which can greatly reduce the size of a DNN [27] by eliminating redundant weights which contribute little to the behaviour of the model. Pruning reduces the density of the neural network, making it more lightweight and easier to compress by traditional compression tools such as `zip`. Which weights get pruned is dictated by the pruning strategy. The most popular approach is *magnitude-based pruning* [7] that eliminates the weights with the lowest absolute value - i.e., the ones whose values are the closest to zero. The proportion of weights that need to be pruned is called the pruning *sparsity* - for example, pruning at 90% sparsity would remove 90% of the connections in a given network.

Weight Clustering. Weight clustering (i.e. *weight sharing* [16]) reduces the size of the model by grouping together weights of similar values. Clustering reduces the model size for two reasons: First, float values only need to be stored to represent the n centroid values. Meanwhile, the entire weight matrix is replaced with pull indices, each index represented by the smaller integer type. And second, the resulting pull indices are more likely to contain repeating values, making standard compression tools (e.g., `zip`) more effective.

3   Implementation

3.1   Data

We use two popular FER datasets for our experiments, CK+ DB [29] and RAF-DB [26], because they are of different nature, and we can get access to the labels not only for expressions but also for sensitive attributes.

Extended Cohn-Kanade Dataset. The Extended Cohn-Kanade Dataset (CK+) has been widely used in the context of facial expression recognition [6,43]. It contains 327 labelled image sequences across 123 unique subjects, expressing one of 8 basic emotions - *"neutral"*, *"anger"*, *"contempt"*, *"disgust"*, *"fear"*, *"happy"*, *"sadness"* and *"surprise"*. Images have been obtained in a controlled lab environment with subjects facing the camera.

In order to examine bias, we need annotations of demographic attributes. CK+ does not provide any annotations in that respect, so we manually annotate all 123 subjects based on their gender appearance. According to our annotation, the dataset consists of 84 female subjects and 39 male subjects.

For each sequence in the dataset, we take the first frame to represent a neutral emotion, and the last 3 frames to represent the emotion which the sequence was annotated with (e.g. "happy", "sad", etc.). That is a common pre-processing step since CK+ sequences *"are from the neutral face to the peak expression"* according to the dataset's documentation. We then use the `dlib` library to detect the faces of the subjects and crop the images around them.

For validation purposes, we split the original CK+ dataset into a *train* and *test* dataset. We use cross-subject validation, allocating 86 subjects to the train dataset and the other 37 to the test dataset. That gives us 924 images in total in the train dataset and 384 images in the test dataset. The train and test dataset follow a similar distribution with respect to the emotion labels. Several data transformations are applied to the images using TensorFlow's `ImageDataGenerator`. Images are scaled down to 48 × 48 pixels and converted to grayscale (since CK+ contains some RGB images). To compensate for the relatively small size of the dataset, we augment the data by applying random horizontal flipping and random rotation in the range $[-10°, 10°]$.

Real-World Affective Faces Database. The Real-World Affective Faces Database (RAF-DB) [26] is another dataset of human faces which has been commonly used in the field of FER [40,42]. It provides 15,339 RGB images of human faces, aligned into squares of 100 × 100 pixels. Each image depicts one of seven basic emotions: *"surprise"*, *"fear"*, *"disgust"*, *"happiness"*, *"sadness"*, *"anger"* and *"neutral"*. Unlike CK+ images, RAF-DB images are *"in-the-wild"* - they have not been recorded in a controlled environment, emotions are expressed more subtly, lighting can vary and faces may be obfuscated. Additionally, the RAF-DB dataset provides labels across three demographic categories - gender, race and age. We form the train and test dataset preserving the original split defined by the authors [26]. This gives us 12,271 training images and 3,068 test images.

3.2 Baseline Models

We implement one FER classifier per dataset to serve as baseline to which we will apply the compression strategies. The neural architecture is inspired by a study by Goodfellow et al. [14] and contains 4 convolutional layers, followed by 2 hidden fully-connected layers (with pooling and dropout layers in-between). The exact model architecture is illustrated in Table 4 of the Appendix. At the time of its publication, the architecture achieved a then state-of-the-art performance of around 65% on the FER-2013 dataset [3,14].

We compile the baseline models using an Adam optimiser [21] and a categorical cross-entropy loss [15]. We train each model for 20 iterations keeping track of training and validation accuracy, and training and validation loss. Figures 7 and 8 in the Appendix show that validation loss stops decreasing before the 20th iteration. At every iteration, we store the "best" weights observed so far (i.e., the ones associated with the highest validation accuracy).

3.3 Model Compression Implementation

We implement three model compression strategies - magnitude-based weight pruning, post-training quantisation and weight clustering. To do this, we make use of TensorFlow's *Model Optimization Toolkit*. After applying each compression technique, we store the model on disk and compress it using the `zip` compression tool so that we are able to observe the change in size that quantisation has introduced.

Quantisation. We convert the pre-trained Keras baseline to a TFLite model and apply the default TFLite optimisation strategy which reduces the model representation to 8 bits.

Pruning. We apply pruning using TFLite's `ConstantSparsity` prnuing schedule. Our implementation is parameterised by the pruning sparsity - we observe the effect of this parameter on compression. After pruning has been applied, we fine-tune the pruned model for 2 iterations as suggested by the TFLite documentation.

Weight Clustering. We implement weight clustering using TFLite's `cluster_weights` module and parameterise it by the number of clusters.

Combined Compression. Additionally, our implementation allows applying quantisation on top of a pruned or a weight clustered model. This gives us two additional "hybrid" compression strategies - *pruning with quantisation*, and *weight clustering with quantisation*.

4   Experiments

4.1   Metrics

In our experiments, we compare the uncompressed baseline model against compressed versions of it using a number of metrics:

- **Model size** - that is the size of the model on disk in megabytes. This metric measures how effective a compression strategy is in reducing the storage requirement of the model since all three compression techniques are primarily used to reduce storage consumption.
- **Overall accuracy** - this is the overall accuracy a model achieves on the test dataset. We use this metric as an indicator of how compression has impacted predictive accuracy.
- **Gender/race/age accuracy** - we adopt the fairness definition of *overall accuracy equality* [39] which states that *a fair algorithm should have the same predictive accuracy regardless of any underlying sensitive attributes.* To express this formally, assume we have a facial expression recognition model that aims to predict a subject's true expression Y by producing a prediction $\hat{Y}$. Let us consider the subject's *gender*, which can be denoted by G and be equal to either m (male) or f (female). In that case, we expect that a fair model would have the following property:

$$P(Y = \hat{Y}|G = m) = P(Y = \hat{Y}|G = f) \tag{1}$$

That is, we expect that a fair FER model would classify the expressions of male and female subjects with the same accuracy, and we call this gender accuracy. *Race* and *age* accuracy are calculated in a similar manner.

4.2   CK+ Experiments

Baseline Performance. The baseline model reports an overall accuracy of **67.96%** on the test dataset. We measure the baseline's size in the same way we measure the size of the compressed models. and we find that the baseline's model size on disk is around **16.51 megabytes**. We find that the female accuracy of the baseline model is **67.08%** and the male accuracy is **69.44%**. This is interesting because the CK+ dataset is imbalanced in favour of female subjects and therefore we would expect the baseline model to classify females more accurately. One reason why the classifier might perform slightly better on male faces is the slight difference in the distribution of emotions across males and females in CK+ - for instance, only 2.1% of male subjects have expressed "contempt" while female subjects have expressed this emotion more than twice more frequently (5.02%). If contempt is an emotion that is inherently harder to classify, then this difference could translate into a minor advantage for classifying male subjects. In any case, though, the gap between male and female accuracy is too minor to conclude the baseline model is biased.

Quantisation Results. We evaluate quantisation by quantising the baseline model 3 times and reporting the mean values for each metric. After applying quantisation to the baseline model, we observe a 4× reduction in the model size as illustrated in Fig. 6 in the Appendix. Moreover, this compression comes at no cost - there is no change in the predictive accuracy or fairness: Overall accuracy, female and male accuracy have all remained identical to those of the baseline model. Quantisation therefore preserves the fairness and predictive accuracy of the model.

Pruning Results. We evaluate the pruning strategy at 6 different levels of sparsity: 10%, 20%, 30%, 40%, 50% and 60% (we do not consider higher levels of sparsity as those result in impractically low model accuracies). For each level of sparsity, we prune the baseline model three times and report the mean values for each metric. We observe the trade-off that pruning sparsity introduces in Fig. 1: As sparsity increases, the model size decreases linearly, reducing the model size by a half at 60% sparsity. However, high sparsity also reduces the network capacity which can impact the accuracy of the model [32]. We can see in Fig. 1 (b) that overall accuracy steadily starts to decrease at 40% and 50% sparsity before plummeting at 60%. Except for the considerable drop of accuracy at 60% sparsity, though, we can conclude that pruning has had little impact on overall accuracy.

Despite the minor drop in overall accuracy, we find that pruning has dramatically increased the discrepancy between female and male accuracy: Table 1 shows that pruning the model tends to keep male accuracy high (in fact, male accuracy has increased for all sparsities up to 50%) while deteriorating female accuracy (which has dropped by 7.22% at 50% sparsity). Interestingly, pruning at 60% actually reports better female than male accuracy. However, at 60%

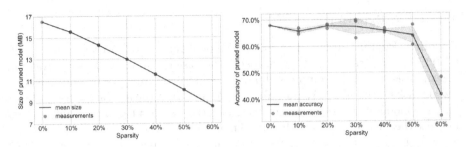

Fig. 1. CK+ DB model size (left) and accuracy (right) after pruning.

sparsity both male and female accuracy are too low for such a model to be of practical use. Those results are in agreement with the study by Hooker et al., which finds that *"minimal changes to overall accuracy hide disproportionately high errors"* [18] in subgroups.

As mentioned previously, we are also interested in the "combined" effect of compression techniques. To this end, we apply quantisation on top of the pruned models. We find that quantisation can greatly enhance the compression effect of pruning: Quantising the pruned models has decreased their size by a further 3.5 times on average. Meanwhile, quantisation has not changed the overall accuracy, male or female accuracy of the pruned models by more than 1%.

Table 1. Pruning's effect on fairness for CK+ DB.

Sparsity	Female accuracy	Male accuracy	Gap
0% (baseline)	67.08%	69.44%	2.36%
10%	59.86%	75.46%	**15.60%**
20%	62.77%	75.69%	12.92%
30%	62.36%	75.69%	13.33%
40%	63.47%	69.67%	6.20%
50%	59.86%	71.06%	11.20%
60%	44.02%	36.34%	7.68%

Weight Clustering Results. We evaluate weight clustering with 4, 8, 16, 32, 64 and 128 clusters. For each number of clusters, we run weight clustering 3 times and report the mean values for each metric. Similar to pruning, the "number of clusters" parameter introduces a size-accuracy trade-off illustrated in Fig. 2. Decreasing the number of clusters rapidly decreases the baseline model size (shrinking it by almost 14 times at 4 clusters). However, an excessively low number of clusters can decrease accuracy dramatically (with overall accuracy dropping below 45% at 4 clusters). Despite that, we can see that keeping the number of clusters sufficiently high (between 8 and 128) preserves overall accuracy close to the baseline accuracy of 67.96%, while offering a lucrative reduction in model size.

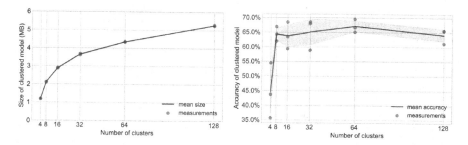

Fig. 2. CK+ DB model size (left) and overall accuracy (right) after weight clustering.

Just like with pruning, though, the overall accuracy of the clustered models is deceptive as it hides an increasing gap between male and female accuracy. Table 2 shows that the baseline 2.36% gap has increased massively, reaching 19.77% in favour of male subjects at 16 clusters. Applying quantisation to the clustered models reduces their size by a further 17% on average - a much smaller reduction than was observed for pruning. Again, though, quantisation comes at no cost for accuracy or fairness - overall accuracy, male accuracy and female accuracy have all stayed within 1.5% of the values for the clustered models.

Table 2. Weight clustering's effect on fairness for CK+ DB.

# of clusters	Female accuracy	Male accuracy	Gap
4	43.05%	47.22%	4.17%
8	59.30%	72.91%	13.61%
16	56.38%	76.15%	**19.77%**
32	60.55%	72.68%	12.13%
64	60.27%	78.47%	18.20%
128	59.16%	72.45%	13.29%

4.3 RAF-DB Experiments

Baseline Performance. The baseline model has a size of **29.80 MB** and reports overall test accuracy of **82.46%** (see Table 3), which seems acceptable given that much larger, state-of-the-art architectures have reported between 86%

and 89% on this dataset [46]. In terms of fairness, the classifier seems to classify female subjects slightly more accurately than male subjects, and African-American subjects better than Caucasian or Asian subjects. However, those differences are minor. A more major classification gap is observed with respect to the age attribute where there is a 19% classification gap between the best classified age group (A0 or 0–3 years old) and the worst classified age group (A4 or 70+ years old). This could be due to the age of the face playing an important role for facial expression decoding, and factors such as lower expressivity and age-related changes in the face may lower decoding accuracy for older faces [13].

Table 3. RAF-DB experiment results in terms of accuracy(%). "+ Q" indicates that quanitsation has been applied and "Ov. acc." stands for *Overall accuracy*. "Female" and "Male" indicate accuracies for female and male subjects. "Cauc.", "Af.-Am." and "Asian" denote accuracies for subjects labelled as Caucasian, African-American and Asian. "A0" to "A4" indicate accuracies across the 5 age groups, 0–3, 4–19, 20–39, 40–69 and 70+.

Model	Size	Ov. acc.	Female	Male	Cauc.	Af.-Am.	Asian	A0	A1	A2	A3	A4
baseline	29.80	82.46	83.33	80.54	81.92	86.75	83.02	89.96	82.92	80.44	85.85	70.78
quantised	6.56	82.46	83.20	80.70	81.92	86.75	83.02	89.96	82.92	80.50	85.65	70.78
prun (10)	28.15	79.51	80.04	78.64	79.00	81.90	80.88	82.57	82.64	78.53	79.88	67.41
prun (20)	26.01	78.30	78.72	77.47	78.10	80.19	78.32	82.16	79.35	77.47	79.34	67.79
prun (30)	23.65	80.84	81.37	79.69	80.44	84.33	81.09	85.51	82.71	78.90	84.32	70.03
prun (40)	21.09	81.38	81.95	79.93	80.97	84.04	82.10	88.34	82.78	79.56	83.79	68.53
prun (50)	18.41	81.11	81.83	79.47	80.85	84.33	80.81	87.03	82.85	79.18	83.59	71.91
prun (60)	15.63	81.64	82.53	79.82	81.18	83.76	82.88	87.03	82.57	80.42	82.73	73.40
prun (10) + Q	6.44	79.54	80.06	78.62	79.05	81.90	80.74	82.67	82.57	78.58	79.94	67.04
prun (20) + Q	6.29	78.32	78.68	77.58	78.16	80.19	78.19	82.06	79.49	77.45	79.54	67.41
prun (30) + Q	6.03	80.85	81.44	79.58	80.50	84.33	80.88	85.71	82.78	78.92	84.19	69.66
prun (40) + Q	5.55	81.46	82.05	79.98	81.05	84.04	82.19	88.34	82.78	79.68	83.86	68.53
prun (50) + Q	5.02	81.04	81.83	79.47	80.78	84.33	80.67	87.03	82.71	79.18	83.20	72.28
prun (60) + Q	4.38	81.64	82.46	79.90	81.19	83.76	82.81	86.93	82.51	80.42	82.86	73.40
clust (4 cl)	1.88	79.22	79.71	78.08	79.05	79.05	80.12	85.61	81.55	76.93	81.80	71.16
clust (8 cl)	2.94	80.18	80.39	79.34	79.75	81.48	81.64	85.10	81.61	78.68	82.27	70.41
clust (16 cl)	4.35	76.54	77.44	75.02	75.92	78.77	78.46	80.64	79.21	75.15	78.55	61.42
clust (32 cl)	5.77	80.56	80.94	79.42	80.13	82.62	81.64	86.32	82.30	78.90	82.60	69.28
clust (64 cl)	7.03	78.03	78.00	77.55	77.38	81.48	79.50	82.97	79.90	76.07	80.94	69.66
clust (128 cl)	8.39	81.27	81.83	80.19	80.77	82.62	83.09	86.72	82.85	79.82	83.06	69.66
clust (4 cl) + Q	1.39	77.89	78.76	76.32	77.62	78.49	78.88	82.57	79.56	76.11	81.07	66.66
clust (8 cl) + Q	2.29	79.97	80.02	79.37	79.46	82.33	81.29	84.80	81.41	78.49	82.33	68.53
clust (16 cl) + Q	3.53	76.44	77.22	74.99	75.86	78.34	78.32	80.54	79.35	75.23	77.49	62.17
clust (32 cl) + Q	4.71	80.62	81.13	79.47	80.15	83.04	81.78	85.71	82.57	79.30	81.80	69.28
clust (64 cl) + Q	5.52	78.00	78.02	77.52	77.37	80.62	79.84	82.57	79.83	76.15	81.07	68.53
clust (128 cl) + Q	5.89	81.13	81.68	80.09	80.74	82.19	82.53	86.01	82.71	79.76	83.20	68.53

Quantisation Results. Figure 6 in the Appendix shows the size of the RAF-DB classifier before and after applying quantisation. We observe that applying quantisation to the baseline classifier reduces the size of the model by around 4.5

times, from 29.80 MB down to 6.56 MB. At the same time, applying quantisation does not impact the predictive performance of the classifier. Table 3 shows that none of the per-class accuracies have changed by more than 0.2%.

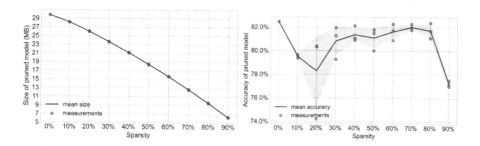

Fig. 3. RAF-DB model size (left) and accuracy (right) after pruning.

Pruning Results. Pruning results are presented in Table 3. Similar to the CK+ experiments, we observe that applying pruning to the RAF-DB classifier translates to a linear reduction in model size as illustrated in Fig. 3. Unlike the CK+ classifier though, the accuracy of the RAF-DB model seems to be much more robust to pruning. Even at 80% sparsity, the overall accuracy has only dropped down to 81.73% compared to the baseline (82.46%). Only when sparsity increases to 90% do we observe a more significant drop in accuracy down to 77.23%. The RAF-DB model is therefore more akin to models such as MNIST classifiers [4] where near-optimal accuracy can be preserved even at 99% sparsity. There is no evidence suggesting that sparsity has negatively impacted fariness across any attribute. For instance, the original 2.8% classification gap in gender classification only varies between 0.2% and 2.7% depending on the sparsity level (Fig. 4).

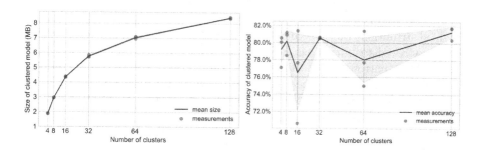

Fig. 4. RAF-DB model size (left) and accuracy (right) after weight clustering.

Weight Clustering Results. Figure 3 shows pruning's effect on model size and accuracy for RAF-DB. In terms of model accuracy, the classifier trained and tested on RAF-DB seems more robust to compression compared to the CK+ experiments. Regardless of the level of sparsity or the number of clusters of the compression strategy, the overall accuracy of the compressed model does not fall below 77%.

5   Discussion

We analysed and compared the effect of model compression on model size, accuracy and fairness in the context of FER on two facial expression datasets. We revisit our research questions:

- **RQ1:** *"How effective is model compression for FER?"* We saw that model compression can dramatically reduce the storage requirements of both FER models. Quantisation alone achieves around $4 - 4.5\times$ reduction in model sizes with minimal impact on overall accuracy for both datasets. Both pruning and clustering progressively decrease the model size on disk as sparsity increases. In terms of model accuracy, the classifier trained and tested on RAF-DB seems more robust to compression compared.
- **RQ2:** *"Do model compression techniques amplify biases?"* Our findings for CK+ DB confirm the claims by previous studies that model compression can amplify existing biases for gender. However our findings for RAF-DB indicate that sparsity does not impact fairness in terms of gender, race or age negatively.
- **RQ3:** *"Is the impact on fairness identical across different compression techniques?"* Our results for CK+ DB suggest that different compression techniques tend to have a highly distinct impact on fairness: Post-training quantisation has no visible effect on baseline fairness. Meanwhile, pruning and weight clustering can severely amplify biases, increasing the initial 2.36% gap between male and female accuracy to 15.60% and 19.77% respectively. On the other hand for RAF-DB we find that the different compression strategies do not seem to increase the gap in predictive performance across any of the three demographic attributes (gender, race and age).

In order to understand the reasons for the different findings, we compare the weight distributions of CK+ and RAF-DB before pruning (See Fig. 5). We see that the CK+ distribution has a 'wider' shape compared to the RAF-DB which is much more 'narrow' and most of its values are located close to its mean at 0.00. As a result, when we prune the two models, we get gaps of different sizes. For the 'wide' CK+ distribution, when we prune at 60%, we need to set 'crop' or zero-out 60% of its weights. However, the CK+ weights are relatively evenly distributed and most of them are located at some (relative) distance from the 0.00 mean. As a result, we need to 'crop' weights which are not located immediately around the centre and that causes a wide gap in the middle. We can expect that a large gap will have a bigger impact on predictive performance since it means values which are further from 0.00 have been set to 0.00. Meanwhile, for the RAF-DB the resulting gap is much smaller. This is because the original distribution is much more 'narrow' in terms of shape with a big share of the weights located at or close to 0.00. Therefore, when we prune at 60%, the 60% of the weights which we set to 0.00 are going to be already equal to or close to 0.00 and therefore we can expect a minor impact on predictive performance.

6   Limitations and Future Work

This work has several limitations. First, the gender annotation of the CK+ dataset was performed manually, labels could be obtained via a crowdsourcing experiment. Second, our baseline model is deliberately selected as a relatively small architecture that could be trained, fine-tuned and evaluated locally. Given more time and computational resources the study could be extended to consider a larger and more modern architecture. This work could also be extended by employing other compression strategies (e.g., quantisation-aware training and various forms of weight sharing [24]) and exploring other system metrics (latency, memory consumption).

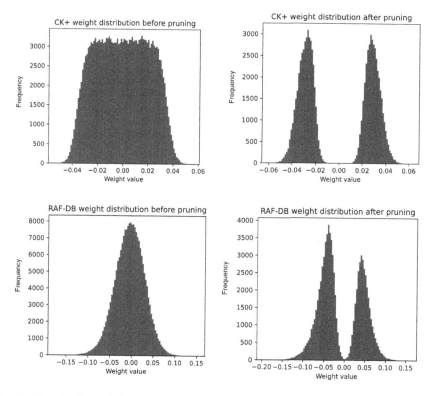

Fig. 5. Distribution of the kernel weights of the `conv2d` layer of the CK+ (top) and RAF-DB (bottom) classifier before (left) and after (right) pruning at 60%.

Acknowledgments. H. Gunes is supported by the EPSRC under grant ref. EP/R030782/1. For the purpose of open access, the authors have applied a Creative Commons Attribution (CC BY) licence to any Author Accepted Manuscript version arising.

Data Availability Statement. This study involved secondary analyses of pre-existing datasets. All datasets are described in the text and cited accordingly.

Code Access:. Code for the experiments is available at: https://github.com/samuilstoychev/model-compression-fer.

Appendinx

Table 4. Summary of the architecture of the CK+ baseline model generated using Keras's `model.summary()`. The `None` values indicate the batch size is flexible.

Layer	Output Shape
conv2d	(None, 48, 48, 64)
batch_normalization	(None, 48, 48, 64)
activation	(None, 48, 48, 64)
max_pooling2d	(None, 24, 24, 64)
dropout	(None, 24, 24, 64)
conv2d_1	(None, 24, 24, 128)
batch_normalization_1	(None, 24, 24, 128)
activation_1	(None, 24, 24, 128)
max_pooling2d_1	(None, 12, 12, 128)
dropout_1	(None, 12, 12, 128)
conv2d_2	(None, 12, 12, 512)
batch_normalization_2	(None, 12, 12, 512)
activation_2	(None, 12, 12, 512)
max_pooling2d_2	(None, 6, 6, 512)
dropout_2	(None, 6, 6, 512)
conv2d_3	(None, 6, 6, 512)
batch_normalization_3	(None, 6, 6, 512)
activation_3	(None, 6, 6, 512)
max_pooling2d_3	(None, 3, 3, 512)
dropout_3	(None, 3, 3, 512)
flatten	(None, 4608)
dense	(None, 256)
batch_normalization_4	(None, 256)
activation_4	(None, 256)
dropout_4	(None, 256)
dense_1	(None, 512)
batch_normalization_5	(None, 512)
activation_5	(None, 512)
dropout_5	(None, 512)
dense_2	(None, 8)
Total trainable parameters:	4,479,240

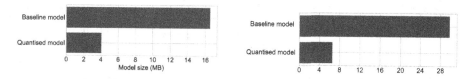

Fig. 6. Size of the CK+ DB (left) and RAF-DB (right) classifiers before and after quantisation.

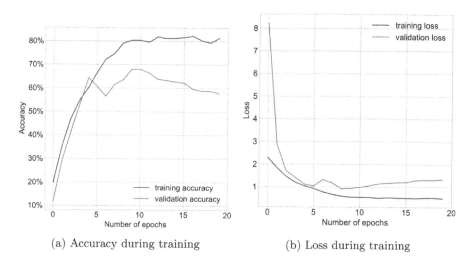

(a) Accuracy during training   (b) Loss during training

Fig. 7. Accuracy and loss during training the baseline CK+ classifier.

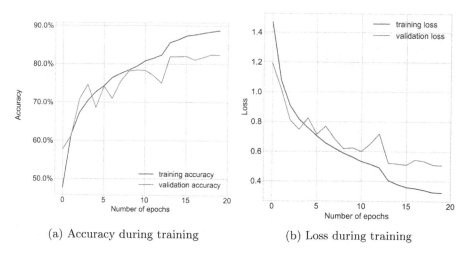

(a) Accuracy during training   (b) Loss during training

Fig. 8. Accuracy and loss during training the baseline RAF-DB classifier.

References

1. Apple's 'sexist' credit card investigated by us regulator, November 2019. https://www.bbc.co.uk/news/business-50365609
2. Introducing AI fairness 360, a step towards trusted AI - IBM research, February 2019. https://www.ibm.com/blogs/research/2018/09/ai-fairness-360/
3. Agrawal, A., Mittal, N.: Using CNN for facial expression recognition: a study of the effects of kernel size and number of filters on accuracy. Vis. Comput. **36**(2), 405–412 (2019). https://doi.org/10.1007/s00371-019-01630-9
4. Alford, S., Robinett, R., Milechin, L., Kepner, J.: Training behavior of sparse neural network topologies. In: 2019 IEEE High Performance Extreme Computing Conference (HPEC), pp. 1–6. IEEE (2019)
5. Barlas, P., Kyriakou, K., Kleanthous, S., Otterbacher, J.: Social b(eye)as: human and machine descriptions of people images. In: Proceedings of the International AAAI Conference on Web and Social Media, vol. 13, no. 01, pp. 583–591, July 2019
6. Bartlett, M., Littlewort, G., Frank, M., Lainscsek, C., Fasel, I., Movellan, J.: Recognizing facial expression: machine learning and application to spontaneous behavior. In: Proceedings of IEEE Conference on Computer Vision and Pattern Recognition, vol. 2, pp. 568–573 (2005)
7. Blalock, D., Ortiz, J.J.G., Frankle, J., Guttag, J.: What is the state of neural network pruning? (2020)
8. Buolamwini, J., Gebru, T.: Gender shades: Intersectional accuracy disparities in commercial gender classification. In: FAT (2018)
9. Capra, M., Bussolino, B., Marchisio, A., Shafique, M., Masera, G., Martina, M.: An updated survey of efficient hardware architectures for accelerating deep convolutional neural networks. Future Internet **12**(7), 113 (2020)
10. Cheng, Y., Wang, D., Zhou, P., Zhang, T.: A survey of model compression and acceleration for deep neural networks. CoRR abs/1710.09282 (2017)
11. Cheong, J., Kalkan, S., Gunes, H.: The hitchhiker's guide to bias and fairness in facial affective signal processing: Overview and techniques. IEEE Signal Process. Mag. **38**(6), 39–49 (2021)
12. Dastin, J.: Amazon scraps secret AI recruiting tool that showed bias against women, October 2018. https://www.reuters.com/article/us-amazon-com-jobs-automation-insight-idUSKCN1MK08G
13. Folster, M., Hess, U., Werheid, K.: Facial age affects emotional expression decoding. Front. Psychol. **5**(30), 1–13 (2014)
14. Goodfellow, I.J., et al.: Challenges in representation learning: a report on three machine learning contests (2013)
15. Gordon-Rodriguez, E., Loaiza-Ganem, G., Pleiss, G., Cunningham, J.P.: Uses and abuses of the cross-entropy loss: case studies in modern deep learning (2020)
16. Han, S., Mao, H., Dally, W.J.: Deep compression: compressing deep neural networks with pruning, trained quantization and huffman coding (2015). https://arxiv.org/abs/1510.00149
17. Heaven, W.D.: Predictive policing algorithms are racist. they need to be dismantled, December 2020. https://www.technologyreview.com/2020/07/17/1005396/predictive-policing-algorithms-racist-dismantled-machine-learning-bias-criminal-justice/
18. Hooker, S., Moorosi, N., Clark, G., Bengio, S., Denton, E.: Characterising bias in compressed models (2020)

19. Jacob, B., et al.: Quantization and training of neural networks for efficient integer-arithmetic-only inference. CoRR abs/1712.05877 (2017)
20. Johnson, K.: Algorithmic justice league protests bias in voice AI and media coverage, April 2020. https://venturebeat.com/2020/03/31/algorithmic-justice-league-protests-bias-voice-ai-and-media-coverage/
21. Kingma, D.P., Ba, J.: Adam: a method for stochastic optimization. In: Bengio, Y., LeCun, Y. (eds.) Proceedings of International Conference on Learning Representations, San Diego, CA, USA, 7–9 May 2015, Conference Track Proceedings (2015)
22. Kleppe, A., Skrede, O.J., De Raedt, S., Liestøl, K., Kerr, D.J., Danielsen, H.E.: Designing deep learning studies in cancer diagnostics. Nat. Rev. Cancer **21**(3), 199–211 (2021)
23. Lee, J., et al.: On-device neural net inference with mobile GPUs. CoRR abs/1907.01989 (2019)
24. Lee, S., Nirjon, S.: Fast and scalable in-memory deep multitask learning via neural weight virtualization. In: Proceedings of International Conference on Mobile Systems, Applications, and Services, pp. 175–190. Association for Computing Machinery, New York, NY, USA (2020)
25. Li, J.P., Mirza, N., Rahat, B., Xiong, D.: Machine learning and credit ratings prediction in the age of fourth industrial revolution. Technol. Forecast. Soc. Change **161**, 120309 (2020)
26. Li, S., Deng, W., Du, J.: Reliable crowdsourcing and deep locality-preserving learning for expression recognition in the wild. In: 2017 IEEE Conference on Computer Vision and Pattern Recognition (CVPR), pp. 2584–2593. IEEE (2017)
27. Liang, T., Glossner, J., Wang, L., Shi, S.: Pruning and quantization for deep neural network acceleration: a survey (2021)
28. Liu, Z., Luo, P., Wang, X., Tang, X.: Deep learning face attributes in the wild. In: Proceedings of International Conference on Computer Vision, December 2015
29. Lucey, P., Cohn, J.F., Kanade, T., Saragih, J., Ambadar, Z., Matthews, I.: The extended cohn-kanade dataset (ck+): a complete dataset for action unit and emotion-specified expression (2010)
30. Nahshan, Y., et al.: Loss aware post-training quantization. CoRR abs/1911.07190 (2019)
31. Oneto, L., Chiappa, S.: Fairness in machine learning. In: Oneto, L., Navarin, N., Sperduti, A., Anguita, D. (eds.) Recent Trends in Learning From Data. SCI, vol. 896, pp. 155–196. Springer, Cham (2020). https://doi.org/10.1007/978-3-030-43883-8_7
32. Paganini, M.: Prune responsibly (2020)
33. Parkhi, O.M., Vedaldi, A., Zisserman, A.: Deep face recognition. In: Xie, X., Jones, M.W., Tam, G.K.L. (eds.) Proceedings of the British Machine Vision Conference (BMVC), pp. 41.1-41.12. BMVA Press, September 2015
34. Schwartz, R., Dodge, J., Smith, N.A., Etzioni, O.: Green AI. CoRR abs/1907.10597 (2019). https://arxiv.org/abs/1907.10597
35. Shuting, J., Zeng, X., Xia, F., Huang, W., Liu, X.: Application of deep learning methods in biological networks. Briefings Bioinform. **22**, 1902–1917 (2020)
36. Swanner, N.: Google's new machine learning curriculum aims to stop bias cold, October 2018. https://insights.dice.com/2018/10/24/google-machine-learning-course-bias/

37. Szydlo, T., Sendorek, J., Brzoza-Woch, R.: Enabling machine learning on resource constrained devices by source code generation of the learned models. In: Shi, Y., et al. (eds.) ICCS 2018. LNCS, vol. 10861, pp. 682–694. Springer, Cham (2018). https://doi.org/10.1007/978-3-319-93701-4_54

38. Talwalkar, A.: Ai in the 2020s must get greener-and here's how, February 2020

39. Verma, S., Rubin, J.: Fairness definitions explained. In: Proceedings of the International Workshop on Software Fairness, pp. 1–7. Association for Computing Machinery, New York, NY, USA (2018)

40. Wang, K., Peng, X., Yang, J., Lu, S., Qiao, Y.: Suppressing uncertainties for large-scale facial expression recognition. In: Proceedings of the IEEE/CVF Conference on Computer Vision and Pattern Recognition (CVPR), June 2020

41. Xu, T., White, J., Kalkan, S., Gunes, H.: Investigating bias and fairness in facial expression recognition. In: Bartoli, A., Fusiello, A. (eds.) ECCV 2020. LNCS, vol. 12540, pp. 506–523. Springer, Cham (2020). https://doi.org/10.1007/978-3-030-65414-6_35

42. Xu, T., White, J., Kalkan, S., Gunes, H.: Investigating bias and fairness in facial expression recognition. In: Bartoli, A., Fusiello, A. (eds.) Computer Vision - ECCV 2020 Workshops. Springer International Publishing (2020)

43. Yan, H., Ang, M.H., Poo, A.N.: Cross-dataset facial expression recognition. In: IEEE International Conference on Robotics and Automation, pp. 5985–5990 (2011)

44. Yan, S., Huang, D., Soleymani, M.: Mitigating biases in multimodal personality assessment. In: Proceedings of International Conference on Multimodal Interaction, pp. 361–369. Association for Computing Machinery, New York, NY, USA (2020)

45. Yeh, I.C., hui Lien, C.: The comparisons of data mining techniques for the predictive accuracy of probability of default of credit card clients. Expert Syst. Appl. **36**(2, Part 1), 2473–2480 (2009)

46. Zhou, H., et al.: Exploring emotion features and fusion strategies for audio-video emotion recognition. In: Proceedings of International Conference on Multimodal Interaction, October 2019

47. Zhu, M., Gupta, S.: To prune, or not to prune: exploring the efficacy of pruning for model compression (2017)

Multimodal Stress State Detection from Facial Videos Using Physiological Signals and Facial Features

Yassine Ouzar$^{(\boxtimes)}$ (ID), Lynda Lagha, Frédéric Bousefsaf (ID),
and Choubeila Maaoui (ID)

Université de Lorraine, LCOMS, 57000 Metz, France
{yassine.ouzar,frederic.bousefsaf,choubeila.maaoui}@univ-lorraine.fr,
laghalynda@outlook.com

Abstract. Stress is a complex phenomenon that affects the body and mind on multiple levels, encompassing both psychological and physiological aspects. Recent studies have used multiple modalities to comprehensively describe stress by exploiting the complementarity of multimodal signals. In this paper, we investigate the feasibility of fusing facial features with physiological cues on human stress state estimation. We adopt a multiple modalities fusion using a camera as a single input source and based on the remote photoplethysmography method for non-contact physiological signals measurement. The frameworks rely on modern AI techniques and the experiments were conducted using the new UBFC-Phys dataset dedicated to multimodal psychophysiological studies of social stress. The experimental results revealed high performance when fusing facial features with remote pulse rate variability with an accuracy of 91.07%.

Keywords: Stress detection · Multimodality · Machine learning · Remote photoplethysmography · Facial features

1 Introduction

Cognitive and mental stress corresponds to an important issue in modern societies. Several studies in this field of research recognize mental stress as a key factor in diseases and pathologies like depression, sleep disorders, stroke and heart attack [9]. These effects are particularly induced by a high and daily mental workload.

Various techniques have been developed for treating or preventing this condition, including stress detection techniques that rely on the processing and the analysis of physiological signals which exhibit a high potential alongside an increasing interest from the scientific community. These methods are based on, among others, heart or pulse rate and its variability, breathing rate, skin temperature, and electrodermal activity (or skin conductance) [3]. These physiological

© Springer Nature Switzerland AG 2023
J.-J. Rousseau and B. Kapralos (Eds.): ICPR 2022 Workshops, LNCS 13646, pp. 139–150, 2023.
https://doi.org/10.1007/978-3-031-37745-7_10

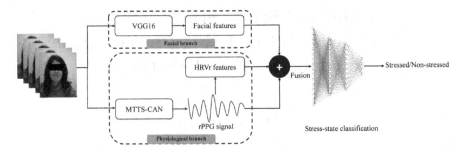

Fig. 1. Overview of the proposed system for multimodal stress state recognition using facial features, rPPG signals, and remote PRV features. It consists of two pipelines. The first one extracts the facial features using a pre-trained VGG16, while the second pipeline extracts physiological signals using a state-of-the-art architecture called MTTS-CAN. The latter recovers the rPPG signal and from which pulse rate variability features can be measured. The extracted features of each modality are then fused and fed to a feed-forward neural network for stressed/non-stressed classification.

signals are also frequently analyzed in the field of affective computing and emotion recognition [26]. The objective consists in automatically processing these signals to predict a stress state or level with a high level of confidence.

Contact sensors are usually employed to record the aforementioned physiological signals. Conventional cameras, through facial video analysis, can also be employed to compute pulse rate, pulse rate variability, peripheral vasomotor activity, and breathing rate to remotely detect mental stress [4,12,14,15], engagement [19] and more generally in applications that relate to the affective computing field of research. Recent techniques include facial features [32], pupil diameter, and blinking rate [20] to strengthen the assessment of stress levels.

According to the recent review of Arsalan et al. [3], most existing studies have examined the use of facial features and physiological cues separately or by combining multiple physiological signals recorded by different sensors. We propose, in this paper, a multimodal video-based method for mental stress state assessment based on facial features and physiological signals. Only a single input source is used to extract features from each modality. Replacing contact intrusive devices with a camera for physiological data measurement may avoid the problems related to asynchrony across modalities, which are usually unaligned. Moreover, it reduces the discomfort caused by the contact sensors that are psychologically stressful. A public dataset, namely UBFC-Phys [17], has been employed to train and evaluate the models proposed in this article. To the best of our knowledge, this is the first study to use this multimodal stress database apart from the original paper.

In the remainder of this paper, stress recognition-related works are presented in Sect. 2. Section 3 details our proposed approach. Then, in Sect. 4, our method is evaluated. Finally, conclusions and future works are given in Sect. 5.

2   Related Works

In recent years, there has been an increasing number of interesting works done in the field of affective computing, including emotion and stress recognition. Despite the distinction between stress and emotion [8], they share some common attributes. Both cause physical and physiological changes in response to a particular stimulus. Just like emotion, various modalities have been used for stress detection either in unimodal [4,6,31,34] or multimodal way [1,10,32]. These modalities can be divided into two classes: external physical cues such as facial expressions, pupil and head movement; internal physiological signals such as heart rate and its variability, breathing rate, skin temperature, and electrodermal activity. Prasetio et al. [23] proposed a stress recognition system based on facial features (such as eyes, nose, and mouth) extracted from face images. Viegas et al. [29] identify the stress state from face videos using 17 action units. An eye tracker device was used by Pedrotti et al. [22] to analyze the correlation between stress and pupil diameter. Physiological signals also have been widely used for stress recognition. They are measured by a contact sensor or remotely using a simple camera. Zubair et al. [35] developed a five-level stress detection system based on PPG signals collected using a pulse sensor on the fingertips. Bousefsaf and al. [4] showed that mental stress can be estimated from pulse rate variability obtained from remote and low-cost devices. Mcduff et al. [16] recently proposed a cognitive stress estimation system based on peripheral hemodynamics and vasomotion power extracted from rPPG amplitudes.

Recent studies have shown that multimodal stress detection systems exceed the performance of unimodal systems [3]. Existing multimodal stress detection schemes can be divided into a fusion of physiological signals only and a fusion of remote modalities with physiological signals acquired from contact sensors. Despite the results obtained, they follow a constrained experimental setup under laboratory conditions due to the use of intrusive and sensitive equipment that is psychologically stressful. In addition, while dealing with multiple signals of different natures gathered from different sources, they may conflict with each other due to asynchrony across modalities and thus lead to misestimation.

3   Materials and Method

3.1   Dataset

We explored the UBFC-Phys [17], a public multimodal database dedicated to psycho-physiological studies. The UBFC-Phys dataset provides data collected from 56 undergraduate psychology student participants, including 46 females and 10 males, all between the ages of 19 and 38 (with a mean age of 21.8 years). Participants underwent a social stress-inducing experiment in three stages: a resting task T1, a speaking task T2, and an arithmetic task T3 (T2 and T3 being the stressful tasks), during which participants were filmed and wore a wristband that allowed the measurement of their blood volume pulse (BVP) and electrodermal activity (EDA) signals. A form for calculating the level of stress (anxiety score) is presented to participants before and after the experiment. For each participant, three videos (one video per task) of 3 min duration were recorded at a frame rate of 35 fps and with a resolution of 1024 × 1024 pixels. BVP and EDA signals for each task as well as their anxiety scores calculated before and after the experiment are publicly available.

3.2 Data Preparation

The conducted experiments include two types of physiological features measured in contact using a wristband or remotely from video recordings. For contact-based physiological features, BVP signals and their derivative contact pulse rate variability (PRVc) features are used. A similar procedure has been conducted for video-based physiological features, rPPG signal, and its derivative remote pulse rate variability (PRVr) are employed. Adding to that the exploitation of the facial features extracted from the video recordings by transfer learning.

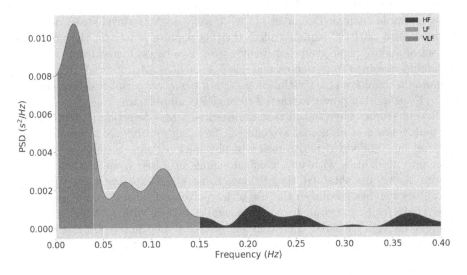

Fig. 2. A representative power spectral density for IBI series showing The areas of VLF, LF, and HF powers of the PRV.

3.2.1 Contact-based Features

First, the ground-truth BVP signals are resampled to the sampling rate of the camera (35 fps). Then, detrending is performed using a smoothness priors approach [28]. After that, we applied a 2nd-order Butterworth band-pass filter with a cutoff frequency of 0.75 and 2.5 Hz to keep only the information related to the pulse waveform. From the filtered BVP signals, 8 contact pulse rate variability

(PRVc) features have been computed. Peak detection is first performed to locate the instant of time at which the heartbeat occurs. The contact pulse rate is computed in the time domain by the inverse of the interbeat interval (IBI) divided by 60 to get the frequency in beats per minute. From the pulse rate variations during the video recording session, we computed the mean (meanHR), standard deviation (stdHR), maximum (maxHR) and minimum (minHR) of the pulse rate series. The root mean square of successive interval differences (RMSSD) is also calculated (see Eq. 1). This parameter gives an evaluation of the vagal activity reflected in pulse variability [25].

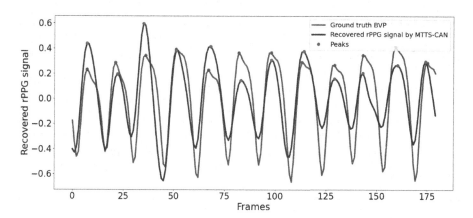

Fig. 3. Comparison between a predicted signal by MTTS-CAN and the ground-truth BVP signal taken from the UBFC-Phys dataset. The amplitudes are different but the peak location seems relevant which is important for IBIs measurement.

Three pulse rate variability features were extracted in the frequency domain. The IBI series were interpolated with cubic Hermite and the power spectra were obtained by employing Welch's method [30]. From the different oscillatory components of the power spectral density (PSD), low frequency (LF) and high frequency (HF) components were computed. The LF component is modulated by baroreflex activity and contains both sympathetic and parasympathetic activity, while the HF component reflects the parasympathetic branch of the autonomic nervous system [2]. The LF and HF powers of the pulse rate variability were computed as the area under the PSD curve corresponding to 0.04–0.15 Hz and 0.15–0.4 Hz respectively (see Fig. 2). The LF/HF, which represents the sympatho-vagal balance [5] has also been computed. The very low frequency (VLF) components were not employed in our experiments.

$$RMSSD = \sqrt{\frac{1}{N-1}\sum_{i=1}^{N-1}(IBI_{i+1} - IBI_i)^2} \qquad (1)$$

3.2.2   Video-based Physiological Features

Remote photoplethysmography (rPPG) and ballistocardiography (BCG) are the two main methods for measuring physiological signals by camera [13]. In our experiment, we used the rPPG technique for the estimation of pulse signals. Despite the advantages and limitations of each method, the BCG has been less exploited in recent years for different reasons. Compared to rPPG method, BCG is more difficult to implement because of its morphology which varies according to the subjects and the sensor used adding to that its sensitivity to noise and artifacts of movements.

rPPG is an optical technique that captures cardiac signals by observing the variation of blood volume on the person's face using a camera. The captured light reflected from the skin is translated into a variation of the rPPG signal. Same to BVP signal, several characteristics can be derived from the rPPG signal such as pulse rate, breathing rate, and remote pulse rate variability (PRVr).

Among the popular methods in the state-of-the-art, we used the Multi-Task Sequential Shift Convolutional Network (MTTS-CAN) proposed by Liu et al. [11] for rPPG signals extraction. MTTS-CAN is an end-to-end deep neural network that combines a convolutional attention mechanism with a time-shifting module. For a better appreciation of the quality of the rPPG signal, we present in Fig. 3 an overlay of a BVP ground truth signal in contact and an rPPG signal predicted by the MTTS-CAN network. We clearly observe a correlation between the estimated rPPG signal and the ground truth, moreover, the peaks are very close which is important for IBIs measurement.

For PRVr features extraction, we processed the raw rPPG signals and extracted the same parameters as for contact signals (see Sect. 3.2.3).

3.2.3   Facial Features

Deep learning models have proven efficient for general-purpose 2D image tasks compared to traditional machine learning algorithms. However, a large amount of data is required to train the model properly in order to achieve high performance. Due to data scarcity, we looked at the transfer learning approach as a viable alternative and to reduce the development effort at the same time. A pre-trained VGG16 model [27] is adopted as facial features extractor. VGG16 is very popular and has proved to be very efficient and achieve high recognition accuracy in computer vision tasks [7]. The network consists of a features extraction block based on convolution layers and the classifier block that consists of dense layers. The features extraction block is frozen, while the classifier block is modified by replacing the upper dense layers compatible with stressed/non-stressed classification. Afterward, the network is fine-tuned with UBFC-Phys data dedicated to stress recognition.

4 Results and Discussion

The experiments were carried out using the same specifications presented in the original article of the UBFC-Phys dataset [17]. Using the supplementary material II provided with the paper[1], 101 of 168 tasks were selected. The 67 removed tasks were eliminated by testing the correlation between BVP and rPPG signals to detect the corrupted signals. We used 7-fold subject-independent cross-validation strategy on both separate and fused modalities. We randomly created 7-fold using 85% of the data for training and the remaining 15% for testing. The average accuracy across each fold is reported in Table 1 and 2.

Three different experiments were performed for stress state detection: a) using physiological modalities only (contact and non-contact), b) using facial features only, and c) merging physiological signals and facial features. The non-stress is represented by task T1, while T2 and T3 represent the stress state.

Table 1. Non-stress vs stress state classification results based on physiological signals

Features	Classifiers	Accuracy (%)
BVP	SVM RBF Kernel	69.72
	SVM Poly Kernel	58.58
	NB	**72.61**
	RF	66.96
	KNN	44.22
rPPG	SVM RBF Kernel	57.81
	SVM Poly Kernel	57.81
	NB	61.82
	RF	**62.40**
	KNN	59.96
PRVc	SVM RBF Kernel	72.74
	SVM Poly Kernel	74.55
	NB	**78.16**
	RF	58.58
	KNN	73.64
PRVr	SVM RBF Kernel	58.58
	SVM Poly Kernel	57.61
	NB	56.92
	RF	58.58
	KNN	**72.22**

---

[1] https://ieeexplore.ieee.org/ielx7/5165369/10056372/9346017/supp2-3056960.pdf?arnumber=9346017.

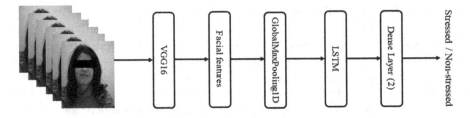

Fig. 4. stress state recognition system using facial features.

4.1   Stress Recognition from Physiological Signals

We used machine learning algorithms and ideas proposed in the original article of the UBFC-Phys dataset to compare the performance of the different features [17]. Five classifiers were considered: Support Vector Machine (SVM) with a polynomial kernel, SVM with Radial Basis Function (RBF), Random Forest (RF), Naive Bayes (NB), and K-Nearest Neighbors (KNN). We conducted the same 7-fold cross-validation on the five algorithms. Each classifier was trained with 85% of the signals, and the remaining 15% were used for testing.

Table 1 provides the recognition accuracy using contact (BVP and PRVc) and non-contact (rPPG and PRVr) features. In this experiment, the best result was achieved by contact-based physiological features. PRVc features reached the highest accuracy at 78.16%, followed by BVP signals with an accuracy of 72.61%. The best performance for contact-based physiological features was obtained with the Naive Bayes classifier. By comparing the obtained results, we note that the stress state recognition accuracy with the BVP signal outperforms the rPPG one. A similar observation can be drawn for the contact and non-contact PRV features, better accuracy was achieved with the contact features compared to the remote ones. These observations are in the line with what has been reported in previous studies [21] but in contradiction with the results presented in the article that introduced the UBFC-Phys [17]. The authors reported higher accuracies with video-based physiological modalities than with contact-based physiological features. We suppose that the performance of each modality depends on the type of classifier and its parameters, as well as the rPPG signal recovering method. In their experiments [17], a conventional framework consisting of several signal and image processing steps was used. Here, we choose to adopt a novel end-to-end deep learning approach that extracts the rPPG waveform automatically without any additional pre-processing or post-processing steps [11].

4.2   Stress State Recognition from Facial Features

A transfer learning strategy is adopted in this experiment to leverage the knowledge from the object recognition domain to stress recognition by replacing the upper dense layers and fine-tuning the network with UBFC-Phys data dedicated to stress recognition. The proposed system is illustrated in Fig. 4. First, each frame of the videos is resized to ($224 \times 224 \times 3$ and then passed to the pre-trained VGG16 model [27], which is initially trained with the ImageNet dataset for object recognition. The output features of VGG16 (before the dense layers) are extracted and then vectorized using GlobalMaxPooling1D to obtain the facial feature vector. This vector is passed to an LSTM layer to consider the temporal dimension. Finally, it is passed to a dense layer composed of 2 neurons for classification. For this purpose, a sigmoid activation function is applied to the dense layer, enabling binary stress classification (stress/non-stress).

The result presented in Table 2 shows that facial features-based stress state recognition outperforms physiological features either measured in contact or non-contact. This confirms the results reported in previous studies where recognition accuracy of affects/emotions using visual features (e.g. facial expressions) outperforms physiological modalities [21].

4.3   Stress State Recognition from Facial Features and Physiological Signals

Figure 1 presents the overall architecture of the proposed multimodal stress recognition system. It includes two pipelines to extract the features of each modality from facial video recordings. Each video of the UBFC-Phys dataset is fed to the facial features network and to the rPPG extractor network (MTTS-CAN). The first pipeline extracts the features vector after the flatten layer using the pre-trained weights of VGG16 (See Fig. 4), while the second pipeline returns either the rPPG signal recovered through the MTTS-CAN network [11] or PRVr features. We conducted two experiments on our multimodal stress recognition system. The first one combined the facial features with the PRVr features only, then with the rPPG signal only. The concatenation result vector of the two modalities is passed into two dense layers with 256 and 2 neurons respectively. The first layer takes the rectified linear units as the hidden units while the second one uses the sigmoid activation function to predict the corresponding stress class either stress or non-stress state.

The average accuracies of fusing the facial features with the PRVr features and with the rPPG signals are shown in Table 2. As we can see, combining facial features with PRVr features improve significantly the classification accuracy and deliver better accuracy (91.07%) compared to using facial or PRVr features separately. The fusion of facial features and the rPPG signals slightly improves performance, achieving an accuracy of 83.12%.

Table 2. Non-stress vs stress state classification results based on facial features only and on a fusion between facial features and remote physiological signals

Method	Accuracy (%)
Facial features	82.48
Facial features + rPPG	83.12
Facial features + PRVr	**91.07**

5   Conclusion

A multimodal approach to stress state recognition through video-based physiological signals and facial features has been proposed. Physiological cues are measured remotely from facial video recordings using the rPPG technique, while facial features were extracted by transfer learning. In such a manner, only a single input source was utilized to extract features from each modality. Both unimodal and multimodal experiments were performed. Analysis has shown that facial features are more relevant and allow for the highest level of accuracy. Compared to performance using only facial features, merging facial features with physiological signals provided a more accurate estimation, indicating the effectiveness of multimodal analysis.

Future tasks are to further improve the method's accuracy and to use other physiological modalities such as electrodermal activity and respiratory rate and rPPG waveform-based features linked to vasomotor activity and blood pressure. We also aim to use the stress score provided by the UBFC-Phys dataset and move to other approaches for facial features extraction using action units and facial landmarks. Furthermore, we intend to extend our work to other datasets such as RECOLA [24], AMIGOS [18] and BP4D+ [33] databases. The RECOLA dataset [24] can directly be used as it is annotated with stress labels and provides videos and the corresponding physiological signals. We plan to annotate the other two databases by exploiting other emotion label classes or by using electrodermal activity signals that correlate strongly with stress. We also plan to improve and search for the best features extractor model by comparing the most commonly employed neural architectures (e.g. ResNet, Xception, Inception).

References

1. Almeida., J., Rodrigues., F.: Facial expression recognition system for stress detection with deep learning. In: Proceedings of the 23rd International Conference on Enterprise Information Systems - Volume 1: ICEIS, pp. 256–263. INSTICC, SciTePress (2021). https://doi.org/10.5220/0010474202560263
2. Appelhans, B., Luecken, L.: Heart rate variability as an index of regulated emotional responding. Rev. Gen. Psychol. **10**(3), 229–240 (2006). https://doi.org/10.1037/1089-2680.10.3.229
3. Arsalan, A., Anwar, S.M., Majid, M.: Mental stress detection using data from wearable and non-wearable sensors: a review. arXiv preprint arXiv:2202.03033 (2022)
4. Bousefsaf, F., Maaoui, C., Pruski, A.: Remote detection of mental workload changes using cardiac parameters assessed with a low-cost webcam. Comput. Biol. Med. **53**, 154–163 (2014). https://doi.org/10.1016/j.compbiomed.2014.07.014
5. Burr, R.L.: Interpretation of normalized spectral heart rate variability indices in sleep research: a critical review. Sleep **30**(7), 913–919 (2007)
6. Cinaz, B., Arnrich, B., Marca, R.L., Tröster, G.: Monitoring of mental workload levels during an everyday life office-work scenario. Pers. Ubiquit. Comput. **17**, 229–239 (2011)
7. Dubey, A.K., Jain, V.: Automatic facial recognition using vgg16 based transfer learning model. J. Inf. Optim. Sci. **41**(7), 1589–1596 (2020). https://doi.org/10.1080/02522667.2020.1809126

8. Epel, E.S., et al.: More than a feeling: a unified view of stress measurement for population science. Front. Neuroendocrinol. **49**, 146–169 (2018). https://doi.org/10.1016/j.yfrne.2018.03.001, https://www.sciencedirect.com/science/article/pii/S0091302218300219, stress and the Brain

9. Giannakakis, G., Grigoriadis, D., Giannakaki, K., Simantiraki, O., Roniotis, A., Tsiknakis, M.: Review on psychological stress detection using biosignals. IEEE Trans. Affect. Comput. **13**(1), 440–460 (2022). https://doi.org/10.1109/TAFFC.2019.2927337

10. Kurniawan, H., Maslov, A.V., Pechenizkiy, M.: Stress detection from speech and galvanic skin response signals. In: Proceedings of the 26th IEEE International Symposium on Computer-Based Medical Systems, pp. 209–214 (2013). https://doi.org/10.1109/CBMS.2013.6627790

11. Liu, X., Fromm, J., Patel, S., McDuff, D.: Multi-task temporal shift attention networks for on-device contactless vitals measurement. Adv. Neural Inf. Process. Syst. **33**, 19400–19411 (2020)

12. Maaoui, C., Bousefsaf, F., Pruski, A.: Automatic human stress detection based on webcam photoplethysmographic signals. J. Mech. Med. Biol. **16**, 1650039 (2016)

13. McDuff, D.: Camera measurement of physiological vital signs. arXiv preprint arXiv:2111.11547 (2021)

14. McDuff, D.J., Gontarek, S., Picard, R.W.: Remote measurement of cognitive stress via heart rate variability. 2014 36th Annual International Conference of the IEEE Engineering in Medicine and Biology Society, pp. 2957–2960 (2014)

15. McDuff, D.J., Hernández, J., Gontarek, S., Picard, R.W.: Cogcam: contact-free measurement of cognitive stress during computer tasks with a digital camera. In: Proceedings of the 2016 CHI Conference on Human Factors in Computing Systems (2016)

16. McDuff, D.J., et al.: Non-contact imaging of peripheral hemodynamics during cognitive and psychological stressors. Sci. Rep. **10**, 10887 (2020)

17. Meziati Sabour, R., Benezeth, Y., De Oliveira, P., Chappe, J., Yang, F.: Ubfc-phys: a multimodal database for psychophysiological studies of social stress. IEEE Trans. Affect. Comput. 1 (2021). https://doi.org/10.1109/TAFFC.2021.3056960

18. Miranda-Correa, J.A., Abadi, M.K., Sebe, N., Patras, I.: Amigos: a dataset for affect, personality and mood research on individuals and groups. IEEE Trans. Affect. Comput. **12**(2), 479–493 (2021). https://doi.org/10.1109/TAFFC.2018.2884461

19. Monkaresi, H., Bosch, N., Calvo, R.A., D'Mello, S.K.: Automated detection of engagement using video-based estimation of facial expressions and heart rate. IEEE Trans. Affect. Comput. **8**(1), 15–28 (2017). https://doi.org/10.1109/TAFFC.2016.2515084

20. Nagasawa, T., Takahashi, R., Koopipat, C., Tsumura, N.: Stress estimation using multimodal biosignal information from RGB facial video. In: 2020 IEEE/CVF Conference on Computer Vision and Pattern Recognition Workshops (CVPRW), pp. 1181–1187 (2020). https://doi.org/10.1109/CVPRW50498.2020.00154

21. Ouzar, Y., Bousefsaf, F., Djeldjli, D., Maaoui, C.: Video-based multimodal spontaneous emotion recognition using facial expressions and physiological signals. In: Proceedings of the IEEE/CVF Conference on Computer Vision and Pattern Recognition (CVPR) Workshops, pp. 2460–2469, June 2022

22. Pedrotti, M., et al.: Automatic stress classification with pupil diameter analysis. Int. J. Hum.-Comput. Interact. **30**, 220–236 (2014)

23. Prasetio, B.H., Tamura, H., Tanno, K.: The facial stress recognition based on multi-histogram features and convolutional neural network. In: 2018 IEEE International Conference on Systems, Man, and Cybernetics (SMC), pp. 881–887 (2018). https://doi.org/10.1109/SMC.2018.00157

24. Ringeval, F., Sonderegger, A., Sauer, J.S., Lalanne, D.: Introducing the recola multimodal corpus of remote collaborative and affective interactions. 2013 10th IEEE International Conference and Workshops on Automatic Face and Gesture Recognition (FG), pp. 1–8 (2013)

25. Shaffer, F., Ginsberg, J.P.: An overview of heart rate variability metrics and norms. Front. Public Health 5, 258 (2017)

26. Shu, L., et al.: A review of emotion recognition using physiological signals. Sensors 18(7) (2018). https://doi.org/10.3390/s18072074, https://www.mdpi.com/1424-8220/18/7/2074

27. Simonyan, K., Zisserman, A.: Very deep convolutional networks for large-scale image recognition. arXiv preprint arXiv:1409.1556 (2014)

28. Tarvainen, M.P., Ranta-aho, P.O., Karjalainen, P.A.: An advanced detrending method with application to HRV analysis. IEEE Trans. Biomed. Eng. 49, 172–175 (2002)

29. Viegas, C., Lau, S.H., Maxion, R., Hauptmann, A.: Towards independent stress detection: a dependent model using facial action units. In: 2018 International Conference on Content-Based Multimedia Indexing (CBMI), pp. 1–6 (2018). https://doi.org/10.1109/CBMI.2018.8516497

30. Welch, P.: The use of fast fourier transform for the estimation of power spectra: a method based on time averaging over short, modified periodograms. IEEE Trans. Audio Electroacoust. 15(2), 70–73 (1967)

31. Zhang, H., Zhu, Y., Maniyeri, J., Guan, C.: Detection of variations in cognitive workload using multi-modality physiological sensors and a large margin unbiased regression machine. In: 2014 36th Annual International Conference of the IEEE Engineering in Medicine and Biology Society, pp. 2985–2988 (2014). https://doi.org/10.1109/EMBC.2014.6944250

32. Zhang, H., Feng, L., Li, N., Jin, Z., Cao, L.: Video-based stress detection through deep learning. Sensors 20(19) (2020). https://www.mdpi.com/1424-8220/20/19/5552

33. Zhang, Z., et al.: Multimodal spontaneous emotion corpus for human behavior analysis. In: 2016 IEEE Conference on Computer Vision and Pattern Recognition (CVPR), pp. 3438–3446 (2016)

34. Zhou, G., Hansen, J., Kaiser, J.: Nonlinear feature based classification of speech under stress. IEEE Trans. Speech Audio Process. 9(3), 201–216 (2001). https://doi.org/10.1109/89.905995

35. Zubair, M., Yoon, C.: Multilevel mental stress detection using ultra-short pulse rate variability series. Biomed. Signal Process. Control. 57, 101736 (2020)

Expression Recognition Using a Flow-Based Latent-Space Representation

Saandeep Aathreya and Shaun Canavan[✉]

University of South Florida, Tampa, FL 33620, USA
scanavan@usf.edu

Abstract. Facial expression Recognition is a growing and important field that has applications in fields such as medicine, security, education, and entertainment. While there have been encouraging approaches that have shown accurate results on a wide variety of datasets, in many cases it is still a difficult problem to explain the results. To enable deployment of expression recognition applications in-the-wild, being able to explain why an particular expression is classified is an important task. Considering this, we propose to model flow-based latent representations of facial expressions, which allows us to further analyze the features and grants us more granular control over which features are produced for recognition. Our work is focused on posed facial expressions with a tractable density of the latent space. We investigate the behaviour of these tractable latent space features in the case of subject dependent and independent expression recognition. We employ a flow-based generative approach with minimal supervision introduced during training and observe that traditional metrics give encouraging results. When subject independent expressions are evaluated, a shift towards a stochastic nature, in the probability space, is observed. We evaluate our flow-based representation on the BU-EEG dataset showing our approach provides good separation of classes, resulting in more explainable results.

Keywords: Flow-based · Latent-space · Expression Recognition

1 Introduction

Facial expression recognition (FER) has a broad range of applications in medicine [35], security [1], and education [22] to name a few. There have been encouraging results in the field through investigation of computer vision and machine learning to encode expression information from facial features [28]. Earlier methods were devised with the notion of Ekman and Friesen [9], that stated emotions are perceived in the same way regardless of the culture. Conversely, recent developments in psychology and neuroscience argue otherwise which indicates that emotions are not universal and are highly subjective per person, context, and expression [3,20]. The attempt to generalize expression is

J.-J. Rousseau and B. Kapralos (Eds.): ICPR 2022 Workshops, LNCS 13646, pp. 151–165, 2023.
https://doi.org/10.1007/978-3-031-37745-7_11

a challenging problem [10], however, to have real-world applications in human affect analysis [30] and human-computer interactions [49], it is a necessary step. With the advent of deep learning, researchers have been able to achieve state-of-the-art results on FER problems [16, 34, 48], but the interpretation of the complex relationship between the deep features, of different classes, is still a black-box concept. Although most of the literature has shown to perform reliably even on in-the-wild data [47] [44], these methods primarily focus on the output and the validation of the their output. This paper deviates from this traditional approach towards a more explicit way of modelling facial expressions with more control over the deep features that the model is able to produce and classify.

Traditional classification methods [40] [32] make the underlying assumption that the given dataset is a normal distribution. This is mostly false for high-dimensional natural signals such as images [26], which can result in an overall decrease in the accuracy of recognition models [45]. Recent advances in generative modelling has taken the field one step closer to a more tractable density estimation of high-dimensional images. For this purpose, we employ state-of-the-art generative models because of their ability to find meaningful distributions in the latent space [5, 36]. Specifically, flow-based generative models [25] have gained traction in recent years due to their ability to find explicit densities of the given dataset. Normalizing flows [41] are a simple, yet powerful technique which are capable of transforming densities of complex data into simpler forms using bijective and differentiable series of functions. Once the multiplex data has been transformed to a simple distribution, techniques such as Gaussian mixture modelling, and maximizing the log likelihood can be applied for classfication problems (see Sect. 3.1). Considering this, the contributions of this work are 3-fold:

1. A flow-based latent representation of facial expression is proposed. We model these representations for the task of expression recognition, in both a subject dependent and independent manner.
2. We visualize the high-dimensional features in the latent space and explore the subjective nature of expressions and observe notable differences between expressions of different subjects.
3. Using a state-of-the-art generative model, GLOW [23], we demonstrate the ability to interpolate between different expressions validating that the flow-based latent vectors form meaningful representations of expression.

2   Related Works

2.1   Generative Models

A range of generative models for classification purposes have been explored. GANs [14] work by finding the implicit density of the dataset through their adverserial structure and classification is done via the discriminator. Another

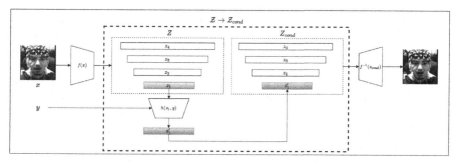

(a) Proposed flow-based latent space representation.

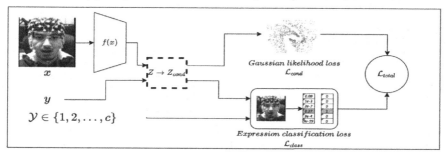

(b) Training for facial expression recognition.

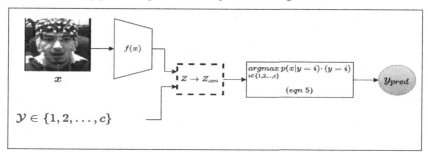

(c) Testing for facial expression recognition.

Fig. 1. Overview of proposed architecture for flow-based latent space representation of facial expressions. (a) $f(x)$ is the original Glow model [23] which outputs the latent vector $Z = \{z_4, z_3, z_2, z_1\}$. $h(z_1, y)$ is a conditional flow model which takes as input the latent sub-vector z_1 and the one-hot encoded class label y and outputs z_1', which is then used as a sub-vector in the new latent space Z_{cond}. (b) x is the batch of input images and y is the set of known expression classes (e.g. happy) which are fed into the proposed model. Each iteration outputs two loss values, $\mathcal{L}_{cond}$ is the conditional loss (Eq. 2) and $\mathcal{L}_{class}$ is the class loss (Eq. 4). $\mathcal{L}_{total}$ is the combination of L_{cond} and $\mathcal{L}_{class}$ (Eq. 5). (c) y_{pred} is computed by running the test input x_{test} through $f(x)$ once and $h(z_1, y_c)$ c times where $c \in \{1, 2, .., c\}$ and taking the argmax of the probabilities of the models output (Eq. 3). See Sect. 3 for more details.

type of generative models are VAEs [24], which inexplicitly optimize the log-likelihood by maximizing the ELBO. These models are not suitable for classification as they suffer from posterior collapse [29] wherein the density of the model closely matches the uninformative prior of the subset of latent data.

Yang et al. [53] used conditional generative adversarial networks to generate six prototypical expressions, which are then used to fine-tune convolutional neural networks. They look at the minimum distance between an input image and the generated images for classification. They report state-of-the-art results on multiple publicly available datasets. Xie et al. [52] proposed a 2-branch generative adverserial network that disentangles identity and expression information. They showed that this approach learns a discriminative representation of expression that is well suited for classfication.

2.2   Flow-Based Modeling

Semi-conditional Normalizing flows [2] employed a combination of unconditional (f_w) and conditional flows (h_θ) wherein they concatenated the hidden features with the one-hot encoded vector of labels. This new vector was then passed on to the conditional flow (h_θ) which was used for classification purposes. This is similar to semi-supervised conditional GANs [46]. Experiments were performed on toy datasets and the MNIST classification problem. Inspired by the findings of this work which utilizes only last k dimensions of hidden data for conditional flow transformation, we employ a similar approach to avoid overfitting the model and maintain the balance between maximizing likelihood and minimizing the classification loss. Given k classes, this approach requires only 1 forward pass to classify a new test data.

FlowGMM [19] utilized the RealNVP [8] model to train each class to be associated with a different mean (μ_k) and standard deviation (σ_k). Post training, Bayes' decision rule was applied on any new test point to gather the class with max probability. This involved random generation of means and standard deviation to be assigned to different classes. Training was semi-supervised with only 10% of the data being labelled at each epoch. They were also able to retain the quality of the generated images and applied the method on several image classification problems (e.g. MNIST [7]). They also show that classification can be extended beyond images by performing text classification on different dataset such as UCI, AG-News, Yahoo answers and found that the methods outperform other traditional classification methods.

2.3   Expression and Explainability

Although there are less works that focus on explainability and expression, there are some interesting works that do focus on this area. For example, Kandeel et al. [21] used explainability to determine the best convolutional neural network architecture for recognizing the expression of drivers. They investigated the saliency maps of the output from the networks to determine the best architecture to use.

They found that using this approach resulting in improved architecture selection, which ultimately lead to improved driver expression recognition accuracy. Weitz et al. [50] investigated using Layer-wise Relevant Propagation and Local Interpretable Model-agnostic Explanations to help explain how neural networks distinguished between expressions of pain and other expressions such as happy. They were able to distinguish key areas of the face that separated painful expressions from the other expression classes. Escalante et al. [11] designed a challenge around explaining video interviews. Their challenge proposes that an explainable system must be understandable by people in affective computing, signal processing social sciences, and psychology. Considering this, the challenge evaluation criteria included clarity, explainability, and soundness of the result.

We are motivated by these works, as being able to explain how different facial expressions are recognized can help the system better communicate with it's users [13], which can lead to more public trust in real-world affective systems [6]. Considering this we extend the state of the art by incorporating generative models, along with flow-based models to give more robust visualizations and explanations for facial expression recognition. We show that the proposed approach allows for clear visualization of clusters of subject's expressions.

3   Flow-Based Latent Representation of Facial Expressions

3.1   Normalizing Flows

Normalizing flows [41] are powerful distribution approximators which are comprised of a chain of transformations that transform a complex distribution into a simple one. Mathematically, it is defined as a bijective mapping $f : \mathcal{X} \to \mathcal{Z}$, where $\mathcal{X}$ defines the data space and $\mathcal{Z}$ defines the density of the latent space, which is typically chosen to be Gaussian. To infer the unknown probability density $\mathcal{X}$, we apply the inverse of the transformations $f^{-1} : \mathcal{Z} \to \mathcal{X}$ to generate new data from the data space $\mathcal{X}$ using change of variables theorem. Figure 1 provides a brief description of the functioning of normalizing flows, as applied to facial expressions.

Given a multivariate random variable z with a probability density $z \sim \pi(z)$, which is a function of unknown variable x given by $z = f(x)$ (and so, $x = f^{-1}(z)$), we need to infer the probability density of $x \sim p(x)$. *Change of Variable* theorem states that during any transformation, the total probability mass must be preserved, therefore the density of both z and x must always sum up to 1.

$$\int p(x)dx = \int \pi(z)dz = 1$$

The new density $p(x)$ is then the product of original density $\pi(z)$ and ratio of the volumes, which is typically given by calculating the determinant of Jacobian dz/dx.

$$p(x) = \pi(z) \cdot \left| det \frac{dz}{dx} \right|$$

Substituting $z = f(x)$, we get

$$p(x) = \pi(z) \cdot \left| det \frac{df(x)}{dx} \right|$$

Applying log on both sides, we get

$$\log(p(x)) = \log(\pi(z)) + \log \left| det \frac{df(x)}{dx} \right|$$

The calculation of log determinant at each step is expensive and therefore research involves finding an efficient way to avoid the direct calculation of log determinants. The functions $f(x)$ and $f^{-1}(z)$ are parametrized by deep neural networks whose core components are called *affine coupling layers*. These layers are defined by affine transformations of the input x as $y = s \odot x + t$, where s and t are neural networks. For more details on normalizing flows, we refer the reader to works from Dinh et al. [8], Kobyzev et al. [25], and Kingma et al. [23].

3.2 Supervised Learning

We examine the conditions where we are trying to solve a supervised classification task and learn a generative model simultaneously. For example, we may want to be able to generate new face images with an arbitrary expression and be able to classify the kind of expression that was generated. Subsequently, we use the feature space generated by Glow [23] to take full advantage of the labelled data available to us. Current works include the multi-scale architecture of Glow where the latent space Z is comprised of multiple sub-vectors $Z = \{z_4, z_3, z_2, z_1\}$. This kind of architecture enables fine-grained intermediate features which adds value to the intermediary representations [8]. We use this to add conditionality and supervision to the model. The overall architecture is shown in Fig. 1. It's a three-fold approach consisting of modifying the current architecture to include *conditionality and supervision*, *training* the modified architecture and *inferring* class labels from the final model.

Figure 1a shows the overview of the proposed architecture. Similar to the work from Atanov et al. [2], the architecture consists of two parts, the original flow model $f(x)$ which maps $x \rightarrow Z$ and the smaller, conditional flow model $h(z_1, y)$ which maps $z_1 \rightarrow z_1'$. Here, h is a subset of f with much fewer layers and blocks (Sect. 4.2). We use a one-hot encoded vector of labels $\mathbf{y}$ and concatenate it with the latent sub-vector as $z_1 = concat(z_1, \mathbf{y})$ before passing it through h. Once we have the new latent sub-vector z_1', we concatenate it back with the original Z vector which now becomes $Z = \{z_4, z_3, z_2, z_1'\}$. The proposed approach extends the work of Atanov et al. [2] in terms of optimizations. They compute the marginal likelihood $p(x)$ by optimizing the joint density $E_y p(x, y)$. We split this approach by first optimizing the conditional likelihood $p(x|y)$ through the loss function $\mathcal{L}_{cond}$ and implicitly optimizing $p(y)$ by minimizing the classification loss $\mathcal{L}_{class}$. This kind of decoupled approach allows us to independently monitor the key objectives involved in classification tasks, which in this case are the two losses $\mathcal{L}_{cond}$ and $\mathcal{L}_{class}$.

Training the model consists of maximizing the log likelihood in Eq. 1 and also minimizing the classification loss at each epoch. We now focus on formulating the two losses $\mathcal{L}_{cond}$ and $\mathcal{L}_{class}$ under the new supervised conditions. Figure 1b shows the overview of model training with 2 different losses while adopting the $\mathcal{Z} \rightarrow \mathcal{Z}_{cond}$ module from Fig. 1a. The new model h has dependence on the label y, so instead of maximizing the likelihood $\log p(x)$ from Eq. 1, we now maximize the conditional $\log p(x|y)$ as

$$\log(p(x|y)) = \log(\pi(z)) + \log \left|det\frac{\partial f(x)}{\partial x}\right| + \log \left|det\frac{\partial h(z,y)}{\partial z}\right|. \tag{1}$$

This likelihood is then maximized by minimizing the conditional loss which is given by

$$\mathcal{L}_{cond} = -\log(p(x|y)). \tag{2}$$

Next, the classification loss, during training, is obtained by evaluating $p(y|x)$, on each of the c classes as

$$y_{pred} = \underset{i \in \{1,2,...c\}}{argmax}\; p(x|y=i)p(y=i), \tag{3}$$

where c is the total number of classes. It's important to note that the first two terms of $p(x|y=i)$, in Eq. 1, undergo only one forward pass as it's independent of y. This approach accounts for relatively inexpensive calculations of log determinants multiple times [2].

The class loss is then calculated using the cross entropy loss on the prediction and labels

$$\mathcal{L}_{class} = CrossEntropy(y_{pred}, y). \tag{4}$$

The overall loss is given by the equation

$$\mathcal{L}_{total} = \mathcal{L}_{cond} + \lambda \mathcal{L}_{class}. \tag{5}$$

For our experiments, we have empirically found a λ of 0.3 to optimize both losses equally since the conditional loss $\mathcal{L}_{cond}$ and the classification loss $\mathcal{L}_{class}$ must converge synchronously. Fast convergence of $\mathcal{L}_{cond}$ might lead to model under-fitting on classification and faster convergence of $\mathcal{L}_{class}$ might lead to overfitting the classification with poorly preserved probability density. See Fig. 1b for an overview of training. During *testing*, a new face image x_{test} is fed into f once and h for a total of c times, where we obtain the prediction by using Eq. 3. See Fig. 1c for an overview of testing.

4 Experimental Design and Results

4.1 Dataset

To validate the proposed flow-based latent representation of facial expressions, we evaluate the BU EEG [27] dataset. It is a multimodal emotion dataset which comprises of posed and authentic facial expressions, facial action units (FACS) [42] and EEG signals. The dataset contains data collected from 29 subjects of various ethnicity and backgrounds with 22 Asian, 2 White, 4 Mid-eastern and 1 from other ethnicity. For the facial features, there are 29 videos, for each subject, which is ~25 min in length at 24 fps with size $250 \times 350 \times 3$. Facial expression segments have been extracted from the videos as part of data preprocessing using the metadata files for 6 prototypical expressions - Anger, Disgust, Fear, Happiness, Sadness and Surprise, with a total of 54511 frames. These expressions are posed under the lab environment. The sequence of frames have been run through DeepFaceLab [39] face detector and cropped to a size of 256×256. The final size of the images have been kept at $64 \times 64 \times 3$. It is important to note that there is some imbalance, in terms of total number of frames for each expression, with $\sim 9\%$ difference in the minimum and maximum number of frames (surprise and disgust, respectively).

4.2   Implementation Details

The code is implemented in the PyTorch framework [38]. The model has been trained on 8 NVIDIA GPUs for a total of 1200 epochs with a learning rate of 1e-4 for both f and h. The batch size was kept at 32 with image size of $64 \times 64 \times 3$. The Glow model f consisted of 4 blocks of 32 stacked Conv-Relu-Conv layer (called flows). Output of each block corresponds to the latent sub-vector of $Z = \{z_4, z_3, z_2, z_1\}$. Similarly, the unconditional model h is the subset of f which consisted of 4 flows and 1 block. The model architecture has been adapted from Rosanality's[1] implementation of Glow.

4.3   Expression Recognition Results

Table 1. Accuracy score on different classifiers using z data and t-SNE embeddings of z data

Data type	Classifier	Accuracy (in %)
z-(latent)	Flow based classifier (ours)	87.5
t-SNE embeddings	Random Forest	96.5
	Extra Trees	89.23
	AdaBoost	69.12
	Decision Tree	94.12

The proposed approach can be *applied* to facial expression recognition, as can be seen in Table 1. It is noteworthy to point out that to the best our knowledge,

---

[1] https://github.com/rosinality/glow-pytorch

Table 2. Average confusion matrix of facial expression recognition for 10-fold cross validation.

	Anger	Disgust	Fear	Happiness	Sadness	Surprise
Anger	820	90	12	2	7	0
Disgust	107	944	50	14	11	0
Fear	4	23	629	63	6	7
Happiness	2	10	49	926	10	3
Sadness	17	14	16	20	826	9
Surprise	6	22	67	38	27	882

this is the first work that performs facial expression recognition using normalizing flows. Since our focus is to showcase the potential *applications* of these techniques in the domain of affective computing, we present our results along with other experiments extended through our work. The first row of Table 1 presents average accuracy of 10-fold cross validation on uniform folds of the entire BU EEG [27] dataset. As can be seen in Table 2, the majority of expressions were recognized with relatively high accuracy. Overall, surprise had the lowest average misclassification error compared to other expressions. This can be explained, in part, by the large visual differences between surprise, and the other expressions, as can be seen in Fig. 4. These results are encouraging and further validate that meaningful information can be extracted from the low dimensional representations of the data.

4.4 Visualization and Explainability

We hypothesize that the proposed flow-based latent representation of facial expressions will provide accurate visualization and greater explainability. To test this hypothesis, we embed the latent representation of the z_1' latent vector into 2D space using the t-SNE method [31]. Figure 2a shows the plot of test images belonging to 6 different expressions from 29 subjects. Each color corresponds to an expression class and it can be seen that 29 clusters are formed denoting each subject, with their expressions, per cluster. This naturally leads to the question, is this visualization any better than what we get with deep features? To answer this question, we juxtapose Fig. 2a with Fig. 2b, which is a t-SNE output of deep features. We used a convolutional neural network (CNN), on the same test data, which comprises of four stacks of residual blocks. Each block contains a pair of Conv-BatchNorm-ReLU layers followed by two dense connections. This model performed reasonably well, obtaining an accuracy of 74% on the test set, however, we can see no discernible pattern in the plot compared to the latent representation. Even though it has formed different clusters, they do not associate with either subjects or different expressions.

Explainability of AI, especially in deep learning, is quite important when solving and realizing real-world problems. The proposed method is a step towards tackling the black box nature of neural networks which restricts the entry of AI into key fields such as medicine and security. The flow-based visualization can give us key insight into the subjective nature of expression [3]. We are able to see that the flow-based latent approach to represent expression was able to extract meaningful information such as each subject and their corresponding expressions are separable, therefore they are largely unique and can be easily classified. On the other hand, the visualization of the deep features does not offer this same insight as the clusters contain both subjects, and similar and different expressions.

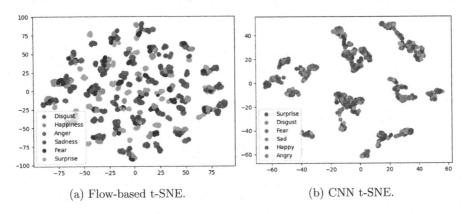

(a) Flow-based t-SNE.   (b) CNN t-SNE.

Fig. 2. Flow-based vs CNN comparison of t-SNE embeddings of latent data during subject dependent classification.

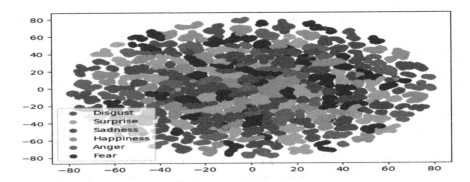

Fig. 3. Flow-based t-SNE embeddings of test data during subject independent classification.

To further explore this phenomenon of the latent space visualization we asked the question, will this specific clustering hold when subject independent experiments are conducted? To answer this question, we trained on 28 subjects of the BU-EEG dataset, and left one out (subject 29) for testing. The t-SNE plot for the latent vector of this test subject can be seen in Fig. 3. We see that the patterns veers away from the deterministic nature (Fig. 2a) to a more stochastic behaviour. This again aligns with work that details the biased and subjective nature of human emotions (e.g. expression) [37]. This visualization allows insight into the difficulties associated with generalization of facial expressions, such as different expressions of emotion are fuzzy, and can overlap (i.e. they are similar) [51].

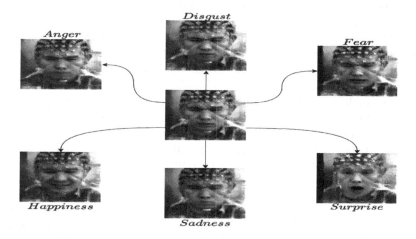

Fig. 4. Interpolation of 6 prototypical expressions from neutral.

In addition to this, we use an extended application of Glow [23] to visualize the interpolation of a test face image to other prototypical expressions. To generate high quality facial expressions, we zero out the z_1 of the latent vector Z from our model and run it for a total of 6000 epochs. This has to do with the fact that retaining the z_1' sub-vector in Z_{cond} deters the reconstructed image. Then, for each expression class c, we calculate pairs of averages in the latent space $(z_{avg}^c, z_{avg}^{other})$ for all the training data, where z_{avg}^{other} is the average of all the other classes combined except c. To interpolate to a specific expression for an arbitrary image x_{test}, we add the corresponding z_{test} with the difference of the z_{avg}^c and z_{avg}^{other}. See Fig. 4 for generation of the 6 prototypical expression from a neutral expression. This experiment was conducted to highlight the potential use cases of this approach in generating new facial expression to accommodate for class imbalance problems. As our model is able to distinguish between different expressions subjectively, the generated expressions for subjects will be in close proximity of the subject's original expression.

5   Discussion

We detail some of the potential use-cases of the proposed method in the context of ethics and privacy for applications in affective computing. To be able to enhance a machine's ability to decode and respond to the affective states of a human, there is potential breach of privacy involved [18]. With the high quality generative ability of flow-based models, it is possible to address some of these ethical concerns and simultaneously leverage the full extent of meaningful classification that it performs. Federated learning [43] can be incorporated in the current method to have a more personalized and secure system in place. Only the deepest latent features z can be processed centrally and rest of the modules, f and h can be trained locally avoiding any bottlenecks. These latent features z, although play a significant role in modelling the true data, are usually considered *Gaussian noise* in the outside world. Moreover, the encoder-decoder nature of $f(x)$ and $f^{-1}(z)$ can be employed as encryption and decryption keys [15] further bolstering the security aspects.

A difficult task in affective computing is the collection of robust, accurate data [33]. Collecting data with true annotations, be it for expression or emotion, involves immense amounts of labor. Due to the flow-based model's ability to interpolate between the latent space to produce meaningful facial images [23] (as shown in Sect. 4.4), we can potentially impart subjective attributes of the facial features without the need of the original data. This reduces the need for copious amounts of data where relevant tasks can then be managed only through sample data. This also gives the opportunity to steer clear from some of the ethical concerns encountered along the way, such as collecting data of painful expressions [4]. This has the potential to support these future applications (e.g., pain recognition) of affective computing.

The proposed approach has broad impacts in fields such as medicine, security, and defense. We hypothesize that the latent space representations are useful for medical applications such as recognition of disorders including, but not limited to, Autism Spectrum Disorder and Post Traumatic Stress Disorder. As previously mentioned, using Federated Learning along with the proposed method can significantly improve security and user privacy. We also hypothesize that the latent space can be used to represent different signals aside from images. This can include physiological signals such as heart rate and EEG, thermal images, and 3D and 4D facial models. Considering this, our future work includes investigating the flow-based latent representation of EEG data, which may allow for a less noisy representation of the signal [12]. Along with this, we will also investigate adding more generalizability to the model, however, the subjective nature of facial expressions and emotions have been explored before. Our findings align with that of Hinduja et. al. [17] which statistically showed, by evaluating facial expressions, that self-reported emotions are different and subjective compared to expected emotions.

6 Conclusion

This work investigates the idea of using generative flow-based models for performing interpretable and comprehensible modeling of latent representations in the domain of affective computing. We show that these models are able to transform the image signals into clear, segregated clusters in the latent space. Our results suggest the subjective nature of expression giving insight into how expression clusters by subject facilitating accurate recognition. We also explore the applicability of this work to perform supervised expression recognition on a posed facial expression dataset (BU-EEG). Finally, we detail potential use cases and broader impacts, to establish the proposed method in real-world applications by addressing some of the ethical and privacy concerns.

Acknowledgement. This material is based upon the work supported in part by the National Science Foundation under grant CNS-2039373. Any opinions, findings, and conclusions or recommendations expressed in this material are those of the author(s) and do not necessarily reflect the views of the National Science Foundation.

References

1. Al-modwahi, A.A.M., et al.: Facial expression recognition intelligent security system for real time surveillance. In: World Congress in Computer Science, Computer Engineering, and Applied Computing (2012)
2. Atanov, A., et al.: Semi-conditional normalizing flows for semi-supervised learning (2020)
3. Barrett, L.F., et al.: Emotional expressions reconsidered: challenges to inferring emotion from human facial movements. Psychol. Sci. Publ. Interest **20**(1), 1–68 (2019)
4. Berthouze, N., et al.: Emopain challenge 2020: Multimodal pain evaluation from facial and bodily expressions. arXiv preprint arXiv:2001.07739 (2020)
5. Bojanowski, P., Joulin, A., Lopez-Paz, D., Szlam, A.: Optimizing the latent space of generative networks (2019)
6. Cowie, R.: Ethical issues in affective computing. In: The Oxford handbook of AC, pp. 334–348. Oxford University Press (2015)
7. Deng, L.: The MNIST database of handwritten digit images for machine learning research. IEEE Signal Process. Mag. **29**(6), 141–142 (2012)
8. Dinh, L., Sohl-Dickstein, J., Bengio, S.: Density estimation using real NVP. CoRR abs/1605.08803 (2016). http://arxiv.org/abs/1605.08803
9. Ekman, P., Friesen, W.V.: Constants across cultures in the face and emotion. J. Pers. Soc. Psychol. **17**(2), 124 (1971)
10. Ertugrul, I.O., et al.: Cross-domain au detection: Domains, learning approaches, and measures. In: FG, pp. 1–8. IEEE (2019)
11. Escalante, H.J., et al.: Design of an explainable machine learning challenge for video interviews. In: IJCNN (2017)
12. Fabiano, D., Canavan, S.: Emotion recognition using fused physiological signals. In: ACII, pp. 42–48. IEEE (2019)
13. Goebel, R., et al.: Explainable AI: the new 42? In: Holzinger, A., Kieseberg, P., Tjoa, A.M., Weippl, E. (eds.) CD-MAKE 2018. LNCS, vol. 11015, pp. 295–303. Springer, Cham (2018). https://doi.org/10.1007/978-3-319-99740-7_21

14. Goodfellow, I.J., et al.: Generative adversarial networks (2014)
15. Habler, E., Shabtai, A.: Using LSTM encoder-decoder algorithm for detecting anomalous ADS-B messages. Comput. Secur. **78**, 155–173 (2018)
16. Hasani, B., Mahoor, M.H.: Facial expression recognition using enhanced deep 3d convolutional neural networks. In: CVPRW (2017)
17. Hinduja, S., Canavan, S., Yin, L.: Recognizing perceived emotions from facial expressions. In: FG (2020)
18. Hu, X., et al.: Ten challenges for EEG-based affective computing. Brain Science Advances **5**(1), 1–20 (2019). https://doi.org/10.1177/2096595819896200
19. Izmailov, P., et al.: Semi-supervised learning with normalizing flows (2019)
20. Jack, R.E., Garrod, O.G., Yu, H., Caldara, R., Schyns, P.G.: Facial expressions of emotion are not culturally universal. Proc. Natl. Acad. Sci. **109**(19), 7241–7244 (2012)
21. Kandeel, A.A., et al.: Explainable model selection of a CNN for driver's facial emotion identification. In: ICPRW (2021)
22. Khalfallah, J., Slama, J.B.H.: Facial expression recognition for intelligent tutoring systems in remote laboratories platform. Proc. Comput. Sci. **73**, 274–281 (2015)
23. Kingma, D.P., Dhariwal, P.: Glow: Generative flow with invertible 1×1 convolutions (2018)
24. Kingma, D.P., Welling, M.: Auto-encoding variational bayes (2014)
25. Kobyzev, I., Prince, S., Brubaker, M.: Normalizing flows: an introduction and review of current methods. IEEE Trans. Pattern Anal. Mach. Intell. 1 (2020). https://doi.org/10.1109/TPAMI.2020.2992934
26. Li, S., Deng, W.: A deeper look at facial expression dataset bias. IEEE Trans. Affect. Comput. (2020)
27. Li, X., et al.: An EEG-based multi-modal emotion database with both posed and authentic facial actions for emotion analysis. In: FG (2020)
28. Liu, M., Li, S., Shan, S., Wang, R., Chen, X.: Deeply learning deformable facial action parts model for dynamic expression analysis. In: Cremers, D., Reid, I., Saito, H., Yang, M.-H. (eds.) ACCV 2014. LNCS, vol. 9006, pp. 143–157. Springer, Cham (2015). https://doi.org/10.1007/978-3-319-16817-3_10
29. Lucas, J., Tucker, G., Grosse, R., Norouzi, M.: Understanding posterior collapse in generative latent variable models (2019)
30. Lucey, P., Cohn, J., Lucey, S., Matthews, I., Sridharan, S., Prkachin, K.M.: Automatically detecting pain using facial actions. In: ACIIW, pp. 1–8 (2009). https://doi.org/10.1109/ACII.2009.5349321
31. Van der Maaten, L., Hinton, G.: Visualizing data using T-SNE. J. Mach. Learn. Res. **9**(11) (2008)
32. McGarigal, K., Stafford, S., Cushman, S.: Discriminant Analysis, pp. 129–187 (2000)
33. Melhart, D., Liapis, A., Yannakakis, G.N.: The affect game annotation (again) dataset. arXiv preprint arXiv:2104.02643 (2021)
34. Minaee, S., Abdolrashidi, A.: Deep-emotion: Facial expression recognition using attentional convolutional network. arXiv preprint arXiv:1902.01019 (2019)
35. Muhammad, G., Alsulaiman, M., Amin, S.U., Ghoneim, A., Alhamid, M.F.: A facial-expression monitoring system for improved healthcare in smart cities. IEEE Access **5**, 10871–10881 (2017). https://doi.org/10.1109/ACCESS.2017.2712788
36. Nguyen, A., et al.: Plug & play generative networks: conditional iterative generation of images in latent space. In: CVPR (2017)

37. Nummenmaa, L., Hari, R., Hietanen, J.K., Glerean, E.: Maps of subjective feelings. Proc. Natl. Acad. Sci. **115**(37), 9198–9203 (2018). https://doi.org/10.1073/pnas. 1807390115, https://www.pnas.org/content/115/37/9198

38. Paszke, A., et al.: Pytorch: an imperative style, high-performance deep learning library. In: Wallach, H., Larochelle, H., Beygelzimer, A., d'Alché-Buc, F., Fox, E., Garnett, R. (eds.) Advances in Neural Information Processing Systems, vol. 32, pp. 8024–8035. Curran Associates, Inc. (2019)

39. Perov, I., et al.: Deepfacelab: a simple, flexible and extensible face swapping framework (2020)

40. Reynolds, D.: Gaussian Mixture Models, pp. 659–663. Springer, US (2009). https://doi.org/10.1007/978-0-387-73003-5_196

41. Rezende, D., Mohamed, S.: Variational inference with normalizing flows. In: ICML (2015)

42. Rothkrantz, L., et al.: Facs-coding of facial expressions. Association for Computing Machinery (2009)

43. Rudovic, O., et al.: Personalized federated deep learning for pain estimation from face images. arXiv preprint arXiv:2101.04800 (2021)

44. Shao, J., Qian, Y.: Three convolutional neural network models for facial expression recognition in the wild. Neurocomputing. **355**, 82–92 (2019). https://doi.org/10. 1016/j.neucom.2019.05.005, https://www.sciencedirect.com/science/article/pii/ S0925231219306137

45. Song, Y., Morency, L.P., Davis, R.: Distribution-sensitive learning for imbalanced datasets. In: FGW (2013)

46. Sricharan, K., et al.: Semi-supervised conditional gans. arXiv preprint arXiv:1708.05789 (2017)

47. Sun, B., Li, L., Zhou, G., He, J.: Facial expression recognition in the wild based on multimodal texture features. J. Electron. Imaging **25**(6), 1–8 (2016)

48. Takalkar, M.A., Xu, M.: Image based facial micro-expression recognition using deep learning on small datasets. In: 2017 International Conference on Digital Image Computing: Techniques and Applications (DICTA), pp. 1–7. IEEE (2017)

49. Vinciarelli, A., Pantic, M., Bourlard, H.: Social signal processing: survey of an emerging domain. Image Vision Comput. **27**(12), 1743–1759 (2009)

50. Weitz, K., et al.: Deep-learned faces of pain and emotions: elucidating the differences of facial expressions with the help of explainable AI methods. tm-Technisches Messen. **86**(7–8), 404–412 (2019)

51. Widen, S.C., et al.: Anger and disgust: discrete or overlapping categories. In: APS Annual Convention (2004)

52. Xie, S., Hu, H., Chen, Y.: Facial expression recognition with two-branch disentangled generative adversarial network. IEEE Trans. Circuits Syst. Video Technol. (2020)

53. Yang, H., et al.: Identity-adaptive facial expression recognition through expression regeneration using conditional generative adversarial networks. In: FG (2018)

An Ethical Discussion on BCI-Based Authentication

Tyree Lewis$^{(\boxtimes)}$, Rupal Agarwal , and Marvin Andujar

University of South Florida, Tampa, FL 33620, USA
tlewis10@usf.edu

Abstract. In recent times, Brain Computer Interface (BCI) applications have progressed as biometric authentication systems. Existing systems each follow the fundamental concepts of ensuring a user can be successfully authenticated into it. This comes with the complexity of developing systems that prevent a user's data from being at risk. Furthermore, with each new integration to make these systems more secure, they may lead to ethical concerns that should be discussed to better understand if they will be beneficial to individuals in their daily life. The discussion of ethical concerns of BCI authentication systems is the primary purpose of this paper. We also present an implemented prototype and discuss its potential ethical concerns that could be addressed in future work.

Keywords: Brain Computer Interfaces · Biometric Authentication · Electroencephalogram

1 Introduction

Brain-Computer Interface (BCI)-based authentication systems allow users to interact with BCI technology, by using their brain data as a form of biometric authentication to enable participants to access systems securely. This brain activity, also known as Electroencephalogram (EEG), has been adapted to authentication, due to the properties in brain data that make it effective, compared to other authentication methods, such as universality and uniqueness. The traditional forms of user authentication are passwords and identification cards. While they were relied upon in the past, these methods have weaknesses in our modern era, as passwords can be easily forgotten and identification cards are always at risk of being lost or stolen. Furthermore, biometric-based authentication systems that use fingerprint and facial recognition have potential challenges, as well. They can resolve the issues of remembrance and misplacement, but are susceptible to replay attacks and the disclosure of a user's private biometric information when they try to access a system [12]. Incorporating EEG into a biometric system can lead to ethical concerns for users, especially when making this technology available to the public. As a result, this paper aims to discuss these ethical challenges, so that they could be considered in future BCI-based authentication systems.

J.-J. Rousseau and B. Kapralos (Eds.): ICPR 2022 Workshops, LNCS 13646, pp. 166–178, 2023.
https://doi.org/10.1007/978-3-031-37745-7_12

As our BCI-based authentication application is currently in its prototype phase, this paper focuses on the evaluations on ethical concerns in BCI. Current results will be presented in a later section.

The main contributions of the paper are as follows:

- Provide an ethical discussion on a BCI-based authentication system
- Present a prototype implementation of a BCI-based authentication system

2   Related Works

Various studies have researched ethical concerns in biometric systems, that are applicable to BCI, and BCI technology. Informed consent, as described by [9], entails that a participant in a BCI study should be provided details about the goal of the research being conducted, the length of the subject's involvement in the work, a description of the process, and identification of any experimental procedures throughout their participation. By engaging with the subject and ensuring they understand the capabilities and limitations of the BCI system, this can work to avoid this ethical concern. Furthermore, this paper describes the importance of communication between the researchers and media as it relates to the future developments of BCI. Ethical concerns can arise if details about the expectations for the system, that are shared with journalists, are not reachable in the near future. If developmental challenges that can occur in the BCI system are not identified, there will be a disconnect between the assumed expectations and the actual progress of the BCI system. As a result, researchers should outline expectations in the near future and discuss potential solutions to prevent issues from happening. This is important to avoid unpredictable circumstances during project development that can lead to misleading information shared publicly.

The work by [4] presents the ethical issues in BCI technology, by mapping them into three categories. These consist of physical, psychological, and social factors, which are the overarching themes of BCI ethics. User safety is the physical factor, which comprises of identifying the physical harms that can be afflicted on a user, while they interact with the system. This is important to avoid unexpected issues that can occur when using BCI technology and understand how to proceed if it were to fail. This also includes the possible exertion on a participant both mentally and physically, while learning to use a BCI. Humanity and Personhood and autonomy are the psychological factors that can be ethical concerns. Potential users interacting with a BCI system may be concerned about the BCI technology becoming apart of themselves and possibly causing a loss of their sense of self. For example, the paper mentions participants in a study that used BCI technology felt more confident, independent, or as if the BCI technology were an extension of oneself. This idea ties into autonomy, as users could become increasingly more dependent on using a BCI in their daily lives to perform tasks.

The paper mentions that if performing tasks is only possible with a BCI, this could create the concern of harming an individual's ability to act independently without a BCI. The social factors that can be ethical issues in BCI technology, as referred by the paper, are Stigma and Normality, Privacy and Security, Research Ethics and Informed Consent, Responsibility and Regulation, and Justice. There is the possibility that a user may feel stigmatized by a disability, and will consent to use of a BCI to prevent it. As it relates to privacy and security, hacking becomes an ethical concern, since BCI technology transmits brain data to a computer to be processed. If a BCI has the ability to extract information from participants, such as their affective state, this could be used to harm them or affect their environment in a negative way.

The applications of informed consent require subjects to understand the risks of using a BCI, before interacting with the system. Another ethical concern in social factors are the possibilities of the user of a BCI performing negative actions while using the system. The paper states researchers believe the legal system is not equipped for determining if either the user or the system itself is at fault if this occurs. Justice in BCI technology is considered, when it comes to the accessibility of BCI devices for everyone. Questions are brought up about the fairness of limited access to BCI's for users. For example, one of the many uses of BCI is to enhance users. If the ability to enhance oneself is restricted to only the wealthy, this leads to inequality and injustice within research to benefit all users.

There are many discussions on the ethical guidelines for BCI, however this paper provides an ethical discussion on a BCI-based authentication system, which was not presented before in literature. Combining the use of BCI technology with biometric authentication brings the ethical concerns that exist in BCI and biometrics together, which is important to consider for developing applications that can be used by everyone.

3   BCI Methods for Authentication

The following section will discuss how users could interact with a BCI-based authentication application, and the process in which the data is acquired and post-processed for the corresponding BCI methods. Furthermore, the ethical concerns and how they can be addressed will be presented.

3.1   Motor Imagery

The act of imagining the movement of an object to perform an action is referred to as motor imagery. As shown in Fig. 1, within the standardized 10–20 international system, the electrode channels that can be used for motor imagery studies are located around the motor cortex of the brain, which are shown in blue. EEG data for motor imagery-based tasks are collected, by giving users an interface to control different types of applications and devices, such as quadcopter drones, wheelchairs, and virtual reality [2]. After the data is acquired, they are post-processed through feature extraction techniques to classify the type of motor imagery performed, such as hand movements, foot movements, and word generation [2]. There are various types of feature extraction techniques, such as

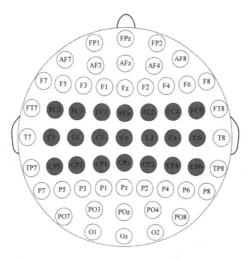

Fig. 1. EEG electrode placement related to motor imagery. Source: Adapted from [3]

Fourier transform, wavelet transform, and common spatial pattern to obtain this information from EEG data. Furthermore, classifiers that have been used for motor-imagery BCI studies include deep neural networks, linear discriminate analysis (LDA), and support vector machines (SVMs). The purpose of these post-processing steps, are to pass these extracted features to the classifier to translate the motor imagery commands a user may have desired to evoke onto an object, based on the classification's predictions.

Ethical concerns in motor imagery can arise from individuals interacting with a BCI system attempting to authenticate themselves. To incorporate motor imagery into authentication, subjects will need to continuously train themselves to perform motor imagery tasks. The more they practice and get accustomed to performing motor imagery, it will become easier for them to authenticate into the system. Due to the length of time this could take, providing informed consent to each participant will be important to prevent subjects from being unaware of the extent of their participation in the study. Privacy and security concerns can occur when communicating with media. When authenticating using motor imagery, the imagined movement thoughts that a participant may have are private. In the case of an interview, to understand how an individual accomplished a motor imagery task, they may be asked what movement they attempted to imagine to perform the action. This creates an ethical concern, because this personal information should be kept secret from anyone other than the user of the system, to avoid knowledge of how to access their account.

3.2   Event-Related Potentials

Event-related potentials (ERPs) refer to a response in the electrical activity of a user's brain, as a result of interacting with a system that evokes a stimulus event. One of these evoked signals, is known as the P300 wave. A P300 is an ERP that is generated in a person's EEG data, which occurs around 300ms, following a visual display of a stimulus that a participant has concentrated on. A P300 speller is an example of this visual display, which is configured in the form of a matrix. The rows and columns of this matrix flash in a random pattern, called the oddball paradigm, to illicit this P300 response. In order to improve the classification performance of the EEG data, it is post-processed through Independent Component Analysis (ICA) to remove artefacts. In general, artefacts are noise that is unwanted data mixed into EEG data. They come from external sources outside of EEG data and can exist in the forms of electrooculography (EOG), electromyogram (EMG), and electrocardiogram (EKG), which are the result of eye blinks, muscle movement, and heart rate, respectively. After ICA is performed, this information is passed to a classifier, such as an LDA classifier, or Quadratic Discriminant Analysis (QDA) to receive predictions on which option out of the matrix a user was focusing on.

As it relates to the use of ERPs in BCI, possible ethical concerns can happen, due to the user's experience with the system. ERP-based BCI systems require a lot of training in order for the classifiers to improve their accuracies over time. If this type of system were to be applicable to daily life, the training times would need to be reduced, while maintaining optimal performance to allow for BCI's to be more appropriate for practical use [15]. The solution would be to adapt these systems with BCIs that are based on evoked potentials, such as steady state visual evoked potentials (SSVEPs), as they do not require as much user training.

3.3 SSVEPs

SSVEPs are incorporated into BCI systems, by enabling relatively accurate and fast input commands with lower amounts of training needed by the user [11]. Data acquisition through an SSVEP-based BCI application consists of providing subjects with several options on a display as stimulus. The user will focus on one of these options, while they are flashing in a random frequency. There may be several frequencies collected, but a specific target frequency would be identified using post-processing techniques on the EEG data. Methods, such as conventional canonical correlation analysis (CCA), can be implemented to recognize the desired target frequency, using correlation values obtained by CCA [13].

In BCI research, ethical concerns can occur as a result of the effectiveness of BCI to classify a user's EEG data, as they are interacting with the system. One issue in BCI research is called, BCI illiteracy, where the classification methods are unable to detect the intentions of a user [7]. This problem appears when the user would need to focus on a specific target in a system that has multiple simultaneously flashing objects on a single display. In an authentication system, a user may select a single option out of multiple choices at a time in order for the application to determine what the user may have selected. If the system is unable to do this, this causes BCI illiteracy, because the classifier will have issues understanding the target the user is concentrating on. As a result, it will affect the classification accuracy and overall system performance. SSVEPs address this issue, as they have been used in studies with lower numbers of stable stimulation frequencies and obtained high classification accuracies and minimal BCI illiterates [7]. Photosensitivity is another ethical concern, where light from photic or pattern-based stimulation systems can causes seizures [6]. Due to the requirement of needing to focus on a flashing target, someone who is more sensitive to the light can be negatively impacted by this system. To avoid these concerns, these applications can incorporate fewer stimulus on screen and also lower amounts of training sessions to expose a user to minimal flashing.

4 Our BCI Authentication Application

Our BCI authentication application is based on the P300 event-related potentials of the user's brain. It creates a direct interaction link between the user's brain and the authentication application, allowing the former to authenticate into the system using the P300 component of their EEG brain activity.

4.1 Application User Interface

The user interface of the application consists of a 2×2 matrix of images, presented on the screen to the user. In our design, the matrix consists of images of four superhero characters: supergirl, superman, black widow and wolverine, as shown in Fig. 2. Each of these images represent the different options that users can select to formulate their password. While they are initially displayed in grey color, during the authentication process each image will transition between grey images and colored images in the flashing state. The rows and columns in the matrix flash according to the oddball paradigm and P300 event-related potentials are elicited in the user when they focus their attention on the flashing row and column containing the target image. The specific images selected by the subjects in the matrix represent their registration and login password that they can use to authenticate into the system. After login, the users receive feedback on the screen, via a pop-up message, indicating if the images they selected during registration and login are a match, and if they were able to successfully login or not. The users interact with the application by participating in four different phases: training, registration, login and authentication

The architecture of our BCI authentication application is shown in Fig. 3 and it details the entire user authentication process. First, the electrical brain activity of the user is acquired from their scalp while they wear the EEG headset and interact with the application. Next, the collected EEG data is cleaned from noise through artefact removal techniques. Then, the acquired EEG data, collected during registration and login is classified to obtain an accuracy of how likely the data is a match. Feedback is also presented to the users in the form of a pop-up display message, indicating if they have successfully authenticated into the system or not. The entire process is described in detail below.

Fig. 2. Concept design for 2×2 Matrix P300 interface, consisting of four superhero images.

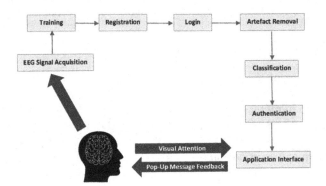

Fig. 3. BCI authentication flowchart.

4.2   Training Phase

As mentioned previously, before beginning the training phase, the user is introduced to the system and how the P300 speller works. This process also includes how to focus on the P300 matrix to perform password selection, by counting the number of flashes to stay engaged, and asking if they have any questions. Once training commences, they will undergo six training sessions, where their EEG data can be recorded, while they concentrate on the images in the P300 speller. We believe that six training sessions is sufficient to acquire enough data to use for the classifier in the back-end at a later stage, and also prevent the participant from getting exhausted from longer session periods. Figure 4 displays a subject undergoing the training session, focusing on the P300 matrix shown on the computer monitor. During training, the users are guided on which specific image to focus on at a time, by indicating the desired image with a red box overlaying it in the matrix. This occurs for a brief moment, before all the images start to

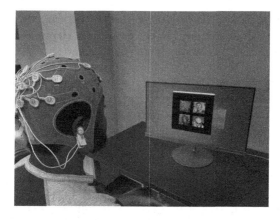

Fig. 4. User interaction with BCI Authentication system.

flash to give participants enough time to switch target images. Over the course of the session, all the images will remain static, one image will be overlaid with a red box for the user to know where to look at, then all of the images displayed on the P300 speller will flash in a random pattern using the oddball paradigm. Each time throughout the process, the user will switch from one random target to the next. Once all training sessions have completed, users will stop focusing on the P300 speller. Their EEG data is passed into a Linear Discriminant Analysis (LDA) classifier to generate a model based on their training data, to be saved for use in the registration and login phases.

4.3   Registration Phase

The registration phase is initiated, by first instructing participants of how they will interact with the system and the differences between this and the training phase. When the phase is ready to begin, they will need to enter a username into the system, using a keyboard connected to the monitor. A pop-up message is shown on screen, which asks for the participants to select a username to register their account for the first time. There will be an input field available at this time for them to enter their username and they will press the "Enter" key on the keyboard to continue and close the message. By requesting users to create a username before EEG collection starts, we can use this information during the login phase to confirm if the user presently exists in the system or not. After the message has closed, the P300 matrix will appear and follow a similar behavior to the training phase. This time, however, there would not be a target stimulus shown on screen, using a red box to guide them on where to focus. Instead, the user would be given the option to determine which password they would like to select from the images in the P300 matrix. These images would be the same ones used in the P300 speller for training, as we must maintain consistency between each phase for proper classification in the future.

The registration password selection consists of selecting two options from the matrix, but not at the same time. For the first image they choose, they will focus on it, while each of the rows and columns of the matrix flash. The flashing will stop after a while, and a red image will overlay the specific image the algorithm has predicted was the image they chose as the password. Then the process repeats while the subjects will either continue looking at the same image to choose it again, or switch targets to select a different image for their second password. We identify the images they decided on, by loading their training model, passing their EEG data recorded during registration as testing data to the model, and then classify the data to make a prediction on which positions in the matrix were the ones they focused on. For example, since our P300 speller is a 2×2 matrix, the images will be predicted by [0,0], [0,1], [1,0], [1,1], corresponding to the top left, top right, bottom left, and bottom right images, respectively. Once the two passwords have been confirmed for registration, the subject's username, EEG data, and the row and column information that corresponds to the images they selected, are saved to a database. A database is useful, as it allows for us to maintain a record of who has accessed the system for registration and to know what their password is. Afterwards, they will proceed to the login phase of the application.

4.4   Login Phase

When the login phase begins, the subjects will be shown another pop-up message, where they will be asked to input their username created during the registration phase. If the username is successfully found, the P300 matrix will appear on screen and the same process will follow as in registration. In the case that the username fails, they will be prompted to try again or to return to registration. While the users focus on the P300 matrix in the login phase, they must make sure to focus on the same set of images that they previously chose for registration. After the two passwords have been confirmed once again, then the authentication phase will commence.

4.5   Authentication Phase

The authentication phase ensures that the individual that is accessing the account is the genuine person it belongs to, and not a potential imposter. After the login phase ends, the EEG data recorded in both the registration and login phases are passed into an independent component analysis (ICA) algorithm in order to remove artefacts. By processing EEG data through ICA, we are capable of obtaining cleaner data and improve the classification performance. When ICA is complete, the participant's registration data is matched with their login data using the cosine similarity to determine if they are the genuine user to the account. The cosine similarity is applicable for classification, because EEG data can be reshaped into a vector and computed to measure the similarity between the two vectors from registration and login. The result found from the cosine similarity gives a matching score between -1 and 1, to identify the probability of the two compared vectors being closely related, independent, or unrelated. The following equation represents the cosine similarity, which is the ratio of the dot product of these two vectors and the product of magnitude of these vectors:

$$similarity(u, v) = \frac{u.v}{\|u\| \|v\|}$$

Based on our current results, we have established a threshold accuracy of 95% for authenticating a subject. This means that if a genuine subject is attempting to access their account, they must obtain a classification accuracy of 95% or higher to successfully login. When an imposter attempts to access a genuine subject's account, our results have shown that they are unable to achieve an accuracy higher than 95%. The highest accuracy obtained by an imposter was 92% when attempting to login as a genuine user. As we continue to improve our system, it will be possible to increase this threshold accuracy for a genuine subject accessing their account. Furthermore, this will widen the gap between the ability for an imposter to try to use their brain data to login as the genuine user, because their accuracy would not be as high. If the authentication is successful, the user will receive feedback consisting of a message on screen indicating the login worked and they will be allowed into their account. However, a failed authentication will proceed with two possible options. If the cosine similarity obtained is close to the 95% threshold, for example between 85% and 94%, they can be given a pop-up message displayed on screen saying the login failed, and also ask them if they are interested in learning more about why their attempt failed. It is possible that the subject attempting to login may not be as focused as they were during registration compared to login, so their affective state can be checked. Their EEG data for both registration and login will be separated into alpha, beta, and theta bands, and the cosine similarity would be performed on each individual band. If they obtain high similarity scores between each band, they will be allowed to login using their affective state instead of their EEG data. Furthermore, depending on the specific results of each band, a display message is shown on screen, to inform the user on why their authentication may have failed. Possible reasons for their failed attempt can include that they were either lacking focus, they were too relaxed, or they were too drowsy during their login attempt. Any of these states can affect their EEG data and prevent them from achieving a high enough similarity score. On the other hand, if the cosine similarity results are still very different, they will not be allowed to access the account and will be given a display message to try again.

4.6 Ethical Challenges

This system is susceptible to the ethical concerns that exist in both biometrics and BCI technology, but they have not been previously discussed for BCI-based authentication. The method for password selection depends on how focused the user was during training, registration, and login. If a user is successful in the registration phase, but fails often in login, they may become frustrated with the system. As a result, this will make it even less likely they will be able to authenticate themselves, due to the changes in their affective state. Informed consent will be needed to allow participants to be aware of the limitations of the system and the areas where they may have to spend additional time interacting with the system to attempt to login. To maintain privacy and security, the system will have to ensure that a user's EEG data is securely stored as to prevent ethical issue as a result of potential exposure of their personal information. For justice concerns, this authentication system must be accessible to any user who would desire to create a password using their EEG data to authenticate themselves.

5   BCI Authentication Ethical Concerns

The brain signals of each individual are unique and therefore, they can be effectively used for person authentication [10]. Many researchers have identified the potential benefits of using brain signals, particularly the EEG signals, for user authentication and have developed several BCI-based applications to achieve this. These BCI devices potentially increase the quality of life, however, they are not without risks as they pose various ethical concerns. The ethical issues inevitably bring about debates on what should be restricted and what is acceptable by the public in our society [14].

5.1   Privacy

User authentication using EEG activity, requires the BCI system to collect brain data from the users. The streamed data contains a lot of personal information of the users that can potentially be exploited by others to derive one's emotional reactions, conscious/unconscious interests and memory. To prevent this, strong security measures should be put in place to stop unauthorized access to extract, add, duplicate and modify the data [1]. The stored brain data should not contain any personal identifiable information such as names, addresses and contact information including email id's and phone numbers. The data should be anonymized by using a person identification number instead of using names so that no person can be identified based on their data in the event of an information breach or system hacking. The data should be stored in an encrypted form in a password protected hard drive and should require authentication by people who have clearance to access it.

5.2   Physical Characteristics

The non-invasive BCI's also pose some ethical concerns related to the physical characteristics of the users such as their hair length, hair type, head shape and head size. The non-invasive BCI's use both commercial and research grade BCI headsets to collect brain data. Past research has shown that the time needed to record the minimal brain signals was much longer for some participants than for others [5]. This inconsistency was directly related to the density and length of the participant's hair. It was found out that the participant's with no hair required the shortest preparation times whereas longer preparation times were required for participants with longer and coarser hair. Another major concern with the non-invasive BCI's is the use of conductive gel that is needed to get a good contact between the electrodes and the scalp. To ensure the collection of good quality brain data, sometimes the skin under the electrodes is abraded and electrode gel is put under the electrodes. Under some conditions, the skin abrasions become painful and increase the skin sensitivity. Moreover, the gel is found to be uncomfortable to many subjects and it needs to washed out of the hair after each session which is quite cumbersome [8].

5.3   Affective State Change

Recording the changes in user's affect can lead to ethical concerns because the person's affective state is recorded. Affective states correspond to user's concentration, relaxation, drowsiness, etc. When a user performs a demanding BCI task, their affective states can vary over time. Therefore, in research, the user's state could be recorded over time to establish patterns between the changes in their affective state and their BCI-task performance. Such recorded data can be accessed by hackers and unauthorized personnel who can use it to identify the private affective information of other users and even gain unauthorized control of their BCI application. To prevent this, the stored affective data of the users should be anonymized by using person identification numbers instead of using their names and email ids.

The user's affective state can also vary while interacting with a BCI authentication application, affecting their ability to authenticate successfully and leading to various ethical issues such as physical and emotional burdens. These applications may require more cognitive attention from the users than what they can attain on a daily basis, giving rise to frustration and eventually causing unsuccessful authentication.

6   Conclusion

In conclusion, we anticipate that our design for a BCI-based authentication system can improve the facets of biometric authentication, as it relates to the challenges faced by other forms of authentication, due to the properties of EEG data. Although this system has its own ethical challenges, many of these issues can be resolved through the development process and future work, depending on how the system would be integrated into different domains. The BCI-based authentication system is a prototype implementation, therefore our current results indicate that the system is able to authenticate users within a threshold accuracy of 95%. For future work, we will address the ethical concerns discussed in this paper and those that occur in the prototype system that we have. As there are already many considered ethical guidelines for BCI technology, this discussion aimed to bring into perspective how applying BCI to the area of biometric authentication will bring up those ethical concerns, as well as those that exist in biometrics.

References

1. Abouelmehdi, K., Beni-Hessane, A., Khaloufi, H.: Big healthcare data: preserving security and privacy. J. Big Data **5**(1), 1–18 (2018). https://doi.org/10.1186/s40537-017-0110-7
2. Aggarwal, S., Chugh, N.: Signal processing techniques for motor imagery brain computer interface: a review. Array **1**, 100003 (2019)
3. Al-Saegh, A., Dawwd, S.A., Abdul-Jabbar, J.M.: Deep learning for motor imagery EEG-based classification: a review. Biomed. Signal Process. Control **63**, 102172 (2021)
4. Coin, A., Mulder, M., Dubljević, V.: Ethical aspects of BCI technology: what is the state of the art? Philosophies **5**(4), 31 (2020)
5. Ekandem, J.I., Davis, T.A., Alvarez, I., James, M.T., Gilbert, J.E.: Evaluating the ergonomics of BCI devices for research and experimentation. Ergonomics **55**(5), 592–598 (2012)
6. Fisher, R.S., Harding, G., Erba, G., Barkley, G.L., Wilkins, A.: Photic-and pattern-induced seizures: a review for the epilepsy foundation of America working group. Epilepsia **46**(9), 1426–1441 (2005)
7. Gembler, F., Stawicki, P., Volosyak, I.: Exploring the possibilities and limitations of multitarget SSVEP-based BCI applications. In: 2016 38th Annual International Conference of the IEEE Engineering in Medicine and Biology Society (EMBC), pp. 1488–1491. IEEE (2016)
8. Guger, C., Krausz, G., Allison, B.Z., Edlinger, G.: Comparison of dry and gel based electrodes for p300 brain-computer interfaces. Front. Neurosci. **6**, 60 (2012)
9. Haselager, P., Vlek, R., Hill, J., Nijboer, F.: A note on ethical aspects of BCI. Neural Netw. **22**(9), 1352–1357 (2009)
10. Marcel, S., Millán, J.d.R.: Person authentication using brainwaves (EEG) and maximum a posteriori model adaptation. IEEE Trans. Pattern Anal. Mach. Intell. **29**(4), 743–752 (2007)
11. Padfield, N., Zabalza, J., Zhao, H., Masero, V., Ren, J.: EEG-based brain-computer interfaces using motor-imagery: techniques and challenges. Sensors **19**(6), 1423 (2019)
12. Rui, Z., Yan, Z.: A survey on biometric authentication: toward secure and privacy-preserving identification. IEEE Access **7**, 5994–6009 (2018)
13. Sadeghi, S., Maleki, A.: Adaptive canonical correlation analysis for harmonic stimulation frequencies recognition in SSVEP-based BCIS. Turkish J. Elect. Eng. Comput. Sci. **27**(5), 3729–3740 (2019)
14. Vlek, R.J., et al.: Ethical issues in brain-computer interface research, development, and dissemination. J. Neurol. Phys. Ther. **36**(2), 94–99 (2012)
15. Zerafa, R., Camilleri, T., Falzon, O., Camilleri, K.P.: To train or not to train? A survey on training of feature extraction methods for SSVEP-based BCIS. J. Neural Eng. **15**(5), 051001 (2018)

Author Index

A

Aathreya, Saandeep 151
Abbate, Giovanbattista 3
Agarwal, Rupal 166
Amerini, Irene 3, 17
Andujar, Marvin 166

B

Bhargava, Kartikeya 106
Bousefsaf, Frédéric 139

C

Caldelli, Roberto 3
Canavan, Shaun 151
Chandola, Deeksha 89
Coustaty, Mickaël 57
Craig, Stephanie G. 89

D

d'Andecy, Vincent Poulain 57

E

Elder, James H. 106

F

Faizi, Adnan 89
Filho, Helio Perroni 106

G

Gunes, Hatice 121

J

Javed, Nizwa 106
Jenkin, Michael 89

K

Kébairi, Saddok 57
Khan, Walleed 89
Kotegar, Karunakar A. 32
Krämer, Petra Gomez 57

L

Lagha, Lynda 139
Lewis, Tyree 166
Li, Chang-Tsun 32, 46

M

Maaoui, Choubeila 139
Maiano, Luca 17
Manisha 32

N

Naheyan, Tasneem 106

O

Ouzar, Yassine 139

P

Papa, Lorenzo 17

Q

Quan, Yijun 46

R

Rouis, Kais 57
Rousseau, Jean-Jacques 89

S

Sidère, Nicolas 57
Stamm, Matthew C. 70
Stoychev, Samuil 121

T

Taburet, Théo 57
Tarawneh, Enas 89
Trajcevski, Aleksander 106

V

Vocaj, Ketbjano 17

Z

Zhao, Xinwei 70

© Springer Nature Switzerland AG 2023
J.-J. Rousseau and B. Kapralos (Eds.): ICPR 2022 Workshops, LNCS 13646, p. 179, 2023.
https://doi.org/10.1007/978-3-031-37745-7

Printed in the United States
by Baker & Taylor Publisher Services